Labour and Society in Britain
1918–1979

James E. Cronin

BATSFORD ACADEMIC AND EDUCATIONAL
LONDON

To Mary

© James E. Cronin 1984

First published 1984

All rights reserved. No part of this
publication may be reproduced, in any form
or by any means, without permission from
the Publisher

Typeset by Progress Filmsetting Ltd
E.C.2.
and printed in Great Britain by
Biddles Ltd
Guildford and Kings Lynn
for the publishers
Batsford Academic and Educational,
an imprint of B.T. Batsford Ltd,
4 Fitzhardinge Street, London W1H 0AH

British Library Cataloguing in Publication
Data

Cronin, James E.
    Labour and society in Britain, 1918–1979.
    1. Labor and laboring classes—Great
    Britain—History   2. Great Britain—
    Social conditions—History
    I. Title
    305.5'62'0941   HD8391
    ISBN 0 7134 4395 2
    ISBN 0 7134 4396 0 (Pbk)

Contents

Preface

This book began simply enough. There seemed a need to push the insights generated by historians of labour in the eighteenth and nineteenth centuries beyond 1914, where most such research normally stops. In the process of doing that, I hoped to create an intellectual bridge of sorts between the historical understanding of the evolution of the working class since the early industrial era and the theoretical debates and empirical investigations of class undertaken by social scientists since 1945.

As research and writing progressed, the task became both more urgent and more difficult. More urgent because the most intensive phase of work on this project coincided with the onset of by far the most serious of the Labour party's recurring crises. The new crisis served to reopen all the debates of the 1950s and 1960s concerning the changing shape of the British working class and its altered relationship to Labour. Curiously, the 'affluent worker' debate came back into fashion at precisely the moment when affluence itself began to disappear.

One of the issues at the centre of this study – the shifting link between working people as a social class and Labour as a political party – therefore became a matter of enormous contemporary import as I was putting it all together. This had two effects upon the book itself. First, it served to concentrate my attention more directly upon that network of formal and informal institutions in which working-class culture has been embodied, and that has helped – indirectly at least – to translate class membership into political allegiance. Second, the renewed focus on the old issues of affluence and class politics somehow led me to conclude that much of the recent debate was miscast, primarily because it was focused too narrowly either on the class or on the party, rather than on the connections between the two.

On balance, therefore, the recent crisis has probably made the argument advanced here both clearer and also less embedded in the current discourse. It did not make the research any easier, however. The basic problem was that key aspects of labour history since the First World War remain virtually untouched by researchers. A few topics, like unemployment or the formation of unions in the new industries, have begun to attract interest, but the best of this work is still in the form of unpublished dissertations. Worse still is the wholesale absence of studies of the larger working-class communities, of women workers, of family life and leisure, and on work itself between the wars. Fortunately, there is a good deal of contemporary documentation on these matters that I have been able to use to fill some of the worst gaps, but we clearly need to know a great deal more.

If historical research is scant for the interwar decades, it simply does not exist at all for the postwar period. Once again, however, this is to some degree compensated for by the existence of a large body of social scientific literature devoted to studying the working class. The use of this material presents quite serious problems for the historian, however, for it is profoundly influenced by the short-term preoccupations of the various disciplines in which most of it was conceived and executed, and these preoccupations are usually far removed from our concerns here. It is necessary, therefore, to 'historicise' and to decode most of this material in order to make proper use of it. In consequence, there is a bit more discussion of 'the sociology of sociology' in the last several chapters than is normal in historical accounts. Still, it was the precondition for getting access to the rich store of information gathered by postwar investigators operating within these disciplines.

Fortunately, we have a surprising amount of useful and quite accessible data available on the decade in between these two periods. The social history of the Second World War has attracted some very good researchers, and the upheavals of war and of postwar reconstruction unleashed a flood of documentation on British society that has still not been fully utilized. This has been a great boon to my research, for the high quality of the sources for the 1940s has helped to illuminate, by contrast and comparison, both the earlier and later eras.

As the argument in the book has evolved and as the diversity and unevenness of the sources have become clear, it has been necessary as well to make some hard choices regarding presentation. More specifically, in order to make the argument about the changing nature of the link between class and politics with sufficient force, I felt the need to sacrifice some detail and description. It became impossible in particular to do proper justice to the considerable regional and ethnic diversity that is still so much a part of working-class life in Britain. I have also sacrificed any sustained discussion of theories of class structure, of labour markets and 'the labour process', and of class formation, despite the importance such work has had in shaping my own thoughts.

The nature of the sources and of the argument has also guaranteed the contracting of a rather large number of debts on my part, larger than can be conveyed in references alone. For that reason, I want to conclude this preface by expressing my gratitude to a number of people and institutions. To begin, welcome financial support for a year of research was provided by a fellowship from the National Endowment for the Humanities. Additional support for research, research assistance, copying and typing came from the Graduate School, the Urban Research Center, the Social Science Research Facility and the History Department of the University of Wisconsin-Milwaukee.

My intellectual debts are greater still. For directing me to various documents and archives, or for giving me access to them, I thank Raphael Samuel, Paul Thompson, Eric Hobsbawm, John Field, Ruth and Edmund Frow, Catherine Burke and Dermot Healy. I particularly want to thank Angus Calder and Dorothy Wainwright for help with the Mass-Observation material at the University of Sussex. For offering guidance through the maze of postwar studies of class structure and working-class culture, I am indebted to Bob Blackburn, Colin Crouch, Richard Hoggart and Richard Johnson, to George Bain, who kindly provided me with copies of the relevant sections of his bibliography of British industrial relations prior to publication, and to Howard Newby, whose grant proposal on the changing class structure afforded me such an insightful review of the literature. My research was also facilitated by several scholars who gave me copies of unpublished articles or theses, including Nina Fishman, Steve Tolliday and Jonathan Zeitlin, and by Howard Gospel, who invited me to the 1981 SSRC conference on business and labour history from which I learned so much. I also profited from having the opportunity to present arguments and findings from this project at seminars or conferences organized by Bob Moeller, Helmut Gruber, Frank Longstreth, John Styles, Eric Hobsbawm, Pat Thane, Gareth Stedman Jones, Alastair Reid, Ron Aminzade and Erik Wright. The actual writing of the text was improved by careful readings of all or part of it by Bob Moeller, Richard Price, Margo Conk and Reginald Horsman.

The person to whom I feel I owe the most is Mary Cronin, to whom I have dedicated this book. There is no easy and straightforward way to summarize her contribution, however, for it involves a great deal more than mere collegial assistance. By this I do not mean that she gave up her career or social life or took over all domestic responsibilities so as to aid my research and writing. On the contrary, in the years I have devoted to this book she has undoubtedly achieved more professionally and personally than I have. But somehow she did find the time and energy to criticise the original grant proposal from which the book grew, to offer sage advice at each stage of research, and to undertake a close and extremely helpful reading of the entire manuscript.

Finally, I want to find some reason to mention and thank my daughters, Rebecca and Johanna. Though they did very little proof-reading, and indeed did not contribute in any tangible way to the book, they did, by their presence, help me to put this modest effort into perspective.

1

Introduction: The Working Class in the Twentieth Century

The working class thrust itself into the centre of Britain's social and political life during an upsurge of militancy lasting from 1910 to the early 1920s. In 1910, the unions numbered just over 2.5 million; by 1920, over 8.3 million. At the elections of December, 1910, 370,000 voted for Labour candidates and the party won 42 seats. By 1922, over four hundred candidates standing for Labour received more than four million votes, nearly 30% of those cast; 142 Labour members entered Parliament.

This massive growth in the industrial and political strength of the workers established the twentieth-century pattern of British politics. Henceforth, support for the Labour party, together with membership of the unions, would be seen as part of what it meant to be working class. More importantly, the representation of the class would come to depend upon the combined fate of the workers' industrial organizations, of their political party, and of the links that held together the unions, the party and the class. For a generation after 1920, that fate was a happy one, as the party and the unions rose together in membership, competence and clout. In 1950, 9.3 million were in unions, 13.2 million voting Labour. Progress seemed steady and assured, an inevitable consequence of the very formation of the working class.

Since 1950, the labour movement has appeared to stumble. For many years union membership stagnated, though it rose again in the 1960s. Allegiance to the Labour party also waned in the 1950s and, instead of picking up in the 1960s, began an even more serious decline. At first, Labour's problems appeared to be the product of exhaustion and the petering out of imaginative new ideas as the welfare state began actually to work. But by 1960 the 'visible moral decline of the labour movement' and its electoral impasse were reinterpreted as merely

1

surface manifestations of deeper processes leading to the decomposition of the working class itself.[1] The disappointments of the Wilson-Callaghan years, culminating in the catastrophes of 1979 and 1983, have reinforced the sense of failure and confirmed the most pessimistic predictions of the future of labour politics.

Gloom over the fate of labour is now pervasive. And it is not just the critics of Labour who, gloatingly, join in announcing its demise. Such thoughtful and sympathetic analysts as Eric Hobsbawm, Samuel Beer and Ralf Dahrendorf, among many others, have come to the conclusion that working-class politics are in deep crisis. Hobsbawm, for example, was moved to ask in 1978 why 'the forward march of labour and the labour movement . . . appears to have come to a halt in this country about twenty-five or thirty years ago'. To him, the disarray of labour was characterized first and foremost by a weakening of 'support for the Labour party'; and certainly the pattern of elections and polls since 1978 has reinforced that diagnosis. The crisis of labour has been manifest also, Hobsbawm feels, in the changed tone of other aspects of the movement. The conduct of strikes, for example, has altered so that now 'the strength of a group lies not in the amount of loss they can cause to the employer, but in the inconvenience they can cause to the public, i.e., to other workers . . .' The very demands of strikes seem particularly lacking in nobility. Inflation and full employment have eroded the old sense of 'a fair day's pay for a fair day's work', and have taught workers the amoral values of the market. Wage demands have escalated, and the combination of seemingly limitless claims and sectional styles of protest has strained the ties of class loyalty among workers while alienating the broader, middle-class public.[2]

Beer and Dahrendorf would concur, and add that the problem of the working class is actually the key to the much broader crisis affecting contemporary Britain. To Dahrendorf, the distinguishing feature of British society and politics over the years has been solidarity. Underpinning this civic solidarity was the cohesiveness of social class: 'The working class', he argues, 'epitomises what such solidarity means'. Present difficulties stem from a loosening of that 'glue which binds social groups together'. The 'bonds of class . . . are weakening', and workers have begun to act as individuals or, more often, as sectional groupings pursuing their narrow interests with little regard either for the common welfare or the interests of the class.[3]

Samuel Beer takes the diagnosis a step further, and produces from it a new label for the malaise gripping Britain: he calls it 'pluralist stagnation' and attributes it largely to the process of class decomposition. Where class loyalties once provided the basis of stable politics, now the fading of class loyalties has produced the 'paralysis of public choice' that has marked recent British history and doomed the efforts at economic management of Labour and the Conservatives alike. This has been caused primarily by the long-term process of 'class decomposition', set in motion by the rising prosperity of the welfare state and culminating in the transformation of the solidaristic working class of the 1940s and 1950s into the competing syndicalist groups that now represent the bulk of the country's workforce. While '[s]ectionalism has always plagued the labour movement', Beer explains, 'from one generation to another the broad direction toward or away from solidarity has shifted profoundly'; in the most recent phase, 'Class composition was succeeded by class decomposition into local and occupational fragments.'[4]

The sense of decay, of disintegration, has found echoes among many workers as well. One working-class woman, from among the many interviewed recently by Jeremy Seabrook, expressed poignantly the 'dislocation in working-class tradition' when she explained: 'What we've got now, it's nothing to do with socialism. It's a mocking of all the things we fought for . . . I don't know what's happened to folk. They've all got greedy-grabbing, that's the trouble.' A worker from Nottingham put it more concisely: 'When we had nowt, we threatened the rich. Now we act like they did.' And another expressed bitter disappointment at the futility of chasing after wages when he commented, 'You can't ruin the capitalist system simply by taking money off it, and that's what the working class is doing. You can't beat them economically. There's got to be an awakening of the working class, a spiritual awakening. I don't know whether it will come.' A somewhat younger worker from the East Midlands conveyed a near-total disillusion: 'In my lifetime I've seen working-class people become more cynical. People actually get through their lives without believing in anything. Now when I was young, the labour movement had a meaning; it had a moral content. It could challenge the morality of capitalism, and appeal to something in us that was generous and magnanimous. . . . What the working-class had to oppose to capitalism is running pretty thin now.'[5]

The malaise which Hobsbawm, Dahrendorf, Beer and Seabrook's informants describe may be real or imagined, but the perception that it is real pervades political discourse and social analysis alike in contemporary Britain. It constitutes, for good or ill, an important aspect of the context in which this study has been conceived and executed.

For the recent dilemmas of the Labour party, the unions and the working class itself raise a variety of questions about how it all came to be. Indeed, an integral part of the current crisis is the sense that it represents a descent from some better, healthier past, and the very terms used to describe it – 'the forward march . . . halted', 'what went wrong?', 'class decomposition' – all conjure up notions of historical transformation. If the diagnoses have any validity for today, they must mean that yesterday, or some time before yesterday, there was in fact a 'forward march', a period when things went right, an era of class composition or formation, against which more recent developments can be compared and found wanting. The recent troubles of the British labour movement thus not only constitute the end point of the evolution to be traced out in the following pages; they also, by their dramatic quality, shape the questions to be asked of that evolution. The discussion of the working class in present-day Britain is profoundly, deeply historical in its structure, and it requires an evaluation based upon an historical reckoning.

Of course, it is not possible to accept the terms of the discussion in quite the way they have been used to date. The simplifications common in engaged polemics clearly cannot be imported into history without dire consequences. It is necessary as the first step in this study of the changing relationship between the working class and its main social, industrial and political institutions, to attend to the formulation of the contemporary argument in order to restate the issues in more neutral and useful terms.

That is best done through an examination of the analyses currently on offer about the causes of labour's decline. To begin, Hobsbawm and the others are generally quite critical of the narrow minds that have dominated the Labour party and the unions in the postwar years, and would locate some of the problem in their activity, or in most cases, planned inactivity. However, they would hesitate to attribute major significance to failures of leadership and would prefer to focus upon the alleged fragmentation of the traditional working class. For Hobsbawm, for example, the starting point for analysis is the simple failure of the manual workers to continue their numerical growth and the consequent rise within the work force of white-collar and service-sector employees. Even among manual workers, as he explains, there have been shifts away from the old centres of union strength and working-class culture, like textiles, mining and shipbuilding, and a tendency for adult men to be replaced by women who, Hobsbawm fears, may be less committed to the 'common style of proletarian life' or the values of trade unionism.

The dispersal of old working-class neighbourhoods and their replacement by blocks of flats or council estates are also said to have lessened solidarity. Years ago the working class was 'a collection of localised communities locally rooted to a much greater extent than the middle classes'. But this comfortable, older pattern has been replaced by a newer social ecology that has produced 'the desolation of ruined communities and broken associations' which Seabrook claims now characterizes urban Britain. The destruction of community, so the argument runs, has reinforced the transformation of the economy so as to marginalize, isolate and 'privatize' the working class.

While these factors have been fragmenting the class, rising living standards have removed the edge from workers' material grievances. Thus to the extent that workers still pursue wage gains, as the record of strikes indicates they do, this very expression of militancy is taken as evidence not of 'class consciousness', but as a symptom of the growing acceptance of the culture of consumption. From this perspective, the rise of unofficial strikes and shop-stewards' organization indicates a reversion to sectionalism rather than a challenge to authority, and the militancy they stimulate loses its former meaning as a battle between rich and poor.

Fleshed out in these terms, the argument bears a striking resemblance to theories proposed earlier about 'the affluent worker' or the process of *embourgeoisement*. The notion has indeed made a surprising rebound in the last few years. When first proffered in the wake of Labour's 1959 electoral defeat, it was linked to an explicit political programme. The idea was that, because Labour's traditional working-class base was being eroded by the social trends of an increasingly 'affluent society', the party should be wary of relying upon old-fashioned appeals to 'class-consciousness' and to socialism. The theory became identified in that context with 'revisionism' and the attempt to push Labour towards the political centre. Scholars who did not share that political programme had little difficulty demonstrating the empirical flaws behind such arguments, however. Indeed, successive investigations seriously qualified the theory, replacing the term 'embourgeoisement' with the more limited 'privatization' and substituting for the image of individual advance to middle-class status the much more prosaic notion of a general improvement via 'instrumental collectivism'. This progressive narrowing of the thesis reflected its declining salience, for as the 1960s progressed and workers in ever larger numbers took to defying the government and union leaders first in 'unofficial' and, later, in the 1970s, in a series of 'official' confrontations, the concept appeared more and more irrelevant. By 1980, research into the state of Britain's class structure appeared at an impasse, stalled by the failure of the *embourgeoisement* hypothesis and yet unable to generate an alternative.[6]

Just as sociologists have decided to bury the argument, however, it has been taken up again. To be sure, there are differences. Hobsbawm, for example, does not use the term *embourgeoisement* or the phrase 'the affluent worker'; in fact, he criticizes them for what they imply about white-collar workers. The emphasis upon individual advance or privatization, too, has been replaced by a focus on sectionalism. And certainly there is lacking the celebratory tone which marked at least some of the early expositions of the argument. But the similarities are in the end more striking than the differences. The 'affluent worker thesis', though largely abandoned as social analysis, is therefore alive and well and doing yeoman service as political analysis.

Whether this new version of the affluent worker thesis, this class decomposition argument, can serve as an historical account is more doubtful. Like the older affluent worker thesis, the current class decomposition hypothesis derives its explanatory power and attractiveness from its apparent ability to link social change and political behaviour. This perspective infuses the study of shifting social structures with ready political import and offers thereby an integrated account that links up changes in working-class life and organization, industrial relations, and politics. The major deficiency in the argument, however, is that it does not in any fashion address the question of how it is that these various aspects of class formation or, as the case may be, decomposition, fit together into a coherent phenomenon. The connection has for the most part been assumed, rather than analysed, and it has taken the form of the assumption that, in Hobsbawm's words, 'the political expression of class consciousness . . . means in practice . . . support for the Labour party'.

Is it really logical, however, to move so quickly from political behaviour back to class structure, and vice versa? Is it valid to make the assumption that 'class consciousness', whatever it might mean, and Labour party support go hand in hand? There is, of course, much in the historical record to justify at least some identification of the working class with its class-based institutions and, especially, with the Labour party. The parallel growth of the class itself, of Friendly Societies, co-operatives and trade unions, of distinctly working-class styles of living, and of the Labour party from before the First World War until

1945–51, suggests a solid, and increasingly close, linkage. But was it ever so close as to allow one to assume a virtual identity between class membership, participation in class-based organizations and support for class politics?

Even the most cursory review of the history of the working class in the twentieth century indicates that one cannot. The timing of the growth of the unions and of Labour party support shows, for example, that there were long periods when workers did not choose to adhere to either, and that it required very special circumstances before the presumed potential of working-class mobilization could be realised in gains for the unions or the party. Fortunately for Labour and for the unions, their failure to attract greater working-class support did not translate into a stable, rooted opposition. Non-unionism as an ideology never took root among the workers and has remained a residual attitude produced by cynicism and incapacity. Likewise, Conservatism has never since the Great War seriously penetrated working-class life, certainly not to an extent that could rival the ties between Labour, the unions and the co-ops, or even the pre-1914 relationship between the working class and the Liberals in many parts of the country. The normal choice facing working people has been between participating in and supporting the labour movement broadly defined or not doing so. A more robust alternative, involving the elaboration of working-class institutions oriented towards Conservatism, has not been on offer, at least until very recently. Conservatism among workers has remained a matter of deference, of local factors like the sectarianism of Liverpool or the unique politics of Birmingham, or of isolated individual decisions.

Despite this lack of serious competition, Labour has rarely been able to command majority status in Parliament and has never achieved it among the electorate. Rather, it has routinely obtained from thirty to forty per cent of the total votes cast. Seen in this light, 1945–51 was more of an aberration than it was the norm in Labour's electoral history. Nevertheless, it has been the record of 1945–51 against which Labour's performance since then has been most often compared. But that achievement was produced by a unique combination of social trends and political events that together swelled Labour's support. Indeed, it appears in the long run that the major effective spurs to class expression in British politics in this century have been the two world wars, which apparently had the effect of creating more space within the political arena for class-based alternatives and stimulating working-class activism at both the industrial and political levels. If one

7

further adds to the record the tensions that have regularly characterized relations between the leaders of Labour as a party and the workers themselves – relations marked frequently by cynicism at the base and contempt at the top – then the assumed link between Labour and the working class becomes still more problematic.

Nor was the history of the unions ever so neatly predetermined as present-day debates imply. Union growth was fitful and uneven; severe decline alternated with rapid growth, and long years of stagnation intervened between successive moments of advance and retreat. Union membership jumped dramatically between 1910 and 1920, fell steadily during the 1920s, stabilized in the early 1930s and grew again from 1935 to 1950; it then stagnated for about a decade and a half before beginning another phase of expansion. No timeless model linking class membership to membership in the unions could make sense of that pattern.

Neither the course of Labour party growth nor of union evolution, therefore, justifies the assumption that class membership results in class organization or class politics. Rather, it suggests that the extent to which the material structures of class are expressed in unions and parties depends upon circumstance. It suggests, too, that the very object of an analytical labour history should probably be the manner in which class formation at work and in community translates into organization and politics. That, at any rate, is the primary object of this study.

In order to address this issue seriously, it is necessary to adopt a quite different approach from that embodied in the current debate. It requires, first, a clear rejection of the temptation for premature synthesis, and a decision to pry apart the analysis of political allegiance from that of economic and social change. That separation will have three efforts upon research, all of which will be evident in this study. First, allowing distinct foci on politics, industrial organization, and social structure, forces a recognition of the complexities and contradictions within each of those spheres. Second, decomposing the final product of class formation reveals the myriad layers of working-class life that intervene between the demographic formation of the class in the urban community or the labour market and the articulation of class interests in politics. These, less overtly political, spheres of daily life not only mediate between class membership and politics, they help to define class and infuse it with meaning. They also provide the bonds that make places of shared work or shared residence into groups and communities, producing a basic connectedness upon which social movements and explicitly political mobilizations can be built.

Lastly, such an approach ensures a direct engagement with the question of how the linkages between different spheres of class existence are made or maintained, and how strong and tight they are. Implicit in the question, of course, is the presumption that at different times the various aspects at which class is lived and understood reinforce one another to varying degrees, producing quite different levels of collective organization and class politics. Separating political and social analysis thus provides an impetus to refocusing study upon the historical processes that link social structure, industrial behaviour, cultural patterns and political allegiance, and upon the extent to which these fit together or pull apart at any given moment. Not only are such processes complicated, they are also constantly changing. Just as the social bases of political behaviour alter, so, too, does the way in which they are related and the strength of the connection. A synthetic picture of working-class life and politics can therefore only be successfully approached when it is understood that in reality there may not be synthesis at all, but rather confusion and dissonance. Unfortunately, both the 'embourgeoisement' thesis and much of the labour history that it subsumes and utilizes assume that such a unitary conception of class structure and politics will suffice.[7]

Such a shift in approach is essential for the twentieth century, for the structure of contemporary politics makes the translation of solidarities based upon economic status and social location into political loyalties a difficult process. There is a gross asymmetry between the resources workers can bring to bear in political struggle and what is needed for success in that struggle. Working-class strength is overwhelmingly local in character, centered in the workplace or the community and best tapped by such forms of collective action as strikes or local elections. Projecting such loyalties into the arena of national politics is not so easy. The national organization of unions may help to 'globalize' locally-rooted solidarities, but the unions have never successfully mediated the two levels. Nor has the Labour party.

The increasing involvement of the central state in the economy and in social services since 1945 has further accentuated the imbalance between the strengths of working people and the requirements of politics. Economic management places great strains on all political actors, and dictates a level of expertise that is not highly compatible with the inefficiencies of democratic process. It also taxes the theoretical apparatus of social movements. Labour is forced not simply to identify enemies and injustices or to propose simple, once-and-for-all reforms, but to develop a plan for economic and social development and a set of devices for overcoming bureaucratic inertia and vested interests.

Labour is at a particular disadvantage on issues of economic management, for while the party remains committed to structural reforms whose benefits are evident over the long term, the standards for judging any government's handling of the economy are inevitably short-term. It was Labour's sad fate to preside over structural changes during 1945–51 that no doubt contributed significantly to the maintenance of full employment during the 1950s, but then to watch from the opposition benches as the Conservatives claimed responsibility for the achievement. The belief that growth depends largely upon the confidence of the capitalists also puts constant pressure upon Labour governments to demonstrate fiscal responsibility.

Of course, even to get into the position to confront these difficulties necessitates the elaboration by a class-based political movement of a programme and a set of leaders that can appeal to a broader spectrum of electors than those united by the local solidarities of unambiguous working-class membership. The victory of 1945, after all, was not won by the mobilization of pure working-class support, but by the mixture of working-class loyalty and substantial, if scattered, instances of middle-class disloyalty to their traditional class party. Some non-working class support is critical also for the implementation of a serious package of reforms. Both to get elected and to rule, therefore, Labour must be more than just a working-class party.[8]

The sum of these difficulties would seem to mean that national politics is likely to be the most unreliable index of class formation, for it is the last level at which changes in social structure would be registered. The reductionist assumptions that have informed the contemporary discussion of class decomposition must, therefore, be jettisoned in favour of a much different perspective. That view would preceed from the recognition that it is most rare for working-class movements to succeed in generalizing local or industrial solidarities into a national political challenge. In trying to understand the evolution of the labour movement into the late twentieth-century, therefore, the most useful analytical procedure might well be to turn around the question most regularly asked of that experience – what social processes have caused or are causing the decline of working-class political consciousness? – and to ask instead what special circumstances allowed for such a close, if temporary, identification between membership in the working class and political support for the

Labour party as obtained in 1945–51 and, second, what has brought about the loosening of that connection since 1950?

Simply posing the problem this way suggests a different and more satisfying rendition of labour's evolution. For the moment, an outline will suffice, the full story left to subsequent chapters. From this new perspective, it appears that in roughly the first half of the century, social processes and political events combined to create a growing bond between the workers and the Labour party. Developments since 1950 have had the effect, not of decomposing the class or making it selfish or into a poor copy of its betters, but of allowing working people greater access to the opportunities and goods produced by an expanding economy. Workers become more full-fledged citizens and this 'integration', if that term be allowed, has made their loyalties to Labour, born originally of *de facto* exclusion from the polity, less habitual and instinctive.[9]

More precisely, the working class grew in numbers, in organization and in political competence consistently from late in the nineteenth century to about 1950 and this increased social presence virtually guaranteed an enhanced political voice as well. But during the same period neither of the two established parties – the Liberals or Conservatives – could wrench itself from its class moorings to become the party of the workers. Labour became the vehicle of workers' entry into the polity, and the hostility of the Conservatives and the incoherence of the Liberals meant that there was little genuine competition for the working-class vote. Labour also had the political good fortune not to be identified with the horrors of the Great War, the agony of the slump (after 1931, at least), the foreign policy blunders of the late 1930s or the ineffective prosecution of the Second World War in 1939–40. By 1935, they were the party of the working-class, demobilized and demoralized though the class was at that time. In the next decade they became the party of an increasingly organized and vital working class and, of great importance, of those numerous members of the middle classes determined to discard the old ways of the Tories.

The rise of Labour was based, therefore, primarily upon the formation and self-activity of the working class. It took the form it did, that of an independent political party, largely because of the failure of the established parties. Having established itself by the Second World War as the carrier of workers' interest, however, the Labour party proceeded to become as well the party of national progress behind which many non-working-class voters could unite. For a brief moment, the class interest of workers in social reform and the national interest in reconstruction were united by an implicitly Keynesian programme serving as both economic and political theory. The essence of that programme, as T. H. Marshall perceived at the time, was the extension of citizenship from the realm of politics and civic equality to matters social and economic, which is another way of saying from the upper and middle classes to the workers.[10]

The 'social democratic synthesis' was thus less a blueprint for the new society than a plan for increasing popular participation in what already existed, and for removing the worst penalties previously attached to membership in the working class. Of course, merely beginning to open Britain's class-ridden society to working people was a major feat, and the difficulties faced by social democrats in effecting this opening up – e.g., the long and tortuous battle over the reform of education – proves that it marked a decisive break with the past. Nevertheless, the essence of the achievements of 1945–51, particularly as they worked themselves out over the two decades following, was the granting of effective rights of social citizenship to working people: rights to decent medical care, to genuine literacy, to decent pensions, to jobs, to organize and bargain collectively and, finally, when these elementary needs were satisfied, to participate more thoroughly in the leisure and consumption made possible by their labours.

Inevitably, though, this meant a gradual diminishing of those invidious distinctions that had so long characterized Britain's class structure and that had come for many to embody the very meaning of class. The working class began slowly to be transformed from a set of largely self-contained communities into a more complex assortment of working-class citizens. Class inequalities and antagonisms remained, and class-based struggles at work actually intensified, but many of the markings by which class was symbolized became less visible.

These exterior markings, of course, had helped to impart a common identity to workers, an identity that was based upon a shared exclusion and to which Labour politicians had had frequent recourse before 1950. As this identity faded, the inherited rhetoric of Labour became less meaningful, and the weaknesses in its programme became more apparent as well. Even in the best of times, Labour fudged critical issues of policy and was never united on a detailed vision of the future. Partly because of this, the Labour Party has received solid, but often quite unenthusiastic, support from the majority of the workers during most of its history. And the cynicism of the workers was reciprocated by the aloofness and at times hectoring contempt of their leaders. However firmly anchored in the institutions and life of the class,

Labour remained an ambiguous projection of the culture, interests and aspirations of the workers into politics. Working-class scepticism was strong even in 1945, and Labour's penchant since then for calling upon its keenest supporters for the greatest sacrifices has constantly justified at least than degree of detachment.

Whatever the causes, it was clear by 1948, or at the latest 1951, that the 'social democratic synthesis' had began to crack. Much of Labour's programme had been enacted in its first four years of office and the basis of reconstruction laid. By the 1950s Labour ceased to offer a compelling reformist vision or even a clear alternative to the Tories. Its middle-class supporters soon began to swing back and forth between Labour and the Conservatives depending on the fickle perceptions of the moment, and its working-class base to alternate between abstention and reluctant support. This was not due, however, to the disintegrating effect of social change upon class structure. Rather, from 1950 until the mid-1970s, Britain exhibited a pattern of structural change whose undiluted political effect could well have been to maintain, or possibly to increase, Labour support.[11] For example, the maintenance of full employment and the moderate pace of growth cushioned the impact of industrial shifts upon the economy, the occupational structure and working-class communities. This allowed trade unions – the main correlate of Labour Party voting – to adapt to the changing composition of the working class and to maintain and even slightly increase their membership.

Two other major structural changes effected by postwar economic development, the increase in women's paid employment and the proliferation of white-collar jobs, also resulted in trade union growth. The introduction of women into industry did not, in most cases, lead to a decrease in union density, as many had feared, and although the substitution of women for men has been associated with a decline in average clerical earnings, it did not prevent the spread of organization into these types of employment. On the contrary, white-collar unionization grew in a close relation to the increase in the white collar workers generally from 1948 to approximately 1965 and then, during the late 1960s and early 1970s, took a giant leap forward to encompass over 39% of non-manual employees by 1974, an increase of a third from the level of 1964.[12]

The deepening of organization throughout society, coupled with the resiliency of working-class values but mixed, too, with a measure of increased expectations, led to substantial increases in trade union militancy that came in the waves of strikes of 1957–62 and 1968–72 and that has yet to truly subside even in the depressed years that have followed. The Labour Party, however, has had little to offer in the way of a political programme for the realization of workers' enhanced sense of collective and personal worth. They have been lukewarm at best to the spread of shopfloor organization and antipathetic towards what they see as troublesome wage claims. Towards the numerical strengthening of the unions they have been more favourably disposed, for obvious reasons, but towards the necessary accoutrements of union power – the independent power of shop stewards, the increase of industrial democracy, the politicization and democratization of corporate decisions – they have by and large not been sympathetic. In place of encouragement have come a flawed incomes policy, a restrictive industrial relations bill, and a savage deflation dictated by the International Monetary Fund and administered by the most recent Labour government.

In retrospect, what is surprising about this contradiction between the trends of social change, opinion and action among working people, and the inert (or worse) response of the Labour party is not that it has led to a weakening of the ties between Labour and the working class and, thus, between the direction of class formation and the evolution of politics. Much more surprising is the residual strength of the relationship, and the fact that so many working people still hope and work for a party that has so often failed to live up to the hopes and needs of its supporters.

The main causes of this growing lack of correspondence between social structure and political allegiance or, more precisely, between the possibilities inherent in the shifting social structure and their actual crystallization or mobilization in politics, would seem to be two. First, there are those many features of modern politics that make it so very hard to translate local, or even individual, working-class interests into reforming alternatives that can command support from stable majorities. These are particularly constraining in the absence of the sort of national crisis, such as the two world wars, that has been the precondition for major realignments in this century. Second, the Labour party itself has not grasped the meaning of the changes affecting working-class life since the war, let alone fashioned a programme to reflect them. Such a programme would necessarily have to be based upon a frank recognition of the achievement of genuine citizenship by most working people and of the altered industrial, occupational, regional and sexual composition of the working class, and then proceed to elaborate an appeal based upon the political possibilities and interests of this reconstituted working class. This Labour has clearly failed to do, or at least to do effectively.

In short, the key problem in the twentieth-century history of the British working class has been in properly connecting up the different social levels at which class operates with the political representation of class interests. The shifting connection between the workers, their unions and the party thus helps to explain both the rise of Labour in the years up to 1950 and its apparent decline since then. It also suggests that present political problems are more or less what they seem – political difficulties politically determined and capable, at least in theory, of political resolution. They are not, it seems safe to say, reflections of the declining saliency of class, for if the following chapters show anything, they show the continuing need to place class at the centre of the analysis of the history of British society.

PART ONE
Class Formation and Confrontation

2

The Moment of Insurgency, 1917–20

The First World War changed everything it touched. Apart from the obvious and terrible toll of lost lives, it also toppled governments, ravished economies and re-oriented the consciousness of a generation of Europeans. In Britain, it marked the definitive closing of the Victorian era and the real beginning of the twentieth century. The break was evident in the economy and in the social structure, in government, in literature and the arts, but nowhere was it quite so visible as in the relations between the working class and the rest of society.

The Labour Party, born as the Labour Representation Committee at the turn of the century, had foundered until 1914. The unions, on the defensive since the engineers' defeat in the strike of 1897–8 and the Taff Vale judgement of 1899, had only just begun to grow again during the unrest that preceded the outbreak of war. During the war, however, momentum swung back to the workers and their institutions. The privations of war, the changed balanced within industry and such intangibles as the Russian Revolution and revulsion at the war itself, combined to produce a massive insurgency by 1917–18. That insurgency posed a fundmental challenge to British society. Its broad dimensions betokened the depth of the underlying social antagonisms; while its resolution shaped the course of social relations for a generation or more. The character and consequences of the militancy of 1917–20 thus repay careful attention, and will provide the entry point for this study.

Nothing better suggests the novel quality of the postwar explosion than the reactions of contemporaries, high and low. Since the vantage point from above affords a broader view, it is best to start there. And since the most volatile centre of working-class protest was on the Clyde, perceptions there provide a useful introduction to the reactions of polite society generally. On January 27th, 1919, the *Glasgow Herald* commented on the engineers' strike then in progress. The editors assured readers that the strikers were extremists 'opposed by the great majority of the engineers'. But the argument soon lapsed into dire pessimism: 'Unhappily, the signs of volcanic fire are omnipresent. The country gets deliverance from one trouble only to find itself confronted by others even more complicated and menacing.'[1] Like this anonymous editor, the British establishment as a whole were confused and disturbed by the events of 1919 and 1920. Few would credit the actual possibility of revolution, but faith in the 'sanity of labour' experienced repeated shocks. If no genuine revolution were in the offing, surely some major change seemed to be, and the prospect was deeply unsettling. In the strengthened and aroused labour movement, authorities were confronted with a force that would have to be engaged, and the outcome of the engagement simply could not be foreseen with any confidence.[1]

The sense of crisis was echoed by elites all over the country. A meeting of the North London Manufacturers' Association on July 16, 1918 was told, for example, that 'the industrial system in this country, as we knew it in July 1914, has been suspended'; moreover, it was 'unlikely to be reestablished without modification of a far-reaching nature'. Specifically, 'no part of our pre-war industrial system is more likely to be radically changed in design and practice after the war than the relationship between employers and employed'. Though not all employers were so conciliatory, most did share the belief of one large industrialist that 'the question uppermost in the minds of all Britain to-day . . . is whether, now that the Germans are beaten, there shall be peace or war in industry'.[2]

For men of business, the problem was made more acute by the realization that British industry was ill-equipped to compete in the export markets of the postwar world. Britain's industrial retardation was visible before the war, but prospects after the war were much worse. F. Dudley Docker, first President of the Federation of British Industries, predicted 'that competition in trade will be keener than it has ever been before'. The incentives to evolve 'sound and amicable relations . . . between Capital and Labour' were therefore both political and crudely economic. It was in the national interest to boost 'the produce of labour', and so to reform industrial relations as well. The means to attaining labour's cooperation in production were by no means obvious, however. Not only were workers demanding higher wages, greater control at the workplace, the nationalization of coal and other industries, and a host of social reforms connected with housing, health and employment; in addition, they exhibited a frightening taste for 'direct action' in implementing these goals, a distrust of the political process and a marked independence from any formal leadership.[3]

As Lloyd George's trusted adviser Tom Jones explained in February 1919, 'Much of the present difficulty springs from the mutiny of the rank and file against the old established leaders and there seems to be no machinery for bringing about a quick change of leaders.' The situation was especially troubling to men like Jones and Lloyd George, who had expended considerable effort in building links to the leaders of the unions, only to learn that their labour friends were unable to deliver the allegiance of the membership. As Churchill lamented in February of 1919, 'The curse of trade unionism was that *there was not enough of it*, and it was not highly enough developed to make its branch secretaries [let alone its rank and file] fall into line with the head office.'[4]

The crisis within industry was in this sense a crisis of authority. The men were aggrieved and the restraints of moderate trade unionism were absent. The Government was much dismayed by the situation and by their inability to control discontent. The Minister of Labour worried openly, 'The problem of the basis of the authority of trade union leaders has become a very real one . . .'

The Government's concern was reflected in the analysis of Basil Thomson, director of intelligence in Scotland. His report, 'Revolutionary Feeling during the Year 1919', for example, contained a list of eight powerful factors producing unrest that were only weakly offset by a few stabilizing influences. Among the 'causes which contribute to revolutionary feelings' were:

> Profiteering and high prices . . ., Insufficient and bad housing
> accommodation . . . Class hatred, aggravated by the foolish and
> dangerous ostentation of the rich, the publication of large
> dividends, and distrust of a 'Government of profiteers'.

Balancing these disturbing forces were 'Popularity of the Royal Family . . , Sport' and several lesser factors, none of which seemed capable of providing proper ballast for the ship of state.[5]

What looked from on high to be an absence of order was experienced by those below as a major increment of freedom and self-confidence. The period witnessed an explosion of organization. Overall union membership doubled, rank-and-file activity flourished. An engineering worker from Sheffield remembers how the men in the shops took to the election of shop stewards in 1916: the drive 'went like wildfire. The rank and file knew they were divorced from the officials and that the officials were linked with the Government so far as the war was concerned. The rank and file wanted to express themselves and this was their medium.' Trades councils, cooperatives, and local Labour Parties also grew as never before. Perhaps the most threatening were the Councils of Action that sprang up during the summer of 1920 to protest against plans for intervention in Russia. Even after the prospect of intervention faded, these organs 'would not go away', and instead 'took on a life of their own'.[6]

Such organized strength served to stimulate workers' sense of solidarity and antagonism. As Carter Goodrich noted, the shop stewards 'exercised the greatest degree of control ever held by British workers . . .', and the 'movement was both an expression of the demand for control and an incitement to further demands'. Even a moderate like J.R. Clynes, Labour's leader in Parliament, grasped that 'Labour has been curiously elevated by the demands of war'. The elevation of labour involved not merely an increase in organization but also a transformation of outlook. With greater resources at their disposal, workers' expectations quickly caught up with the expanding limits of their collective power. Of course, the new awareness contained many elements inherited from the past, but its tone and depth were very different. 'Within the lower or broader stages of society', W.A. Orton explained, 'there had been growing for nearly a century a sullen "class-consciousness" founded, for what it was worth, almost entirely on a community of economic disabilities.' By 1918, the disabilities were being matched by sources of strength and the sullen demeanour of labour was becoming more assertive. The context in which this occurred also ensured that the new vision expressed itself in class terms. Thus a Ministry of Labour official discerned in February 1920 an 'increasing tendency for the trade unionists of one shop works or small districts to act together, irrespective of their division into crafts or occupations. What is called "class consciousness" is obliterating the distinction between those who follow different occupations in the same works.'[7]

It is difficult to gauge precisely how much this expanded sense of class differed from pre-war views. It is possible, however, to point to considerable evidence on the structural evolution of the class in the late nineteenth and early twentieth centuries, indicating a waxing of class sentiments. Furthermore, these structural trends were accentuated during the war to produce an intensification of attitudes and activities based upon class.

Briefly, it appears that a variety of technical, social and economic processes combined to create a working class that was, if not more internally homogeneous, at least somewhat less sharply divided within itself, and also more culturally distinct from middle and upper class society, than its Victorian analogue had been. These same forces also strengthened the capacity of different groups of workers to organize and press their interests in collective fashion. The most visible consequence was the steady spread of union organization beyond the relatively small stratum of workers who were unionized in mid-Victorian Britain, to include increasing numbers of the less skilled.

Three distinct sets of changes reshaped the working class. First, the service sector, in which most workers were 'semi-skilled', expanded significantly. Second, developments within manufacturing led to an increasing demand for semi-skilled, as opposed to either skilled or unskilled labour. Third, the social ecology of mid-Victorian cities slowly gave way to a more socially segregated pattern of residence, creating a physical space for the development of a distinctive working-class culture embedded in a broad array of social and political institutions.[8]

Taken together, these changes in the workplace and the community enabled working people to organize themselves in the industrial and political spheres far more effectively than before 1890. This increase in the collective clout of workers, especially in unions, provoked in turn efforts at counter-mobilization from employers that forced people to broaden their efforts still more. By 1914, therefore, unions had been created to service the needs of the bulk of the workers in the major industries, and the unions, largely from self-defence, had created the shell at least of the modern Labour party.

The war brought with it a consolidation, and in some instances an acceleration, of those long-term developments promoting organization. It also created conditions more immediately favourable to the growth of the unions and the Labour party, and to the general intensification of class-based politics. Just how much class feelings were strengthened can be seen very clearly in the remarkable outpouring of books and articles that sought to ascertain just what it was that was agitating 'the worker's mind' after the war.

In reviewing this material, it is perhaps best to begin again with the view from above or, more precisely, from someone quite unsympathetic to the workers' novel pretensions. Lynden Macassey, KC, 'an experienced industrial arbitrator' who boasted participation in 'some three thousand close and intimate conferences during the war with employers' organizations, Trade Union executives, district and branch committees, together with many mass meetings – at all of which careful notes were taken . . .' and who served on various commissions concerned with labour during and after the war, set out in 1922 to define *Labour Policy–False and True*. His notes on the 'outlook of the worker' bespeak a deep frustration at his increasing independence of mind. He complains of British workers' 'appalling ignorance of economic matters . . .', which produces in them numerous 'misconceptions as to Wages'. 'The average workman thought, [even] before the war, that his employer was always able to raise his rate of wages . . . and that only the employer's selfishness stood in the way . . . .' With the war, this opinion became ingrained and no amount of reasoning could make workers grasp 'the futility of the mad race of prices after wages'.

Yet Macassey also understood that the unrest was one of those 'convulsive movements' that 'generally register a forward march' in human welfare. Workers were better educated than ever before and shared 'a new vision' containing both 'aspirations for improvement of material conditions . . .' and a 'desire for mental and cultural improvement'. Nonetheless, they were misled by socialists into believing that the 'denial . . . of a human status in industry' was 'caused by the capitalist organization of industry'. In consequence, 'The strongest sentiment . . . permeating the workshops' was a quite unjustified 'suspicion of employers'.[9]

What disturbed Macassey was more sympathetically observed by others. One was Arthur Gleason, an American journalist of socialist inclinations. A review of labour's public and private utterances convinced him that 'the workers will no longer work for unrestricted "private enterprise", with its profits for a small group, its competing interests . . ., its failure to install modern machinery and to use scientific research, its underpay, overwork, bad housing, preventable accidents, proletarian disease, and its negation of constitutional government in industry'. He believed, as a *Times* leader had recently argued, that 'we are already passing through a social revolution'. However divergent their politics, Macassey's description and Gleason's distillation of opinion concurred in several respects. Both sensed that workers were interested in more than wages, that their list of grievances had been extended and linked to a thorough-going critique of society, and that their political beliefs had come to colour their attitude toward work itself. Gleason adds a further twist, suggesting that workers had become aware of management's reluctance to modernize. The implication is that workers' propensity to output restriction, or 'ca'canny,' was in part a response to the employers' own technological backwardness.[10]

The attitudes picked up by Macassey and Gleason also find their way into Whiting Williams's account of his travels through industrial Britain in the summer of 1920. Most of the tour was taken up with lengthy visits to Wales and Scotland, both hotbeds of left wing sentiment, and his report naturally reflects the militancy of these regions. But even in London, Middlesborough, Barnsley and Sheffield, discontent was very evident. An eminently reasonable smelter in Middlesborough, for instance, felt that 'we must have a new system of society for this one reason: *Management and Capital just can't be trusted*'. A miner from Barnsley agreed: 'Masters and men have come to such a point of suspicion and misunderstanding that the mining industry is at a dead standstill. The only way out is nationalization – an entirely new stand all the way 'round.' In nearby Sheffield, a local official confessed that 'every labour leader 'as to suffer from the distrust of his men', and estimated that among workers locally, 'the majority is more for political action – also, of course, direct action'.[11]

Feelings ran deeper still in Glasgow. The streets there rang with a 'continuous appeal to the "working class" . . . . Everywhere, up and down and across at all times, the current explanation, alibi, or appeal appears to be made in terms of class interests and differences.' An engineer complained, 'It's our government that's betrayin' [us]', while a woman of the working class commented, 'The Kaiser whom we licked buys himself a castle. And you and I of the working classes that licked him, and put our bodies between him and Britain's homes – we have not where to lay our heads.'[12]

The peculiarly brutish conditions of Glasgow – the intolerable housing, the legacy of wartime repression and no doubt the Scottish question itself – imparted to class relations there a nastiness and bitterness that was absent in South Wales, that other centre of revolutionary sentiment. Most striking in Wales was the democratic style of dissent. 'In this country the members do run our unions, they do', claimed an older worker. 'We [all stand] together, we do, and we 'as no "black-legs" amongst [us]!' In this context, agitation took a more open form. Williams reports on the extraordinary atmosphere inside the pits: 'For all day down in the headings 1,000 feet below it has been little but a succession of Bolshevist meetings.' A group of miners 'at the

25

face near us were either arguing lustily or singing most of the day about the beauty of the "red flag of revolution" to the tune of "Maryland, my Maryland."' This ferment obviously won many converts for the left. 'Of one hundred men [you'll] meet 'ere in South Wales – at least among the colliers . . . [you'll] find nine and ninety Socialists', claimed one union man. Inevitably, quite a few of the ninety-nine were socialists only for the moment, but it seems the commitment of many was reinforced by at least a rudimentary social analysis. As one young miner boasted, 'Studying and reading we are, so now we're fit and ready to govern . . . We 'ave classes in Marx and all the others right 'ere and now we're ready to take over the job of runnin' the country. First off, we must make the company by 'ere so much trouble that they will give over the mines to the government.'[13]

Underpinning these sentiments was the more basic sense that workers now had more power and strength: the war, one explained, had awakened the worker to his tremendous power. Put more elegantly, 'the w'ip of the [masters], 'tis [that] we be makin' shorter now and this be the [way] to fight 'um, through the lessenin' of output'. Output was indeed a crucial issue, and the miners' ability to restrict it implies an impressive degree of control at the point of production. Miners themselves regulated the pace of work and provided whatever discipline existed. 'Oh, we've got the owners so scared here they don't trouble us, and it's just our good consciences that [makes] us work at all', explained one. Another told of a manager who had to go way, 'fair sick and like to die o' worry [of] it all with the Bolshies and all, these months'.[14]

The workers also seemed to feel that, by their reluctance to invest in new equipment, the employers had somehow forfeited the right to ask for full cooperation from the men. The head of a rank-and-file committee believed that 'We've all been too busy talkin' wages, wages. But now we're seeing that more wages is impossible unless the masters will do away with some of their obsolete works.' Among both the miners and iron and steel workers, there was frequent complaining that 'most of our mines and steel plants here are pretty old-fashioned and backward', and a sense that, without investment in up-to-date technology, there was nothing for the worker to do but treat the job as 'a form of property'.[15]

Williams, an outsider from America, was certainly not capable of picking up the subtleties of meaning in many of these remarks. But the sincerity of the attempt can hardly be doubted, and the rough fit between his and other accounts suggests that the broad outlines of each were essentially correct. And they show that by 1919–20 large numbers of workers had an intense class awareness that encompassed an elementary critique of capitalism as a social system, a sense that reasonable alternatives existed, and a confidence that labour was solid and strong enough to bring about major change. This accords, too, with the estimates of Scotland Yard that in 1919, 'the number (of workers) who are determined to have a revolution by constitutional means is certainly increasing' and that, by 1920, those who sought social revolution of some sort had become a majority.[16]

The picture that emerges from Macassey, Gleason, Williams and Basil Thomson of Scotland Yard was confirmed in an unusually detailed inquiry into working-class life in Sheffield. It appeared in 1919 with the unalluring title, *The Equipment of the Workers*. It was produced by a voluntary society in Sheffield, and the actual author was Arnold Freeman, head of the St Philip's settlement. His aim was an 'interrogation of the future' involving an assessment of 'what the workers are capable of doing' and of 'what, later on, they are likely to do'. The investigators assumed, as current scholars seem only recently to have learned, that the cause of unrest was neither 'class-hostility' nor material poverty, but rather 'a spiritual stirring . . . for a life bigger than was bounded by twelve hours in a factory followed by supper and sleep in a slum'.[17]

The inquiry went on to determine that, among the manual workers, about one-quarter were 'well-equipped', nearly three-quarters 'inadequately-equipped', and a small portion, about one in fifteen, positively 'mal-equipped'. The terms of this classification are as quaint as they are objectionable, but what is important is how the totals add up. The overwhelming majority were in either of the two top groups. More than 90% of the workers were judged either very aware of their environment and its potential, or at least capable of achieving such a level of personal competence. Only a small fraction were beyond hope. Despite its tone, the *Equipment of the Workers* was far more sensitive to the intelligence running through working-class attitudes than almost all earlier studies of poverty and social life.[18]

The core of the survey involved interviews with 816 working-class men and women, divided by age and occupation in much the same way as the total working population of Sheffield. From these were derived a summary of workers' political attitudes and a detailed picture of their daily lives, and the published volume reproduces sufficient data to bring these together and to suggest what sorts of people held various kinds of politics. Because the interviewing occurred at just about the time that the Government's Commission on Industrial Unrest was conducting its hearings, moreover, a sub-sample of thirty adult males, ten each from engineering, mining and the railways, was devised to compare their attitudes with those recorded in the Commission's report. These results give the flavour of the larger set of interviews, and may serve as an introduction.

'To a man', the report asserted, 'the colliers [were] "fed up" with the war . . .', and 'talk of revolution was quite common among workers'. Similarly, 'All ten of the railwaymen were utterly sick of the War . . .' Industrially, there was 'general distrust of both the companies and the Government', and several prophesied 'trouble ahead': 'If trouble was to break out anywhere on the railways, I can tell you it would spread like wildfire'. The engineers also were angry at the war though not about to oppose it actively. But their political sentiments were clear: 'only one pooh-poohed any talk of a Revolution. Among the other nine the debatable question was whether it would come during or after the War.' 'Revolution is in the air', claimed one; another concurred: 'The men want to have a complete revolution in the present system. . . . Everybody I've met up to now in the last few weeks has spoken that way. . . . They're not so bothered about the War as about the Revolution. . . .'

Disaffection of this sort was extremely widespread among the working people of South Yorkshire. Thus, the main report was forced to conclude that:

> . . . the Well-equipped men and women workers (about one-fourth of the whole) will be intelligently determined, beyond all possibility of statesmanlike denial, to achieve extremely far-reaching changes in the existing civilization; and that the inadequately-equipped workers (comprising the bulk of the remainder), without knowing definitely what they want, and without much willingness for self-discipline and patient endeavour, will violently react against a continuance of the pre-War industrial and social order or of any approximation to it.

These findings contradicted the comforting illusion of the middle and upper classes that discontent found its breeding ground among the poor and those least capable of resisting. Rather, those labelled 'well-equipped' by the rigorous standards of the St Philip's Settlement would certainly have been among the most competent of their class, and their politics were the most left wing. Take Mrs Leaning, a

24-year-old machinist working in a shell factory, whose husband was at the front. Fond of her home and family, she felt that 'nine women out of ten work against their feelings, chiefly because the work is too hard and coarse'. As for politics, she seldom had the time or energy, but when asked her view of Socialism responded that it was 'the greatest and best movement in the whole world. The only hope of the working-classes.' Or Mrs Quarles, aged 28 and a housewife. Knowledgeable and active in local affairs, a member of the Women's Liberal Association, she was no radical, Socialists being in her view 'rather wild and unbalanced people but harmless'. Nevertheless, she was convinced that 'there is likely to be in the near future *Control of Industry by the Democracy*; the workers will never consent to return to pre-War conditions; the wage-system is doomed'.

The 'well-equipped men' exhibited much the same attitudes but were, on the whole, even more active in and integrated into unions, WEA classes and co-ops. Mr Dalson, an engine tester of 27, had been a member of the National Union of General Workers for five years, and 'booms the [Co-operative] Movement at every opportunity'. As for Socialism, he professed to believe that it was 'The only means of establishing the "Kingdom of God" on earth.' A 35-year-old fitter named Youngson was less of an activist but no less militant or self-confident. He had not long before moved to Sheffield from Middlesbrough, where he was actively engaged in the trade union movement. His rent was recently increased but he had refused to pay, and so was now given notice to quit. Nevertheless, he was proud of his home and relatively happy at his work. In politics, he was a committed socialist: 'I disagree entirely with the present constitution, and would abolish the House of Lords' and much else. Socialism was 'The only way for us', and he very much hoped that the present 'trials' would 'awaken' the workers 'to the power they possess'.

Not all of the 'well-equipped' were so articulate, and the views of the not so well equipped were more confused still. And, of course, labour in Sheffield was probably more 'advanced' in 1917 than elsewhere. It had certainly a more developed working-class cultural and institutional life. Nonetheless, the compilers of the Sheffield report were much impressed by the fact that such large numbers of the 'better' workers were possessed of a definite and radical vision of present ills and future solutions, and that this group was strategically located to move the whole class towards that vision. They assumed as well, not unreasonably, that roughly similar processes were having comparable effects throughout Britain. The result could only be a body of 'well-equipped' men and women intent upon social transformation. The report noted loftily:

> Eight millions of workers, each of them effective in trade union, co-operative society, local and national politics; all of them . . . increasingly homogeneous in their political and industrial purposes; these men and women will be the makers of English history from 1920 to 1950; upon a bridge made of their stalwart backs our children will cross from the shame and wretchedness of today to the Land in which the dreams of humanity are coming true.[19]

In sum, these reports on working-class sentiment at the end of the war suggest that a genuine transformation of outlook had occurred. In contrast to the conventional picture of a defensive, resentful class, they portray working people optimistic and quite confident of their own potential. There was still, to be sure, a dose of cynicism, but less of the fatalism that others have found to characterize the pre-war mood of the workers. There are still those who believed 'that tomorrow will in all probability be very like today', still those who, like Will Thorne, 'suffered much in mind and soul just thinking of tomorrow and tomorrow's "morrow", and perhaps many more who feared that this was true. But after the war there seems to have emerged an overwhelming sense that things could and must change.[20]

This expanded sense of the possible was combined with a much enhanced idea of the competence of ordinary people, particularly in relation to the diminished respect that existed for employers and the government. The workers' critique of management for incompetence, lack of interest in productivity and refusal to invest, was especially striking. While such ideas could have been picked up from the broader public discussion of war production, it seems more often to have grown out of the workplace itself, where workers' power had registered a major advance and where working-class capacities and employer incompetence were daily contrasted. The need for workers' control was widely asserted, and captured the imagination of guild socialists, shop stewards, advocates of Whitleyism, and various industrial reformers. G.D.H. Cole, writing in 1919, was so impressed as to claim 'that, so far as the Labour Movement is concerned, the internal battle for the idea of workers' control of industry has been fought and won'.[21]

It would be easy to exaggerate the differences between the workers before and after the war. The men and women who described their daily rounds and personal preferences in *The Equipment of Workers* were very much of a piece with those described by others before the war. There was the same belief in self-respect and improvement, the same concern with home and family, the same ambivalence towards education and the same resentment against the outside world. The church was no more popular, even after the traumas of the Great War, and the pub no less so. The 'pictures' were beginning to compete with the music hall, especially among the young, but cultural patterns were basically the same.

It appears, therefore, that the secular, self-contained working-class culture that was taking root before 1914 was greatly consolidated during the war. Yet in becoming more solid and in coping with the changed external conditions, it became far less defensive than it had been. It thus evolved from being a source of sustenance and protection into a basis of strength and, indeed, of actual organizing and resistance. For this reason, the militancy of 1917–20 transcended the issues of wages and prices and dilution and even war itself. It was, more than any previous or subsequent unrest, a mobilization of the workers as a class and of their institutions and neighbourhoods. It was this that accounted for its breadth and resiliency, its tendency to spill over the boundaries of normal industrial action, its unique ability to involve women as well as men, and its political dimensions.

This helps to explain, moreover, the prominence of protest based in the community both during and after the war. In fact, the labour movement derived considerable strength from the combination of industrial unrest with actions over issues of consumption, which inevitably drew in large numbers of working-class women. Entire communities rose up in protest against exorbitant food prices, rent increases and shortages of food and housing. Tenants' associations mushroomed, and the struggle over housing from 1915 to 1924 meant an effective end to privately-owned accommodation for the working class, even if it did not yet guarantee the provision of an alternative. In this agitation, women were especially prominent, being regularly appointed as the 'street captains' in rent strikes, for example. In Glasgow, Coventry, Woolwich, Rosyth and elsewhere this community-based insurgency merged momentarily with more purely industrial action.[22]

Women also brought their consumer consciousness and enthusiasm into efforts at industrial organization. The spread of unionization during the war was more rapid among women than among any group of men, and as the war progressed, women took an increasing part in strikes. The task of bringing women into the labour movement was shared by the general unions – the National Union of General and Municipal Workers and the Workers' Union – and the National Federation of Women Workers, which had links with existing unions of men, especially the Amalgamated Society of Engineers. Together, they accounted for most of the increase of 750,000, or 270%, in the number of women in unions during 1914–18.

Their approaches were quite different, however, for the general unions were interested in permanently organizing women workers, while the NFWW was willing to accept the prospect of women retreating from industry at the end of the war. Indeed, the Federation made a formal agreement with the ASE to this effect in 1915, simultaneously agreeing to the male engineers' demands to maintain control of the industry and acquiring an important ally in their efforts to organize, particularly in munitions. Paradoxically, the NFWW committed itself immediately to the demand for equal pay, for this guaranteed that women would not replace men in skilled jobs. Activists among the Workers' Union, by contrast, perceived that parity could only be maintained at the expense of women's employment. Nevertheless, as the war progressed and organization expanded, the demand for equal pay took on a more practical aspect and became much more widespread – by 1918 it was part of the panoply of demands embraced by the labour movement as a whole. Arguments about the possible loss of employment opportunities seem to have been ignored, and working women chose to merge their demands with those of men in a programme that at least implicitly identified women's concerns for community and consumption with the interests of the class.[23]

The role of the government during the war both facilitated and reflected the broadening of local and sectional grievances into class antagonisms. By intervening so drastically in the economy, the state ensured that protest over consumption would be directed against itself; and by providing a focus for discontent outside the workplace and the neighbourhood, the government bypassed sectional styles of protest. The Commission on Industrial Unrest of 1917 noted the critical nature of the state's new ties to society in stimulating industrial and community protest. 'The War', according to one Commissioner, 'has introduced a new element into questions affecting Labour, viz., the Government.' More precisely, 'the Munitions of War Acts . . . revolutionized industry', making the state responsible for what went on inside the factory. The 'trade union world' was thus 'in a state of flux and ferment'. By asserting the social control of production during wartime, the government guaranteed a debate about the nature of control after the war had ended; by showing the feasibility of alternatives to the prewar, private organization of society, the state encouraged a rethinking of the possible forms of social organization; and by not managing its intervention into the war economy as equitably and efficiently as a more socially neutral and responsive regime could have, it ensured that the decisions over the shape of the future would be made in the course of violent industrial battles.[24]

The political dimension of labour militancy thus found its ultimate reflection in the form which confrontation generally took. Though a few strikes were fought out between the two sides of industry pure and simple, as in textiles and engineering, the major turning points in the unrest all involved employers, workers *and* the state. Inevitably, the state was drawn into all conflicts before the Armistice. Its actions were directly responsible for the engineering strikes of 1915 on the Clyde and in May 1917 throughout the country, while its ban on strikes had to be reconciled with the strikes of miners and textile operatives. Despite the thrust towards 'decontrol', the state remained a critical factor in the most important postwar contests as well. The Glasgow engineers' strike of January-February, 1919 led to swift intervention, made more urgent by the fact that at almost the same moment, the government was confronted with a possible national strike in the mines over nationalization. Again Lloyd George intervened and appointed the Sankey Commission which in March issued a preliminary report supporting the claims of the men. Lulled into inactivity, the miners were shocked when the Prime Minister refused to accept Sankey's final recommendations in August. By this time, the moment to strike had passed and the Miners' Federation turned instead to a political – note political, not industrial – campaign over 'mines for the Nation', launched officially on December 9th.

Government kept being drawn into conflicts outside the mines as well. In August 1919 the police strike was defeated and the union proscribed. Workers remained on the offensive throughout 1919, however, and forced the government to back down during the railway strike in late September and early October. This strike showed the enormous power of the railwaymen to cripple the nation's economic life and the difficulty of extricating the government from industrial matters. The state continued to be involved in the major disputes of 1920. The 'Hands Off Russia' agitation in the summer was sparked by and aimed at government policy, and even Jimmy Thomas regarded the threatened general strike as a 'challenge to the whole Constitution of the country'. This was followed in the autumn by yet another clash with the miners, leading to the 'datum line' strike on October 16th. Within the week, the railwaymen had resolved to come out in support and the third leg of the Triple Alliance, the transport workers, seemed on the verge of doing so as well. The government responded on the one hand with the Emergency Powers Act, giving itself authority to requisition supplies and transportation and to set up courts of summary jurisdiction, and on the other by negotiating a deal very favourable to the miners on October 28.

As late as the end of 1920, therefore, the state had failed either to decisively defeat the unions or to pull back from industrial affairs. In addition, the apparent effectiveness of the threat of a general strike called by the Triple Alliance actually increased the sense of power and the expectations of the rank-and-file. Soon expectations would be deflated and events would teach workers the underlying weakness of their position, but it was a measure of the depth of the militancy of 1917–20 that it took until 1926 to accomplish this stabilization and, as Sir Philip Gibbs put it, to 'get the working classes back to their kennels'. Even then, the defeat was incomplete and labour would eventually resume the offensive. The outburst of unrest and the explosion of class sentiments that greeted the end of the war were too deeply rooted, too massive, too potent for any return to normal in political or industrial life. Order might well be restored, but it would have to be on a new basis.[25]

3

The Politics and Economics of Stabilization in the 1920s

. . . industry is now too far gone to secure public confidence. The workers of the industrial world may still for some years bear with the existing situation, but they no longer believe that it is inevitable; their faith in the competence of the controllers is shaken, and they no longer fear the dangers with which they used to be threatened . . . . Fear . . . was one of the greatest forces for the maintenance of output in the industrial system: but the workers no longer fear . . ., for they are organized, and even those who should use the lash have lost heart.

C. Delisle Burns, *The Principles of Revolution* (1920)

Delisle Burns was working for the intelligence division of the Ministry of Labour when he penned this passage. He meant merely to describe the newly aggressive and insurgent mood of labour, but embedded in the description was an explanation for its expression: the absence of fear for their jobs and their futures among workers. The insecurity normally so central to working-class life had, however, been banished only temporarily, by an unusually tight labour market. It would return in the 1920s, and dampen hopes and expectations for a generation.[1]

The first signs of slump came in April 1920; by June 1921 unemployment had reached 23% among union members. Industries where organization was most extensive, like engineering and mining, were among the worst hit, and shop-floor activity began to wane. Employers, of course, took advantage of the scarcity of work to rid their shops of troublesome agitators. By late 1922, J.T. Murphy was forced to report that, 'In England we have had a powerful Shop Stewards' movement. But it can and only does exist in given objective conditions.

These necessary conditions at the moment in England do not exist . . . . You cannot build factory organization in empty and depleted workshops . . . .'[2]

The depression of trade slowly reintroduced a sense of contingency into the outlook of working people. The feeling of powerlessness began again to dominate working-class sensibilities by the mid-1920s, and was clearly documented in the accounts of daily life published as *Working Days* in 1926. A 50-year-old fireman for the railways, for example, looked with terror upon the prospect of his next physical examination, for failure would 'hurl him from the position it has taken him thirty years to attain, and turn him from the magnificent engine-man of today into a heartbroken man . . .' Two building workers also stressed the casual nature of their work as its main failing, and a painter was gripped with fear: '. . . no description of a painter's life would be complete without describing the misery and horror of unemployment . . . Unemployment is the lurking phantom that haunts a painter's mind . . . It means no security, no peace of mind, no certainty of the future. . . .' Similarly, T.J., a barrow-man at a blast furnace, appended a bitter afterword to his account: 'At present I am one of the million and a quarter superfluous workers, who is such a nuisance to politicians and the cause of deep concern to statesmen.' The women workers whose accounts were printed were more concerned with problems on the job than with employment itself – perhaps a reflection of the different labour market they confronted – but of the working-class housewives one was reduced to desperation by her husband's lack of work, while the others could only hope against its coming.[3]

The contrast with 1919–20 is striking, and indicates what a potent weapon unemployment could be in a war of attrition between workers and employers. Still, the political crisis of 1919–20 was too severe to wait upon such an outcome and required a more dramatic resolution. The unrest constituted a challenge to the authority of employers and the government alike, and its containment was complicated by the blurring of the line between political and industrial action. Part of the blurring came from the simultaneous advance of workplace organization and Labour party support, part from the unwillingness of militants to defer to the traditional division between politics and 'direct action, and part from the politicizing effect of government intervention'. Whether or not conflict took an explicitly political form, it nevertheless demanded an essentially political solution. This alone made the upsurge of 1917–20 a threatening phenomenon, but it also almost guaranteed an outcome unfavourable to labour, for the bases of workers' strength were local, fragmented and only indirectly political, while the power of its opponents was constituted at a national political level.

The enhanced presence of working people in the shops and communities was projected into the political arena only with great difficulty. The main vehicle was, of course, the Labour party. Because of its historic ties with the unions and its *de facto* recognition by the government as the voice of the working class during wartime, it was much better positioned than either the Independent Labour Party (ILP) or the smaller socialist sects to take advantage of the opportunities created by the increased activism of 1918–20. Conversely, it was the networks of local activitists, often formalized in the trades councils and called into greater prominence by the exigencies of war, that became the core of the new constituency Labour parties and served as the key to the party's electoral success.

The Labour party did not grow, however, as a party with serious prior commitments or clear theoretical orientations. It was the embodiment of a mobilized working-class culture and of the institutions rooted in that culture. As such, it refleted both the institutional strengths and the ideological weaknesses of that tradition. As R.M. Fox explained in a critical appreciation of working-class culture, 'the completely industrialized English worker is practical, matter-of-fact, and has little use for extreme theory or indeed, for theory of any kind'.[4] Not surprisingly, the changes in the Labour party after 1917, dramatic as they were, did not involve a thorough transformation of consciousness. By adopting a new constitution and structure, Labour both fitted itself out for the electoral struggle and linked itself more closely to the culture from which is sprang. To a lesser extent, it was opening itself to middle-class socialists. In adopting the socialist objective as Clause IV, more precisely, the party reflected the left-wing drift of opinion but also acquired a slogan and a programme behind which to fight.

Clause IV did not represent the victory of socialist theory. This is not to minimize the importance of those currents of socialist thought – Fabianism, ethical socialism, and the ILP, secularism, social democracy and the SDF, syndicalism and guild socialism – that competed for influence before and after the war. They provided analysis, inspiration and, through the organizing efforts they spawned, invaluable training for the movement. Nor should their long-term effects on workers' attitudes be entirely denigrated, for there is considerable evidence of their importance in numerous individual instances. But the Labour

37

party of the 1920s, with its minimum of doctrine and its overwhelmingly practical orientation, captured the spirit of the workers more accurately than did those parties and groups more explicitly concerned with ideological matters.[5]

Still, the political affinity was tenuous, and the relationship between the Labour party and its working-class base revealed a mixture of loyalty and cynicism. At the height of militancy in 1919, Whiting Williams found workers extremely sceptical of Labour's representatives in Parliament, and the government was aware of the weak hold of Labour's putative leaders. The distrust was more than reciprocated. Clynes, for example, based his opposition to the use of direct action for political ends on the backwardness of the workers. In 1919, he observed, the party offered 360 candidates to the electorate, but 'Sixty of their men only were returned . . . three hundred were rejected. They were rejected in the main from those great working-class, industrial constituencies where most of their propaganda had been done, and where there was the best opportunity of the working class understanding the Labour men. Let them not deceive themselves by saying that the working men were deceived by designing knaves and politicians. The working men were not ready for their appeal.'[6]

Virtually all of the leaders of Labour exhibited ambivalence towards the class whose interests they sought to articulate and further: Ramsay MacDonald saw Labour's political weakness in 1921 as primarily 'the fault of the minds of the people', while Snowden complained in the same year that if workers 'would spend one-twentieth part of the money they now waste in drinking and gambling on political and publicity organization, the capitalist monopoly of the means of influencing public opinion would be quickly destroyed'. The antipathy of the leaders towards their working-class supporters was undoubtedly itself based in part upon class. The middle classes were surely over-represented in the party's internal hierarchy, and this was accentuated by the infusion of converts from the Liberals after 1918. But more important still was the contempt for working-class culture shared by both middle-class radicals and upwardly-mobile workers. Popular culture and leisure came in for sharp criticism. MacDonald, for example, was convinced that the workers in the main 'retain the love of primitive man for gaudy ornament and sparkling anything', while Minnie Pallister wrote contemptuously of how the workers were consistently tricked by the 'red herrings' of mass culture: 'Sweepstakes, cup-ties, competitions, cross-word puzzles, the dazzling chance of winning someone else's money on one day to compensate for being defrauded of rightful earnings on every other day.'[7]

Such attitudes both derived from, but also reinforced, political moderation. They helped to create a political party whose primary orientation was towards maintaining its ties with the workers, with little time left over for thinking through the problems of economic and social policy that enveloped interwar British politics. Labour constituted itself as the main opposition, but had yet to become the alternative.

The very weakness of Labour's programme and ideology made the institutional connection between the party and the class closer and more valued. This, of course, suited the workers well, for their indifference to ideology did not mean an apathy towards organization. The British working class was extensively organized – most obviously in trade unions and cooperative societies, but also in clubs, tenants' councils, choral groups and countless other formal and informal ways. The dense web of organizations through which British working people met their material and social needs impressed itself upon foreign observers and it forced itself, in curious ways, into the political consciousness of socialist thinkers. Both before and after the war, for example, G.D.H. Cole based his claims for the superiority of the Guild Socialist vision upon its alleged fit with the logical development of trade unions: 'the problem of the transition to Guild Socialism is . . . primarily a problem of Trade Union development', he explained; and elsewhere boasted that 'I am building on the practice of the workers themselves, and not upon a confused, if wide, reading of Nietzsche, Faguet, Dicey, and other indigestible persons'. Delisle Burns likewise was much impressed with the workers' own chosen forms of organization, and so theorized: 'The trade union was a social discovery of the manual workers in the new industrial era; and the experience so consolidated is now the source of increased vitality in the whole community.' Even the Webbs, not easily moved by popular preferences, were willing to base virtually their entire vision of the Socialist Commonwealth upon the collective organizations of ordinary people. It was thus logical that the transformation of Labour politics in the era should take the form, not of an ideological shift, but rather of a marshalling of the various institutions of working-class life behind the Labour party. Viewed this way, the Labour party was a most appropriate vehicle for the entry of working people into the polity, and its doctrinal vacuity a necessary correlate of its institutional resilience.[8]

Regardless of ideology, then, the very fact of a much increased Labour presence necessitated substantial changes in how political business was conducted in Britain. Moreover, the coincidence of this new presence with massive industrial unrest ensured that the transition would be turbulent and troublesome, for there would have to be losers in any realignment. The precise nature of the postwar political system was in fact very much in doubt in 1919–20, and it is important for the understanding of subsequent events to describe the new balance with some care.

What emerged by 1926 was neither 'organised capitalism', as some would have it, with its regular brokering between highly structured groups of workers, businessmen and an interventionist state; nor was it a simple reassertion of old forms of legitimacy. Rather, it was a unique political settlement characterized by several, seemingly contradictory, features. Most prominent were the dominance of finance over industry in the counsels of the state; the presence of national organizations of employers and workers engaging in industry-wide collective bargaining with only modest assistance and informal encouragement from the state; a stable, class-based party system with Labour in a semi-permanent minority status; and a state machinery thoroughly under the domination of the fiscal conservatism of the Treasury. It was a sort of bastardized liberalism or, looking forward, a form of corporatism without Keynes, without the state and thus without the cash. The emergence of this pattern effectively ended the postwar crisis of authority, but before it could take hold, it was necessary to restore order within the labour movement, to secure the orthodoxy of the administrative machine and to re-vitalize Conservative politics.[9]

The severity of the insurgency guaranteed that these preconditions could be achieved only gradually. Indeed, in 1919–20, Britain's rulers were very much on the defensive and policy-making was reduced primarily to the granting of concessions and to stalling for time. Confrontation was postponed, and in the meantime various measures were designed to keep a lid on discontent, especially among ex-servicemen. Rent control, the dole for returning soldiers, and promises of massive efforts at housebuilding all served as interim measures of control.

In the end, however, it would take more than a pitiful 15s per week dole to exorcise the spirit of 'direct action' from the labour movement. By late 1920 sterner measures were contemplated. Officials and employers alike were agreed on the need to discipline the rank-and-file and to shore up the authority of the leaders. The spokesman of one employers' association explained:

We want more power – not less – for the union heads. Then we can work out together the best possible agreements . . . and be sure that those agreements will be kept, without so much troublesome pressure from the union members . . . . Stronger unions rather than fewer unions is what British industry needs.

Another employer, a representative of the National Union of Manufacturers, felt that the object of government policy was, or should be, 'to take the "virus" out of trade unions and leave them useful industrial factors'.[10]

Restoring the authority of leaders meant undercutting the influence of militants among the rank-and-file. In this, the forces of order were aided greatly by unemployment, which tipped the balance of tactical advantage in strikes in the employers' direction after 1920. Lloyd George noted the shift almost immediately, telling Bonar Law in 1920 that the era of compromise was finished. 'It would have been a mistake', he explained, 'if the fight had come sooner – the nation had not settled down', a dangerous 'restlessness' was about, and, most important, the outcome of a potential confrontation could not be predicted with any confidence.

The defeats of the miners in 1921 and of the engineers and textile workers in 1922 began the process of lowering expectations and deflating hopes. But even after the collapse of the Triple Alliance on Black Friday in April 1921, Beatrice Webb confided to her diary that the rank-and-file remained militant and blamed the vacillation of their leaders for the defeat. Because 'direct action' and the general strike had not been tried, she felt, they had not been shown to be folly. All 'those', therefore, 'who believe the strike would have succeeded will go on working for it'. The Government itself was of two minds about the proposed strike. Some clearly wished to avoid it, but Lloyd George preferred a showdown: 'I think we had better have the strike. Let them kick up their heels for a week or fortnight. It will help the moderates against the extremists.'[11]

The General Strike did not come, however, until 1926, by which time all of the other elements in the programme of containment were in place. There is no need to recount the incident here, but a few analytical points are in order. First, it was not sought by the unions. The leaders of the Trades Union Congress did not want it, but neither the Government nor the miners would back away from their positions and the TUC General Council acquiesced. The miners feared that the owners' demands for a reduction in pay and a lengthening of hours

41

would be a great loss and would signal further reductions in standards of living and working conditions.[12]

The position of the government was equally resolute. They had avoided a confrontation with the miners in 1925, but determined not to do so again. After 'Red Friday', they began to dust off the strike-breaking machinery set up earlier, and simultaneously started to cultivate public opinion. Understandings were also reached with the employers' organizations. These preparations suggest that the government very much wanted the General Strike in order to demonstrate conclusively the futility of mass action.[13]

What they did not want was to crush the unions. The aim was to tame them. Even Steel-Maitland, the Conservative Minister of Labour, wrote: 'What is needed is that the position of the leaders should be better safeguarded.' And in this the authorities were partly successful. Predictably, the left saw the General Council's decision to call off the strike on May 13th as abject surrender, but among the rank-and-file feelings about the strike were, it seemed, 'a compound of bitterness and pride: pride in the unselfishness of it, in the skill in organization which their people had shown, in the standing together in a noble cause of their own, not one thrust upon them from above as in a war'. In this rather curious fashion, the General Strike helped to unify the labour movement, prompting most trade unionists to rally round the leaders who, though beaten, appeared to have given it their best effort.[14]

Having restored order in the unions and banished the spectre of direct action, the Government achieved stability of a sort in industrial relations. The outcome of the contest created a sanitized system of free collective bargaining between well-organized employers and responsible and cautious trade unions. On this safe basis, capital and labour could be left to work out their own relations, and the state could withdraw from industrial affairs. Government was able finally to retreat from the exposed position of appearing to be responsible for the problems of industry. One of the spurs to broader class consciousness that had been in operation since the emergence of the war economy was thus removed for the remainder of the interwar period.

The triumph of this particularly limited vision of government's role in society was ensured by the novel political arrangements worked out during the early 1920s. The new system had three key elements – a recharged Conservative party, a crippled and compromised Labour Party, and a chastened state apparatus. The restoration of conservatism as a political force was in some ways the most interesting of these phenomena. It is certainly that which is least well studied by historians, who seem to be endlessly fascinated with the demise of the Liberals and the rise of Labour. But the modernization of conservatism was essential to the emergence of a stable politics and the delay in achieving it points to a genuine crisis of representation affecting the political right during 1910–24.

The problems on both left and right can be traced back to the political stalemate of 1910–14. This was the moment when a significant section of the elite became disillusioned with parties and parliament in general and began to think of alternative forms of leadership that would be 'above politics'. There was growing interest in the possible formation of a coalition to guarantee the rule of 'the competent', in H.G. Wells' phrase, in the interests of the nation and the empire. Lloyd George became the focal point of most such efforts from 1910 until the failure of 'fusion' and the fall of the Coalition in 1922.[15]

What doomed the various schemes for coalition and for the fusion of the forces of order into a new national party was the growing threat from the left. Before the war, coalition had been seen as a way of breaking out of the constraining mould of British politics, of weakening the influence of the 'die-hards' among the Conservatives and of moving towards a state-sponsored, 'efficient' solution of social issues. During the war, coalition was accepted as the means of national survival. After 1918, it came to be valued primarily as a bulwark against socialism. Lloyd George himself was quite unabashed in his willingness to use the prospect of socialism to frighten potential allies into supporting him. By January 1920 he was arguing: 'A Labour Government would land the country in revolution because it would resist direct action by talk and not force. It would be Kerensky all over again. I want strong government. I want private enterprise. But private enterprise must give the workers a change and a certainty.'[16]

The problem with the Lloyd George Coalition was that it was not the best vehicle through which to oppose socialism. Not that it did not try. As Kenneth Morgan has admitted, 'by the time of Black Friday, an anti-labour front was what the government closely resembled'. But because of its origins, its rhetorical commitments, and its personnel, the Coalition could not do the job effectively. By 1919, it also lacked a mass base in the country. The problem was simple enough; the coalition could not compete with Labour except by promises of reform that antagonized important segments of the elite and the middle-class. Lloyd George's animus towards the 'die-hards' among the Conservative party was well-known and so they never accepted him. He was equally disliked by the City, for bankers sensed in him a willingness to flout the doctrines of sound finance for personal political gain. Nor was Lloyd George notably more popular among industrialists. Employers in general tended to overlook the benefits they might receive from government-supported investment and to remember instead his interventions in strikes, which they saw as too favourable towards the unions, and his association with the elaborate network of wartime controls imposed upon industry.[17]

For all these reasons, the prospect offered by some continued form of coalition was less attractive than a revitalization of the Conservative party. The Conservative party could also provide a mechanism for the articulation of explicitly middle class interests. After the war there was noticeable disloyalty and disaffection of the middle and lower-middle classes. One symptom was the alarming increase in white-collar and civil service unionism, and Lloyd George was warned more than once that 'the greatest asset of the Labour Party . . . has been the sympathy which it has received from the middle classes. . . . The middle classes see no solution except by supporting those who have already gained concessions.'[18]

Enrolling these discontented elements on the side of conservatism was essential. The problem was how to make the Conservative party appear responsive to the needs of the 'salaried, rate-paying, owner-occupier' rather than the captive of old-fashioned, backwoods land-lords. It was extremely difficult to reconcile popular appeals to middle-class interest with the rhetoric of the coalition headed by Lloyd George. Faced with the massive growth of the working-class electorate and the appeal of the Labour party, the Conservative party came to be seen as the best means to obtain a popular basis for stabilization. However, the Conservatives were unable to play this role while they remained in the coalition. Of necessity, then, the coalition was jettisoned when the Convervatives decided to fight the 1922 election as an independent party.[19]

The Conservative party would continue to erect defences against socialism, with greater flexibility and with the weight of tradition and the powerful force of inertia behind it. It would also receive the more or less united support of the middle classes, the City of London and the industrialists, who were arrayed behind the party as a result of its adoption of the slogans of fiscal responsibility and its support, during the 1923 election, of a modest measure of protection. By 1924, the party was solid behind Baldwin who, as Cowling has said, would wear 'for the next phase of political activity . . . the mantle Lloyd George had worn in his last two years of office as leader of resistance to "Socialism" '.[20]

Meanwhile, the traditional elements in the hierarchy of finance moved decisively to institutionalize their influence over government policy. State intervention during the war, the creation of new ministries, and uncertainties over Lloyd George and the Coalition were deeply worrying to the City and the Treasury. In response, they acted to restore the Treasury's role in the state and to obtain the government's commitment to return to gold.

The crucial decisions were taken in 1919. Sir Warren Fisher, Permanent Secretary to the Treasury, was formally recognized as 'Head of the Civil Service' and given the major role in advising the Prime Minister on senior departmental appointments. In the same year, the Treasury forbade the practice of recruiting higher officials from outside the ranks of the Civil Service and instituted a requirement that each ministry should appoint an officer for 'finance and establishment' who was to introduce rigorous accounting procedures, oversee staffing arrangements and, one may safely assume, represent the Treasury view inside the department. The Treasury also obtained the right to name a permanent member to the increasingly powerful Cabinet Secretariat. The first of these was Frederick Leith Ross, who later recounted his perception of the job: 'One of the normal duties of the new post was to keep a special watch on all proposals for new expenditure and to make sure that the Chancellor of the Exchequer had had sufficient time to pronounce on their financial implications before they were submitted to the Cabinet for decision.' In 1924, this informal function became a formal requirement that all proposals involving public expenditure had to be submitted first to the Exchequer. By the early 1920s, therefore, the Treasury had effective control of the Cabinet agenda and could virtually guarantee that no initiatives of which it disapproved would become policy.[21]

From such positions of strength, the orthodox men of the Treasury effected the deflation of the economy from 1920 to 1925. With the fall of the Labour government in late 1924, the time had come for the final act in the restoration of fiscal responsibility, the return to gold. By 1925, the acquiescence of the Federation of British Industries was secured, and even Reginald McKenna of the Midland Bank came round, under pressure from the Treasury and the Bank of England, to its inevitability. The arguments made by the proponents of the return to the prewar parity were both economic and political, for a modified gold standard was seen not only as necessary for the revival of world trade but also as a 'knave-proof' guarantee of social discipline and political moderation. It was viewed specifically as a device which would provide a nearly-automatic check on any 'irresponsible' actions which a future government might be tempted to take.[22]

The main contours of stabilization had thus been worked out prior to the confrontation of May, 1926. When that occurred, and resulted in the workers' defeat, the process was essentially complete. The dominance of capital was restored throughout society from the highest levels of politics and policy to the most mundane levels of production and, of necessity, consumption. But such a thorough restoration, so lacking in subtlety or compromise, came at a very high cost. For, though beaten, the workers were not won over; on the contrary, they remained resolutely outside the mainstream of British society, deeply resentful of their employers and of the obviously anti-labour character of Conservative rule.

Most important, there was simply no mass desertion from the ranks of the trade unions. Flushed with victory, many British employers naturally wanted to follow up on the collapse of the General Strike with an all-out assault on the unions. The government toyed with the idea, and in the Trade Disputes and Trade Unions Act of 1927 went so far as to proscribe political strikes, to prohibit public employees from joining the Trades Union Congress and to force union members to 'contract in' to support for the Labour party. Still, this legislation was far milder than the draconian measures advocated by militants in the business community. A delegation from the National Union of Manufacturers, for example, visited the Ministry of Labour on October 12, 1926, and advocated the reform of labour law such that strikes could be called only by secret ballot, that union benefit funds be strictly segregated from strike funds, and that political funds, too, be disbursed only after approval by secret ballot. Picketing would also be strictly curtailed. But the government wished to avoid such entanglements. H.B. Betterton, the Parliamentary Secretary, explained that 'the one thing that is desirable is not to do anything which would tend to bring the State automatically into every trade dispute. . . .'[23]

In support of their proposals, the employers had claimed that the mass of the workers were ready to desert the unions if only given the option. The Ministry of Labour in December, 1926 countered with a series of local reports from the Chief Conciliation Officers in the regions. The latter were asked to assess specifically the impact of the General Strike on trade unionism. In response, the Officer in Birmingham argued that 'the unions are not penitent; there is no change of heart; no goodwill; just exhaustion'. In Glasgow, 'faith in the strike weapon has declined . . .', but this was merely 'a temporary expedient to meet existing circumstances. The ultimate aim is [still] probably reorganization of society.' In London, too, defeat dampened spirits but did not weaken the allegiance of workers to their unions and their current leadership. 'There is no resentment among the rank-and-file against the General Strike', nor any 'general dissatisfaction with the policy of the leaders and no tendency on the part of the rank-and-file to take matters into their own hands'. The government concluded that, though the General Strike had discredited direct action, its failure did not signify a mass reversion to non-unionism and so did not license a wholesale attack upon unions.[24]

The labour movement, for its part, did not veer sharply to the right or left after 1926, but stuck resolutely to the middle as the key to consolidating its resources. For a brief period, it seemed as if the drift would be to the right, towards collaboration with employers in the interests of 'industrial peace'. But such inchoate corporatist tendencies played themselves out with little effect, and the famous Mond-Turner talks of 1928–9 broke down before resolving any major issues. There was perhaps more of a chance for a move to the left, as dissatisfaction with the conduct of the General Strike swelled the ranks of potential dissidents in the unions. The Communist Party did, in fact, take in almost 5000 new members in 1926, due to its own efforts in the strike and the apparent failure of others. But most of the gains were short-lived, and the Party's sectarianism destroyed what potential there might have been.[25]

Given the continuing depression, the string of industrial defeats and the hostility of the employers and the government, the ability of the unions simply to maintain their position must be counted a considerable achievement. It shows the durability of the foundations of the trade union movement and its rootedness in the world of the workers. Add to this the growth of support for the Labour party after 1926, and the refusal of the workers passively to accept the defeat of 1926 looks even more impressive. Though the available data do not permit detailed analyses of class voting between the wars, the gross totals suggest that working people gave their support in ever-increasing numbers to Labour. In 1923, Labour voters totaled 4.4 million; in 1924, almost 5.5 million; by 1929, nearly 8.4 million, or 37.1% of the electorate. In 1923, the figure translated into 191 seats, in 1924 only 151, but in 1929 into 287 MPs, making Labour the largest of the three main parties.[26]

Labour's gains in 1929 were not achieved by any feats of leadership or electioneering. Rather, it was the Liberals who provided the most creative and attractive alternative under Lloyd George's revitalized leadership. They were armed with funds, with ideas developed by Keynes, Lloyd George and an impressive list of collaborators, and with a bold programme: 'We Can Conquer Unemployment'. Labour's response was characteristically confused and contradictory, and its own programme uninspired. Labour's was simply a class appeal to the workers to vote against the party of the capitalists, the Conservatives, and to ignore the Liberals as irrelevant. To the extent that it succeeded in winning almost 40% of the votes, it demonstrated the tremendous saliency of raw class alignments in society and in public life.[27]

By 1929, therefore, the working class challenge had been decisively beaten back on the industrial front, and the structure of the administrative machinery secured so as to frustrate the reforming impulses of even the most zealous Labour Cabinet minister. The remoteness of the possibility of a Labour government that could command a Parliamentary majority also seemed to ensure the future stability of British politics. Still, the enduring strength of the unions and the increasing allegiance of working-class voters to the Labour party demonstrated the persistence, indeed sharpening, of class antagonisms and loyalties and the enormous industrial and political possibilities that a more favourable conjuncture would open up to working men and women.

PART TWO

The Emergence of the Social Democratic Alternative

4
Class and Work, 1921–39

The political settlement of the 1920s could not last. The workers could not be kept at bay indefinitely; the unions would eventually grow again; and the Labour party would at some point work out the secret of its disfranchisement and do something about it. Still, it would take until 1945 for the defeats to be reversed and avenged – two long decades during which working people were forced to endure a painful slump and a gruelling war effort. During the same score of years, the composition and outlook of the working class itself changed. To the extent that the unions and the party sought to speak for and to mobilize the working class, they had to change as well.

Fundamentally, the shape of the working class was dependent upon the types of jobs on offer from employers. Any description of the changes should thus begin with an analysis of the evolving structure of firms and industries that provided employment. It was widely agreed by the end of the First World War that that structure was outdated and ill-fitted to the needs of the postwar world. The British economy retained a Victorian cast; enterprises were small and specialized, methods of working were rooted in custom inherited from the past but frozen in place by strong workplace organization, and entrepreneurs seemed unwilling or unable to introduce rational planning and new techniques into their shops.

There were, to be sure, some changes before the war. Engineering employers experimented with new methods of payment, and fought to break their skilled men's hold over certain jobs; printing employers introduced new processes and linotype machines; large plants with better machines were erected after 1905 in Lancashire textiles; and the notion of 'scientific management' began to penetrate the thinking and discussion of businessmen. But the initiatives were seldom pursued very far, and none of these management efforts served to weaken the power of the skilled workers or to move decisively towards mass production. Nor did the war revolutionize British workshops. Women did replace men in a few classes of jobs, but their presence was sharply circumscribed, and in most jobs limited to the duration of the war. Most important, the exigencies of wartime necessitated a drastic increase in output through an expansion of 'state-of-the-art' techniques, not through experimentation with genuinely novel methods. At the end of the war, therefore, the structure of British industry was not very different from what it had been in 1914, and the first priority during the demobilization was to restore the industrial *status quo* in the interests of returning soldiers. This was facilitated by a short boom, lasting until mid-1920, whose main effect was to draw labour and capital into the oldest, least technically progressive industries, further accentuating Britain's economic backwardness.

By 1921, over 1.2 million were at work in mining and quarrying, about 950,000 in textiles, and another 700,000 in clothing. Transportation occupied another million and a half, building around three-quarters of a million, while the more dynamic chemical industries employed a mere 45,000. The metal, engineering and shipbuilding industries employed over 2 million, but many in the least modern branches. In 1924, establishments in metal manufacturing averaged fewer than 40 workers, those in engineering, shipbuilding and vehicles just 58 workers.

Increases in firm size and industrial concentration, as well as technological modernization, proceeded only gradually from 1919 to 1939. A wave of mergers and combinations began in 1919 and continued through the 1920s, but increased concentration of ownership was not translated immediately into major technical rationalization. Judging from the data on plant size, change was often delayed until the mid-1930s. Between 1924 and 1935, the share of output contributed by firms employing less than 200 persons remained stable, and by 1935, there were only about 1600 manufacturing establishments with 500 or more workers. In aggregate terms, growth and transformation were thus modest and incremental. Workers never experienced economic change in the aggregate, however, but industry by industry depending upon where they worked; and at this level there was considerable variation.

In the older industries – textiles, shipbuilding, and mining – industrial structure changed hardly at all. There was no increase in the scale of enterprise and little in the way of technical innovation. Overcapacity was far more of a problem than productivity – throughout the 1920s, shipbuilders used but a third of existing capacity, in 1933 a mere 7%. Investment in new equipment made little sense in such a context, and little was forthcoming. In textiles, the problem was the same: to consolidate firms, share out markets, stabilize prices and shed excess capacity. These were the aims of the Lancashire Cotton Corporation and of the Cotton Industry (Reorganization) Act of 1936. By the late 1930s, the output of cotton was less than half what it had been in 1913, exports of piece goods but a fifth of their prewar peak.

The growing industries – rayon, chemicals and pharmaceuticals, electrical engineering and appliances, public utilities and, later, building stood in sharp contrast. Except for construction, these were industries noted for the larger size of the typical firm, high rates of investment and advanced methods of production. In motor vehicles, 52.4% of the workers laboured in plants of more than 1500 in 1935, another 10.7% in factories employing between 750 and 1500. Overall, engineering came to be divided between those firms operating plants with 1000 plus workers, with relatively modern techniques and employing about 40% of the workforce, and the older, smaller and more backward companies employing another two-fifths of the labour force in units of under 400 workers, with a quite small number in between.

The uneven character of economic activity from industry to industry during the 1920s and 1930s was especially visible in employment shifts and unemployment rates. Between 1923 and 1939, unemployment averaged 19.6% in coalmining, 36.8% in shipbuilding, and 20.7% in cotton textiles, but only 10% in vehicles. Predictably, from 1920 to 1938, the coal industry lost 400,000 of its insured workers, cotton 230,000, woollens 50,000, shipbuilding 150,000, iron and steel 185,000. During the same period, more than 600,000 had been added to the workforces in chemicals, electrical engineering, vehicles, electricity supply, silk and rayon, and hosiery, plus another 400,000 odd in construction and in building materials. The latter industries increased their percentage of total employment from just above 20% to more than a third. By the outbreak of the Second World War, a notable shift had occurred away from the staple, export industries of the nineteenth century to a complex of industries more closely linked to domestic markets and to the emerging technologies.[1]

The restructuring of the labour force meant also a geographic redistribution of the population. Because different regions specialized in one or another trade or one or another set of industries, the variation among industries in employment led to pockets of severe unemployment and, over the long term, employment loss. For the years 1929–36, unemployed averaged 16.9% across Great Britain, but it ranged from as low as 8.8% for London and 7.8% for the Southeast to as high as 30.1% for Wales, 22.7% for the Northeast, and just under 22% for Scotland and for the Northwest. Over time, people followed jobs and moved from the depressed to the more buoyant areas: between 1924 and 1935, the contribution of firms based in Greater London to total industrial output jumped from 17% to nearly 25%, and the Midlands share increased from 16% to 20%, while that of Lancashire, Cheshire, Wales and Scotland dropped from 37% to under 30%. A census of factories opened and closed during 1932–7 showed a net increase of only 644 in all of Britain, of which 532 were located around London.[2]

It thus mattered a great deal where one lived and to what sort of job one became initially attached. For those in growing industries and areas, regular work and wages combined with falling prices and shorter hours to produce a style of life involving considerable scope for leisure and consumption. For the many who were tied by reasons of training, sentiment or simple inertia to declining industries and stagnant areas, the period between the wars was marked by bitterness and fear, hunger, ill-health and desperation. Thus industry and geography exerted a profound influence on the life chances of individuals. The differences, of course, came on top of, and accentu-ated, other historic divisions in the working class between women and men, manual and white-collar, skilled and not-so-skilled which also circumscribed opportunity. Employment prospects differed markedly for men and women, and followed quite distinct trends during 1919–39. With manufacturing jobs so scarce, positions in the growing white-collar and service sector became more prized and took on greater importance for the shape of the class structure, but the differential access to these relatively secure posts also served as a reminder of the deep cleavages in British society.

Job opportunities for women were extremely limited and improved only very gradually. Despite the massive entry of women into production during World War I, their overall rate of labour force participation declined from over 35% to 33.7% between 1911 and 1921. It rose a bit by 1931, to 34.2%, but by 1951 still had not reached the level attained by 1914. The major cause of the decrease, and later stagnation, was the steady decline of the industries, particularly textiles and clothing, where most women workers were established. Women's options were also curtailed by the fact that those industries that were expanding did so mostly with male labour. There was no noticeable increase in women employed in chemicals, food, drink and tobacco, public utilities or transport from 1923 to 1935, and only a modest 10–15% increase from 1935 to 1939. What few industrial gains were made came in engineering, where women workers incrased over 80% during 1923–39, i.e., by about 200,000. Even this was not enough, however, to overcome the losses from the previous strongholds of women's work.

The only serious gains came in clerical work and in retailing. The First World War marked the onset of the 'feminization' of the office. In 1911, female clerks made up only 20% of the total; by 1921, they were almost 45%. During the 1930s, they became a majority. Before the war, 180,000 worked in clerical jobs, by 1931 their numbers had swelled to nearly 650,000 and by 1951 to more than 1.4 million. Increases were less dramatic within the distributive trades; nonetheless they grew from half a million in 1923 to over 900,000 in 1938.

Women moved rapidly, therefore, into the expanding white-collar and service occupations, but not all such categories were increasing as quickly as routine office work. Probably the best jobs open to many women of working-class backgrounds were in teaching and nursing, the so-called 'lower professions'. Both of these occupations grew rapidly from the late nineteenth century, but the rate of growth slowed after the war. By 1921, there were 115,000 nurses, mostly women, and 287,000 teachers, three-quarters women. The number of nurses increased by a quarter in the next decade, and by nearly a hundred thousand more by 1951, and the great bulk remained women. Teaching also grew, but more slowly – by under 3% to 1931, by 15% more to 1951 – but, more important, absolutely all of this increase was in men teachers.

In sum, although women's employment expanded slightly between the wars, it was probably not growing as fast as women's desire or need to work. Perhaps the best evidence of that was the jump in the number of married women, particularly younger married women, who either wanted to or had to stay in work. The statistics, indeed, reveal an interesting generational difference in this regard. Up to 1921, the participation rate for married women was lowest in the childbearing years, for obvious reasons. Between 1921 and 1931, however, the percentage of married women at work aged 25–34 grew from 9.38% to 13.2%. By 1951, the combined ratio for married women aged 25–44 was over 25%, more than double any previous level. The change was particularly significant because it was in those occupations that were growing most rapidly that the 'marriage bar' was most strictly enforced. Even in the early 1930s, married women were legally forced into retirement in teaching and in the civil service, and the government's ban on married women carried over into many firms in finance, banking and insurance. The first major break came only in 1935, when the London County Council decided to drop the 'bar' for women teachers and medical staff; further progress had to wait until the Second World War.[3]

The long delay in lifting the formal restrictions upon the work of married women reveals the tenacity of established attitudes regarding the proper role of the sexes. The old pattern began to break down, but slowly. Employment trends also eroded the traditional social and cultural differences between those engaged in white-collar and manual work, though, again, change was painfully slow. The share of manufacturing, and of the manual workforce it relied upon, within the entire economy probably peaked about 1914. Since then, if not before, growth has centred in services and in white-collar jobs. Manual workers, according to one estimate, made up 80% of the occupied population in 1911, declined to 77% in 1931 and to less than 70% in 1951. The gap was made up by white-collar workers of one sort or another: teachers, nurses, civil servants, clerical workers, salespeople. Government employment, for example, a major location of white-collar work, increased by 27% between 1920 and 1938.[4]

These positions were filled from three sources, in a slowly changing mix. First, there was a small but steady amount of self-recruitment. Second, there was a drift to white-collar jobs from other non-manual pursuits, like shopkeeping. Third, there were those of working-class origin who had stayed at school and typically received a year or two of grammar school education. In the initial expansion of clerical and lower professional employment, most came from the lower-middle class. In 1907, the President of the National Union of Clerks could still argue that 'as a rule clerks come from the middle-class, a class opposed to the principles of trade unionism. In a middle-class family there are two sons, one goes as a clerk, the other as a teacher.' A survey of 1927–8, however, revealed a markedly increased working-class representation. Out of 746 second-class civil servants, clerks and other salaried officials, 47% came from manual backgrounds, mostly skilled. Among 858 teachers, the majority women, 35% had working-class fathers. The trend was confirmed by the New Survey of London in the late 1920s, from which it was estimated that about 35–40% of young, unmarried clerks were from working class origins. The most reliable inquiry was the massive LSE social mobility study of 1947, which showed that 45% of female and 41% of male clerks were of unambiguously working-class origins.[5]

As working-class children found work in the service sector, these sorts of jobs were drawn slowly within the orbit of working-class life and experience. This did not guarantee any automatic spread of working-class attitudes to non-manual employees, however, nor did it entail their 'proletarianization'. The barriers to trade unionism remained strong among white-collar workers and, however low the wages, the security of employment and the character of the work made possible a lifestyle quite different from that of industrial workers. Still, the rise of these jobs and the transformation in origins of their membership did create the potential for subsequent changes in class outlook and political allegiance.

In fact, none of the shifts in the shape of the class structure were in themselves sufficient to alter attitudes and behaviour. These depended much more on how change was experienced by working people and upon the options for translating problems into grievances and then into forms of collective action. The diversity of industrial change across Britain made the projection of conditions into shared complaints and common programmes exceedingly difficult. British workers did seek, wherever possible, to soften and make more human their conditions of work and to extend their sphere of control, but success varied, depending upon employer resistance, local labour markets and the strength of union organization.

Almost all employers were conscious after 1918 of the need to boost productivity. Industry was also better organized than ever before. During the war, the Federation of British Industries, the National Union of Manufacturers and the National Confederation of Employers' Organizations were erected on top of groups already existing in shipping, shipbuilding, cotton, engineering and other industries. The groups were not always capable of speaking with a unified voice, but they gave industry a stronger national presence than before the war. They were united, in particular, on the need to defeat the postwar challenge of labour, and to present the businessmen's opposition to government interference in economic affairs. On these points, they had their day, and after 1926 their main objectives were accomplished.[6]

These victories were achieved, however, purely on matters of defence. On the offensive, employers were much less successful, partly because they were unsure of their goals and partly because of the economic environment in which they had to operate. The chorus of support for enhanced production broke up into a discordant debate on how to do it. Workers, though on the defensive, still had to be coaxed into cooperating for greater output. This led a few visionaries in the business community to put their faith in plans for a new industrial partnership based upon works councils and 'trade parliaments', but such schemes for industrial reconstruction never commanded majority support among the employers.[7]

A rather tamer variant of reform had somewhat more success. A loose grouping of company welfare officers, personnel managers, industrial psychologists – many of these in association with the Industrial Fatigue Research Board – and 'enlightened' employers, like Cadbury, Leverhulme, and Mond, began to define and argue for a kind of 'welfarism'. Plans for employee participation and stock ownership, for improved conditions in the factories, for holidays and company-sponsored outings were adopted by quite a number of new firms – ICI, and Unilever, for example.

Most employers, however, were interested in more direct ways of getting greater output. The major systematic alternative engaging their attention was 'rationalization' or 'Fordism', the postwar labels attached to scientific management. Lyndall Urwick, Director of the International Management Institute, explained the logic of rationalized production: 'With the advent of the modern industrial group in large factories in urban areas, the whole process of control underwent a fundamental revolution. It was now the owner or manager of a factory, i.e., the employer . . . who had to secure or extract from his employees a level of obedience and/or co-operation which would enable him to exercize control.' The 'Fordist' solution was a system of control based upon time payment, close supervision and machine pacing. Machines were to set the tempo, foremen were to enforce its constant demands, and high hourly or weekly wages were to reward workers for their tolerance of the process. The theory struck a responsive chord in employers beleaguered by strong unions, but its application was distinctly limited. Employers seemed to recognize that workers would not accept such a regimen. 'The human element', it was argued, 'was of far greater importance in England than in America.' Or, as the management at Austin put it, 'The daily task system at fixed wages may perhaps be workable in American, or even Continental factories, but the necessary . . . driving works policy, would not be acceptable either to English labour or management.' Austin chose instead to rely upon a system of payment by results to motivate its workforce. As the head of the cost department explained, 'The remuneration he is able to obtain through

. . . [the piecework system] is a sufficient incentive to the worker to make large output effective with the minimum of supervision.'[8]

Even in the advanced sectors, therefore, British industrialists were reluctant to rely upon the efficacy of machines and preferred to combine technical innovation with piecework methods to obtain maximum output. They did not reject rationalization outright, but sought to temper the domination of the machine with established techniques of labour management. The result was that new work processes were applied with less zeal and with more compromises and survivals from the past than might have been possible or necessary on purely technical grounds alone.

The ambivalence and moderation – or, as some would say, backwardness – of British management was one reason why the transformation of the labour process was so incomplete during the interwar years. The other major reason was money. Profits and investment were notoriously low in the 1920s and 1930s, and lowest in those industries most in need of retooling and re-organization. Technical advance virtually came to a halt in the old industries and employers struggled to survive by cutting wages, speeding up, reducing excess capacity and artificially raising prices; the least promising path to recovery was new investment. In textiles, shipbuilding and coal mining, virtually all of the statistical gains in productivity were due to the closing down of the older and least efficient factories, yards or pits.[9]

In the growing industries located in the more prosperous regions, technical progress was more marked. In the expanding branches of engineering, particularly electrical engineering and the manufacture of motor cars, the typical factory came to employ over a thousand workers. The Engineering Employers' Federation calculated that the percentage of skilled workers in the trade fell from 60% in 1914 to 32% in 1932, while that of semi-skilled workers had risen from 20% to 57%. Mass-production techniques were also applied in such industries as food processing and baking, especially sugar refining, in tobacco, in artificial fibres and in newspaper production. The chemical industry was highly concentrated and heavily capitalized, the plants were correspondingly large, though, of course, the nature of production and the efficiency of the plants kept the numbers employed rather low.[10]

The most advanced firms were those producing automobiles. Despite their scepticism about the Fordist model, motor car companies experimented consciously with variation in pay systems and workplace organization, and introduced a variety of highly rationalized and mechanized systems. Ford itself applied the principles 'perfected' in Detroit to Manchester and later to its massive new plant at Dagenham, east of London. Another American firm, General Motors, purchased the ailing Vauxhall company in 1925 and expanded it along similar lines. As early as 1921 the Vauxhall management closed for a month and a half, undertook 'scientific' studies of 6000 jobs and redesigned the payment system. The first assembly line was introduced in 1925, prior to the GM takeover, and the wage system further refined. After the acquisition by GM, the 'transition to direct control' of men by machines was completed between 1928 and 1930.

The British firms were equally resolute in the pursuit of efficiency. Morris and his associates were machine enthusiasts, hoping to reach a state where 'actual production is automatic'. Morris installed a chassis assembly line in 1919, and mechanized nearly all operations after 1934. Austin adopted a [superficially] different attitude, with stress upon the 'human factor'. Nevertheless, Sir Herbert was much impressed upon his visit to Ford in America by continuous flow production and the constant 'atmosphere of push and go' that it created, and began a massive expansion programme at Longbridge upon his return. During 1923–7, 'moving lines, electric hand-operated hoists, pulleys and conveyors' were installed; while chassis production was thoroughly mechanized after 1928. In 1929, it had become the first British car factory to assemble both the chassis and the body on 'mechanically-driven track'. Labour was closely supervised, fragmented into many grades, and paid on a bonus system – a quintessentially rationalized operation. The smaller British firms were also keen on the latest methods. The Associated Equipment Company, owned by Rover, installed its first assembly line in 1917, while the works manager at its Southall plant, opened in 1926, was accused by the London Engineering Employers of having contracted 'Forditis'. Old methods of work and paternalistic management practices lasted longer at firms like Rolls Royce, but of course Rolls Royce was not competing in the same market as Morris and Austin. Standard, Rootes and Singer, which did aim at a mass market, followed paths similar to those charted by Austin and Morris.[11]

If the motor companies did most to transform the experience of work, other industries were not totally immune. Perhaps the best indication of the extent of 'rationalization' was the popularity of the 'Bedaux system'. Charles Bedaux was an American whose techniques were disseminated by 19 offices in 26 countries. A successor to Frederick Winslow Taylor, Bedaux developed a scheme for calculating effort and payment that managements found extremely attractive. Tasks were to be measured in combined units (B's, after Bedaux) made up of time devoted to work and time required for rest, thus allowing strict comparisons between jobs. This made it possible to establish effort and production norms with which to set bonus rates. In Britain, the Bedaux system was the major carrier of the spirit and practice of scientific management. Approximately 250 firms used it to restructure the workplace, including such leading employers as ICI, Lucas, Joseph Lyons and Wolsey. The strategic position of these companies suggests that the influence of Bedaux, and of the principles upon which it was founded, may have been even more broadly diffused throughout the economy. The spectrum of industries affected points in the same direction: approximately 13% of Bedaux's clients were in food, drink, and tobacco, 16% in engineering, 11% in chemicals, and 10% in metal manufacturing, 21% in textiles and 23% in 'other manufacturing'. The system made sufficient inroads to prompt a special TUC inquiry in 1933 and several disputes.[12]

It is difficult to strike an exact balance in assessing the extent of changes in the workplace during the 1920s and 1930s. Retardation and tradition dominated many shops and the slump held back innovations in many fields. Moreover, in two of the 'growth' sectors of the depression, services and construction, there was little scope or incentive for introducing new technologies. Clearly, too, the industrial changes that did occur had to wait until recovery after 1935 in order to be broadly applied and to register major social consequences. Nevertheless, if one takes into account the decline of the oldest and least technically progressive industries and firms, the high degree of rationalization of production in the new, mass-production industries, like motor cars, and the extent of efforts like Bedaux among the larger, stable and more profitable concerns throughout the economy, the transformation of the labour process during the interwar years begins to look more advanced. Gradually and fitfully, it seems, the economy modernized.

The evidence on work itself and on how people experienced it corroborates this rather mixed assessment. The reality and visibility of technical transformation gave rise to recurring fears of deskilling and job loss, but its modest pace left most unaffected. Even where new machines and processes were put in place, employers seldom capitalized on their potential for control. In such instances workers came to regard the techniques with ambivalence rather than outright hostility. In consequence, there was little overall sense of degradation or deterioration at the workplace, especially among men.

Perhaps the clearest statements on this issue came from W.F. Watson, a long-time engineer, who used his autobiography, published in 1935, to review the history of his chosen trade. 'When labour-saving machinery and mass-production came to be adopted, the doom of craftsmanship was predicted. . .', he recalled. But such prognostications invariably failed to 'appreciate the significant fact that the basis of engineering rests on quality and craftsmanship, that mass-production never was and never *can* be the rule. . . . Nor did we realize that mass-production would produce a new, and equally skilled, type of craftsman; . . . and that the number required may tend to increase with the expansion of mass-production.'[13]

Though he recognized the weakening of apprenticeship and the relentless advance of 'rationalization in car production and heavy engineering', he was more impressed with the continued need for skilled workers in even the most mechanized factories. He was equally struck by the resilience of the small engineering shop, of which, he guessed, there were still two thousand just in Greater London. Throughout the trade, he concluded, 'craftsmanship still predominates'. Indeed, a variety of 'new crafts . . . have sprung up as a result of the machine', and even in motor cars many skilled men were employed. The more advanced the machinery, Watson believed, the more challenging the work, and though he conceded the 'tendency for those employed on monotonous work to develop into automata', he believed that few would be so affected. In the end, 'the human factor in the average British workman – a traditional love of sport, fair-play, freedom, and independence – makes it impossible for him to submit to Robotic influences.'[14]

The logic of Watson's argument is somewhat contradictory. He begins by minimizing the extent of technical change, but gradually shifts his ground to asserting that, widespread as it is, working people remain 'human' and resist degradation. His final refuge is in the vitality of workers' leisure, their non-work pursuits. Such a slippage suggests a hesitancy about his defence as a whole, a sense that things were in fact changing but a vague confidence that the effects would not be as bad as often feared. A similar hesitancy and ambiguity pervaded Alfred Barratt Brown's thoughtful book, *The Machine and the Worker*. Barratt Brown was then principal of Ruskin College, and his contacts there and in WEA classes would have imparted a somewhat broader, if not exactly universal, applicability to his analysis, which was largely based upon the writings and opinions of his working-class students.

Barratt Brown, too, was very interested in the fate of the skilled workman. Acknowledging that 'certainly there are crafts that have been displaced', he nonetheless felt it necessary to assert, first, that much of the romance of craftsmanship was just that, and second, that 'the machine has actually created additional tasks for the hand skills'. In sum, he concluded, '. . . the broad tendency would seem to be one that need cause no fear for the decline of skilled work . . .'; better still, '. . . we may be sure that . . . the proportion of skilled to unskilled workers will steadily increase'.

Behind this broad conclusion, however, was an argument surprisingly similar to Watson's, suggesting that for him, too, the matter was not so simple. For what Barratt Brown really says is that, as industry develops, there are 'both changes in the form of skill and the emergence of new skills'. Examples of both types of change come to him from engineering: 'an increase of skill and accuracy among pattern-makers, and a new class of "semi-skilled" workers in the foundry'. The skilled became more specialized; the hard, dirty work of the unskilled is eliminated; and the semi-skilled play a greater role. The cumulative effect of these three distinct trends is thus towards a general improvement in skills and in the quality of working life.

This occurs, moreover, not so much because of technology itself but because working people constantly seek to appropriate the new technology and make it part of their lives. Hence, the highly ambivalent, but for that reason quite believable, opinions and feelings expressed by Barratt Brown's students towards work and machines. On the negative side, a 45-year old postal employee found 'sorting letters for three or four hours a paralyzing process' that made him feel like 'jumping up and screaming', while a mass-production worker could only tolerate his job by allowing his imagination free rein: 'I have painted pictures, built cabinets, drafted essays and speeches, and a hundred other things in my mind whilst at the bench.' A printer – surely a skilled craftsman by any definition – found the same difficulty and 'very often used to day-dream. The purely mechanical action of picking up a sheet of paper, and setting it against "marks" all day long, brings about a state of coma.' Unfortunately, he once inserted his hand instead of the paper and lost a portion: 'needless to say, I never day-dream now.'

But day-dreaming, dangerous as it was, did reveal that deadening jobs could not totally deaden workers' sensibilities. And, more important, counterbalancing these sentiments were those of workers for whom the machine was a source of attraction, and to whom it gave a sense of moving mountains, of power, of dominating the world. An electrician expressed it most forcefully, explaining that 'There are some machines which I enjoy manipulating. Most men are denied a controlling voice in any part of their lives, and so it is . . . satisfying to one's desire for power to be able to pull a . . . switch, and lo! steel bends like cardboard, or shrieks off in curling blue and orange shavings; or a flat piece of steel is thrown from the "innards" of a machine as a finished article!' Haulage men experienced a similar surge of power, and even a chauffeur confessed to 'a feeling of elation when driving'.[15]

This is surely a rather optimistic reading of the trends in working life, but its very complexity suggests an authenticity. It was based, after all, on a wide experience among working-class adults and upon at least a rudimentary survey of 50 workers which showed that by far the majority held more positive than negative attitudes towards their work – they identified with their trades, were proud of their skills and competence, whether 'skilled' or not, and with few exceptions experienced work not as an imposition but as an opportunity. These attitudes implied a considerable continuity between the sense of power and efficacy expressed by workers in 1919–20, at the height of the postwar insurgency, and their views in the depth of depression. It seems that the assertiveness of workers at the point of production remained strong despite the weakening of organization and the threat of the sack.

This view is largely confirmed by several other studies of work and the workplace dating from the 1930s. Jack Common's collection, *Seven Shifts*, Walter Greenwood's *How the Other Man Lives* and John Hilton's *Are Trade Unions Obstructive?* each provide convincing evidence of the efforts of workers to humanize their work and their modest success and satisfaction in so doing. Hilton, for instance, though eager to acquit the unions of any responsibility for retarding progress, nevertheless found dockers, masons, and printers slowing down the work, enforcing demarcation boundaries and restricting overtime in spite of the unfavourable labour market. He believed, moreover, that the unskilled were as prone to such action as the skilled.[16]

Greenwood, in his investigation, discovered surprisingly high levels of satisfaction among a variety of workers. Among lorry drivers, 'most like their jobs', he explained, and found in the roads they travelled 'something irresistible, something that smacks of adventure. . . .' Greenwood's informant from the docks was also far from complaining. Contrasting the conditions of pre-1914 to those of the 1930s, he offered,

'We've got what we set out for in the union – well, nearly all. Every docker in this port has to be a union member. Overtime is only permitted under certain conditions . . . In every way things are improved. I'm proud of what we've done and the strength we've now got.' A railwayman was somewhat less enthusiastic, but he, too, conceded that 'we're much better off on the railway now than before the war'. In woodworking, part of the trade had been given over to mass-production, but the process had not spread far. In fact, 'The union is sufficiently strong to be able to stipulate to builders that if they wish to use mass-produced joining . . . it must be made by trade union labour.' 'Union control', a woodworker explained, 'is stronger inside a shop than on building jobs. . .', and 'a man who defaults from the union won't get a job in any other union shop in the country'. Among miners, too, physical conditions were much improved, and the working miner claimed that 'many lads who're leaving school want to go into the pit rather than an engineering works'.

There were several exceptions to the generally favourable picture painted by Greenwood. Car workers, for example, seemed to him 'a craven lot, spineless, money-grubbing, selfish'. 'The money's the only thing that keeps me here', one is quoted as saying, noting further that 'I don't know of many fellows who're here now who take the job seriously . . . nobody ever feels settled and permanent. . .' The second black spot was those trades where unemployment, or the fear of it, were most pervasive. An engineering apprentice felt it a terrible waste, 'not finding the boys who've served their time to engineering something to do. In three years, he would be finished with his apprenticeship and out on the street. Nearly all the machinery is automatic and it doesn't need the skilled men . . . then the firm takes on another batch of apprentices'. Among cotton workers, the wasting of life and skill was also palpable: 'Talk about skilled workmen walking the streets. The town is full of them; there's more walking about than you'll find in the mills.'[17]

Work was degraded, then, more in proportion to its scarcity than to its actual content. Much the same conclusion emerges from the life stories assembled by Jack Common. His characters – a plasterer, a railwayman, two steel workers and a gas worker (plus one long-term member of the unemployed) – were overflowing with grievances from their jobs, but still derived an identity and a sense of personal worth from them. A plasterer recounted the beginnings of full-time employment, 'the historic workday of my life', to which he had looked forward as 'the confirmation of my faith – WORK'. The very trials and troubles of work seemed to these writers matters of accomplishment, evidence of virtue and the verities of the 'gospel of callous good-humour and rough and ready common sense'.[18]

It was, of course, a peculiarly masculine virtue that did not apply to women workers. Common at least recognized that his book's 'one serious omission [was that] it does not include any contribution from the woman's side of the world of work'. Accounts of women's work were also absent from most of the other descriptions, though the absence was neither noted nor, it seems, regretted. This suggests that many of the concerns underlying much of the debate about skill, technology and the degradation of work were decidedly male-oriented questions, for women had never been apprenticed and seldom allowed into skilled occupations in the best of times.

The omission is particularly unfortunate because the few brief appearances women do make in these accounts suggest a very different experience at work. Barratt Brown, for example, cites a telegraph operator who finds much less scope for personality in her work than men normally did – 'I do not like operating', she said, 'though I have no lively antipathy to it. I have a distant admiration for . . . the instrument as a technical achievement but cannot identify myself with it in any way. . . There is not the slightest element of craftsmanship.' The detachment of this statement stands in marked contrast to the more violent, if contradictory, reactions of men. Greenwood's few descriptions of the jobs women held were also distinctly less appealing than those of work done by men. The shop assistant, he explained, was overworked, underpaid, spied upon by the company and regularly insulted by customers, with little recourse or defence. The only women for whom work was modestly satisfying were employed by the post office and protected by a union and by civil service provisions. As one older woman explained, 'The most attractive aspect of my job is its security. I am well paid, I get good holidays and when I'm due for retirement there's a pension for me. . . .' No doubt the experience of women in textiles and clothing, where their position was more firmly established, was also reasonably tolerable. Women weavers possessed high levels of skill, and had evolved a female-oriented factory culture which stood up well even to the ravages of the slump. Nevertheless, these industries were in decline, and the newer kinds of work available to women usually involved less skill, more repetition and much closer supervision.

For the bulk of labouring women, in fact, work appears to have held little joy or satisfaction. Most were young and single, and treated as mere 'girls', with few prospects. Employers, by prejudice, custom or rational calculation, had little or no incentive to provide training or benefits. Worse still, women's historic vulnerability made them the target for many of the worst excesses of mechanization and manipulation. The firms that instituted Bedaux, for example, were heavily weighted towards women's work and the most famous strike against the system was fought by women hosiery workers in Leicester. It seems, too, that women were invariably the guinea pigs for experiments by industrial psychologists designed to show the best mix of environmental influences to boost output on boring work. It was assumed that women traditionally did such work, and it is likely that, between the wars, they came to do much more of it.

It turns out, however, that some of the research on women and 'fatigue' also documented in some detail the quite different world of work that existed for women. One study done just after the war showed how 'casual' was much of the work women could secure. Five munitions factories employing primarily women experienced 100% labour turnover in from five to fourteen months; while after the war a biscuit factory lost 66% of its women workers in a year. Married women, of course, 'turned over' even more rapidly than the rest.[19] A study entitled 'The Nervous Temperament' in 1930 turned up consistently higher levels of mental strain for women than for men and much more 'contentment' among the men than the women.[20]

The later 1930s saw two studies of much greater depth and subtlety on the subject of women and work. The first focused upon women in various 'machine-feeding processes' – wrapping chocolate or toffee, cutting buttons, assembling chains or producing cartridges. The women found it no great trouble to keep up with the machine, and many preferred to be able to increase its speed to guarantee making the week's wages. When asked what they liked or disliked about work, the overwhelming majority, almost 80%, were most interested in their friends at work, in the tolerability of the hours (75%) or in the wages (68%). A miniscule proportion perceived the opportunity for promotion; and less than 30% thought the work interesting. These findings echoed a comparable study done a year earlier, except that in the former the women also voiced concern over security. In neither case did they derive satisfaction from the intrinsic character of the work or express a desire for greater control over it.[21]

The most thoughtful analysis of women's work was undoubtedly Marie Jahoda's study of a mass-production factory near London employing about 400 young women, published in 1941. She began by chiding researchers for not listening to what the women were themselves saying. Her own observations revealed a remarkable solidarity and equality among women workers. This 'attitude of solidarity . . . extends even to those who are not liked as individuals'; and it overcame the divisive effects of the piecework system and was linked to a sharp antagonism to the foremen and 'headgirls'. The relationship between the girls and their supervisors was characterized by 'resentment, lack of mutual understanding, a feeling of superiority on the one side, of inferiority on the other'.

This embryonic 'class consciousness' did not carry over into collective organization, however, and unionization remained low. 'Although she might be willing to prove her solidarity in every concrete situation, . . . [the woman worker] refuses to look farther than that'. The reason, it seems, was that, 'Whilst the man has accepted work as a part of his life, "real life" for the factory girl starts with the moment she leaves the factory at the end of the day'. Thus, they seldom took an interest in the details of production or the end product of their work. Rather, attention focused on things that mattered outside – personal appearance, for instance. 'Lipstick, rouge, and powder are commonly used from the early morning onwards; waves and curls become obligatory.' Appearance in turn was linked to boyfriends and these to marriage: 'The expectation of marrying at latest in her twenties is part and parcel of the outlook of a factory girl; she is very conscious of the fact that this is her only means of escape from the routine and monotony of work.'[22]

The contrast between this world of women workers and that of working men could hardly be starker. Where men structured their lives around their identity at work, women drew upon their roles in the family and community for their sense of self, and fitted work around these. When men feared deskilling, women were more likely to welcome any change that lightened their labours so long as it did not reduce earnings. If anyone's work was degraded it was probably that of women factory workers whose defences were weaker than men's and whose outlook on the jobs was shot through with a deep ambivalence. In many cases, then, women's jobs came to approximate most closely to the norm which the rationalizers and scientific managers held out for all of industry, while men continued to inhabit relatively more comfortable and sheltered niches within the production process. And from these more secure positions they could begin, even in the most advanced and rationalized firms, to build up once again those networks of resistance that would crystallize in formal union organization. To be sure, this depended upon having a job, but after 1935 jobs were created. When they were, it quickly emerged that recent changes in the labour process may have been sufficient to heighten resistance to further technical change, but not so dramatic as to wrest control of the shopfloor from the men or to incapacitate their efforts at collective organization.

The less happy fate of working women had rather different consequences. Because the technological domination feared by men so often fell upon women, they did not look to work for meaning and satisfaction. Instead, they coped by constructing their lives around different relationships and values – around the home, around the neighbourhood, around the needs of family members. In so doing, they may have pioneered a path of development for working-class culture as a whole from the sphere of production to that of consumption. Whether that path was one of retreat or of progress may certainly be debated, but it was the path that would ultimately be followed by the entire class when circumstances allowed. Of course, circumstances seldom allowed much advance in patterns of consumption or leisure before 1939, but what little there was set the course for much of what followed. Conversely, the fact that the course was largely set in the depressed context of the 1930s would have great impact upon the subsequent evolution of working-class ways of life.

5

Working-Class Life and Culture between the Wars

The overriding problem faced by workers between the wars was economic. Without prosperity, prospects for improving the quality of life were dim. What little progress there was, was achieved by enormous efforts, and despite the state of the economy. The depression not only undermined workers' collective strength, it also made more or less permanent those outward signs of inequality that branded working people and marked them off from the rest of society.

It is more than a little ironic, therefore, that the great social discovery of the interwar decades was 'the problem of leisure'. The New Survey of London claimed that '. . . all the forces at work are combining to shift the main centre of a worker's life more and more from his daily work to his daily leisure'.[1] This was no doubt aided by the fact that 'Work, once a curse, has become a blessing that – paradoxically enough – is being withheld because the fruits of man's labour are too abundant.'[2] The absence of work focused attention upon the problem of the workless and upon what working men and women did apart from work. The curious connection was made explicitly by Henry Durant, founder of the British Institute of Public Opinion: '. . . since the war', he wrote, 'and . . . the . . . depression. . ., with its vast unemployment and its severe jolt to all social institutions, all the bareness of our institutional life has become visible.'[3]

But was the institutional life of ordinary people in fact really bare, and were they actually left exposed to the rigours and privations of the depression with no social or cultural protection? Or was it more a matter of the commentators from outside the working class failing to see the richness or, as Jack Common put it, the 'good communal stir and warmth' within it?[4] The latter would seem the more likely possibility, for most investigators never considered the normal routines of social interaction among working people as the proper use of leisure or even as genuine friendship. Even sympathetic observers, like Durant, failed to penetrate the habits and mentality of the working class. In a classic instance of class blindness, Innis Pearce and Scott Williamson, founders of the pioneer Peckham Health Centre, completely missed the social networks of the urban workers. They wrote movingly, for example, about 'The state of isolation in which the artisans of the big cities dwell. . .', and felt it to be 'so complete . . . that when faced with some quandary or difficulty there is literally no one to whom [they] can turn . . . [T]he isolation . . . is a specific source of disease', they argued, 'physical, psychological and social alike'.[5]

It is possible, however, to read the apparent impenetrability of working-class life in quite a different way, as proof not of the paucity of friendships and institutions but of their richness. It is clear, after all, that by about 1920, British workers had elaborated a broad array of institutions – unions, cooperatives, local political parties, working-men's clubs and a plethora of groups devoted to sports and hobbies – running through the neighbourhoods and factories and centred upon the family, the pub or the place of work. It is unlikely that this culture disappeared during the interwar period, but it does appear to have become less aggressive and self-confident. The defeats of the early 1920s, of 1926 and of 1931, plus the chronic lack of work, exerted a dampening effect upon attitudes and behaviour, turning workers inward, and making security rather than any notion of collective advance the highest value.

The insurgent working class of postwar was in this way tamed and transformed. 'Among the workers', as Jack Common put it, 'there is little faith. . .'; class sentiments and loyalties were strong, but streaked with a 'primal apathy'.[6] The result was a hardening of class attitudes and relationships. This is revealed graphically in a survey done by Mass-Observation just before the outbreak of war in 1939.[7] A national panel of respondents was sent a questionnaire on class in June, 1939, and usable replies were received from 225 men and about half that number of women. The panel was weighted disproportionately towards the middle and lower-middle classes, but over a third of the men claimed membership of the working class, not enough for a definitive sample but surely enough to indicate the general picture. The tenor of the answers was amazingly 'class-conscious': almost 97% had no difficulty attaching a class label to their work and persons. Nearly all conceded that their social circles were restricted to their own class; a majority were more highly sensitive to class than to regional variations in accent, and a minority admitted having made a conscious effort to modify their own manner of speaking.[8]

Most striking was the way intense class awareness was mixed in with an acceptance of class membership and tolerance towards other classes. A young machinist from Durham, for instance, was utterly content to be a worker and immensely proud of what it meant: 'I belong, quite definitely, to the Working Class, by reason of my income, but mainly of course by my occupation. . . . I should still "class" myself with the workers no matter how much income I had. . . . I am proud of my being a member of the "Working Class", [and] have no desire to be identified in any other class. . .' A middle-aged textile worker from Huddersfield felt much the same sort of identification: 'I somehow feel I have working class in my bones, and if my circumstances were suddenly altered I feel I couldn't be disloyal to that class.' Were he, despite such deep loyalties, nevertheless to be tempted into a new posture, he felt sure that his background would force him back: 'With not having had an upper class grounding in grammar, deportment or speech, I know I could easily make a mistake or slip, which would place me immediately. So I try to be my natural self.'

Aspirations, social intercourse and personality were also coloured by the strength of class feelings and of class boundaries. The idea that money would not suffice to shift a man or woman from one class to another was expressed again and again. This is a curious finding, for there were improvements in living standards between the wars, especially after 1934–5. Yet they did not create among workers any sort of vision of sustained increases in consumption or convince any large number that such a prospect would have altered or muted class differences. A printer's assistant from Bradford expressed the predominant ethos when he wrote that 'Money, of course, is the mainstay of any class. The working-class attitude to it is for the most part indifferent. If a person has a steady job and a decent income he never worries overmuch about saving, except for holidays, etc. There are a good few "grab-alls", of course, but on the whole the average worker is most happy when he can be indifferent.'

The fact that a bit more money and educational opportunity existed in the 1930s probably made working people and their children more aware of the distinctiveness of class culture and outlooks. A young 'works chemist', just beginning to rise above his class roots, figured that since 'At the present time I do not move in a different class to my parents', . . . 'I belong to the working class people.' His view of the role of money revealed a fine sociological sensibility: 'Money, I believe, has a great deal to do with present day class distinctions, not perhaps for the actual bank balance but for the background it can provide.' To have enough money thoroughly to alter lifestyle and background was for most a remote prospect. 'Income', one worker believed, 'does not affect me at present, I would not move to a better house or district unless I had a very substantial increase in income.'

The perception of such a wide gulf between not just the incomes, but the social life of working and middle class people allowed workers to distinguish various grades and types among their own class and yet to retain a broad sense of class identity. A 31-year-old upholsterer from Nottingham, for example, dissected class membership into occupational, economic, social and cultural dimensions and could locate himself precisely on each. 'Myself, I should classify: Skilled artisan by trade; middle working class in living habits and manners; round about £3–£4 in income; the W.E.A. study-in-spare-time class as differing from the pub-dance-and-girl-class of young men.' The same young man expressed his preference for socializing 'with informed, but respectable, working-class people' rather than with those of superior background who 'behave in such a mannerly fashion in which I have no training, who have a code which I do not understand'. His sense of belonging to the working class was thus none the weaker for acknowledging the enormous differences that marked off workers from one another. The women workers on the Mass-Observation panel, though too few to draw truly reliable conclusions, seem also to have combined a keen sense of the differences in outlook and behaviour among workers with a frank acceptance of broad working-class identity. Moreover, charged as they were with the twin duties of physical and cultural reproduction, women were even more aware of the importance of families and family background in determining class position and sentiment. The women much more often mentioned long-term roots in the working class, through grandparents, aunts, uncles and siblings than did the men, and recognized clearly that money gains were evanescent compared to the ingrained habits of thought and behaviour that made one 'working-class' by birth.

Both the men and the women sampled by Mass-Observation thus testified to the persistence, possibly even the strengthening, of class distinctions and loyalties through the 1930s. Nonetheless, the sense of class expressed in 1939 differed in important respects from the meanings attached to class before and after this point in time. In the early postwar years, the recognition of class was coupled with a sense of antipathy, confrontation and crisis. Then the very existence and polarization of class seemed to imply also a bitter class struggle. Later on, the rhetoric of class would become increasingly bound up with notions of change and progress, against which the resiliency of class inequalities would be measured, resented and denounced. In 1939, the reality of class is accepted, not happily, but with a tone of inevitability, and the shape of the class structure remains, in the view of most people, essentially 'immobile'.

It is necessary, therefore, when looking at the details of working-class life in the late 1920s and 1930s, to bear in mind this essential stability in class relations. Though aspects of working class family life, community structure and patterns of consumption and leisure changed significantly, nothing happened that could not be understood and appreciated within the terms then in use for thinking about class. A review of the gains and losses in the various spheres of working-class existence will make this even clearer, and will confirm in local detail the opinions and conclusions of the Mass-Observers of 1939.

The working-class family

When Richard Hoggart set out in the 1950s to describe the working class as he had known it, back in the late 1930s and 1940s, he began with the home and the family. 'The more we look at working-class life', he wrote, 'the more we try to reach the core of working-class attitudes, the more surely does it appear that the core is a sense of the personal, the concrete, the local: it is embodied in the idea of, first, the family and, second, the neighbourhood.'[9] At the centre of the home and the family was, of course, the mother, 'the human anchor which holds it fast . . . without whose labour the whole structure of the family tends to collapse.'[10] The shape of the family and the position of women were thus critical factors in the condition of life for most working people.

Just how important can be seen from the relative contribution of falling family size to standards of living. According to Mark Abrams, nearly one-third of the gains in real income between 1913–14 and 1937–8 were attributable to the decrease in the size of the average worker's family from 4.65 persons before the war to 3.77 in 1937–8. This decline was primarily due to deliberate family limitation by working-class couples, particularly by the women.[11]

Before the First World War, the birth rate for families of semi-skilled workers was more than a third higher than for families of professionals and the upper ranks of business; the rate for unskilled workers was almost double. From that time on, however, it began to fall steadily and, after 1921, sharply. From 1921 to 1931, the birth rate among semi-skilled fell by 50%, among the unskilled by 48% and among the skilled by 28%. The resulting family sizes were correspondingly smaller for both manual and non-manual workers, as Table 5.1 demonstrates.

Table 5.1 *Estimates of Size of Completed Families, by Marriage Date, 1900–1929*

	Family Size among:	
Date of Marriage	Non-Manual Workers	Manual Workers
1900–09	2.79	3.94
1910–14	2.34	3.35
1915–19	2.05	2.91
1920–24	1.89	2.73
1925–29	1.73	2.49

Source: Jane Lewis, *The Politics of Motherhood*, (1980), p.48.

This shrinkage was achieved primarily by conscious efforts at contraception. Table 5.2 shows how few women married before 1910 used the available means of contraception. After the war, however,

Table 5.2 *The Spread of Contraception, 1900–1947*

PERCENTAGE OF WIVES OF MEN IN THE FOLLOWING GROUPS WHO HAD USED BIRTH CONTROL:

Year of Marriage	Higher occupations & Non-Manual Workers	Skilled Manual Workers	Other Manual Workers	All
Before 1910	26	18	4	15
1910–19	60	39	33	40
1920–24	56	60	54	58
1925–29	58	60	63	61
1930–34	64	62	63	63
1935–39	73	68	54	66
1940–47	67	53	47	55

Source: Ronald Fletcher, *The Family and Marriage in Britain*, Third Edition, (Harmondsworth, 1973), p. 125, calculated from the Royal Commission on Population, Vol. 1, 1949, Cmnd. 7695.

some method of family limitation became the norm. This could not have occurred without the assent of a good many husbands, but there can be little doubt that in most cases it was the wife who took the initiative. Women in the working class had long sought to control their fertility, sometimes through abstinence but often through abortion. Among the women textile workers of Lancashire, for example, the birth rate had begun to fall even in the late nineteenth century.

That women themselves were crucial is suggested also by the fact that official attitudes remained distinctly hostile. As late as 1939, a government committee opposed a plan for disseminating birth control information, claiming that 'A proposal making contraception universally available upon request . . . [might well] affect adversely the continuity of the state . . . .' Not merely the 'continuity of the state' but the fate of the race was at stake; surprisingly, these 'eugenic' concerns were echoed by feminists like Eva Hubback and 'progressives' like the founders of Mass-Observation and Keynes. Carr-Saunders, for instance, correctly located the source of declining fertility in the reasoned decision of parents, but could not help but describe it as an essentially anti-social act – i.e., as a strike against the community:

> In part the reason for the small size of the family is that parents have gone on strike in protest against the neglect of their special problems. Parenthood has always involved trials and burdens; formerly, however, they were inescapable. . . . Parents are now becoming free, and they take advantage of this freedom to bring the strike weapon into play.[12]

What surely drove women on, despite official discouragement and, in many cases, the less than enthusiastic support of their husbands, was the pain and drudgery of childbirth and childrearing. Women's own accounts, gathered before the First World War by the Women's Cooperative Guild and published as *Maternity*, and later by the Women's Health Enquiry Committee and issued as *Working-Class Wives* in 1939, show both the enormous hardships born by women in producing children and the persistent efforts by women on their own behalf. The Women's Cooperative Guild played a critical role in arguing that in public policy 'the care of the mother should have equal consideration with that of the infant'. Women in the cooperative movement and in the Labour party insisted that family limitation would be in the clear interest of working people. The 1924 party conference actually set up a 'Workers' Birth Control Group', and if many Labour men could be charged with severe 'backsliding' after

1924, the commitment remained in place. As the 1920s progressed, other groups – the National Union of Societies for Equal Citizenship, the Women's Liberal Association, etc. – also came out for birth control. The main campaigners, of course, were Dr Marie Stopes and her supporters, but the role of working-class organizations was important and indicative of the evolving sentiments of working-class women.[13]

Their views were based largely on the dire consequences to women's health and well-being of frequent childbirth, coupled, as it was so often, with poverty and over-work. Of the 1250 women surveyed by the Women's Health Enquiry Committee in the late 1930s, less than a third were judged in good health, 22.3% in 'indifferent health', 15% in bad health and another 31% 'whose condition is very grave'. 558 women suffered from anaemia, almost 400 from gynaecological troubles; while headaches, toothaches, rheumatism and other ills plagued large numbers as well. Despite these massive rates of illness, health care was abysmal; a mere 13 of the 1250 were covered by national health insurance; the rest had to pay or take what was offered by the local council or parish. Most ailments went untreated and women's overall health slowly deteriorated, as bad housing, under-nourishment and unremitting household toil took their toll. As the report concluded,

> All except a very few . . . are too poor. Nearly all are too poor to buy the healthy satisfaction even of their primary needs, food, fuel and light, decent housing and a minimum of clothing and household equipment.[14]

What is most interesting about this evidence is how late it comes to us. It is based upon conditions of the late 1930s, after the sustained increase in living standards and the revival of the mid-'30s had begun to lift substantial numbers out of primary poverty. The health of working-class women appears to have been almost impervious to economic improvement. This accords with the abundant testimony on the tendency of working-class women to sacrifice their own health, nutrition and amenities for their husbands and children. In view of this, the equanimity with which women spoke of their troubles and the generosity which they expressed towards their husbands was in fact quite remarkable. One example will suffice:

> I believe myself that one of the biggest difficulties our mothers have is our husbands do not realise we ever need any leisure time. My life for many years consisted of being penned in a kitchen 9 feet

square, every fourteen months a baby, as I had five babies in five years at first, until what with the struggle to live and no leisure I used to feel I was just a machine, until I had my first breakdown, and as dark as it was and as hard as it was it gave me the freedom and privilege of having an hour's fresh air. And so I truly know this is the lot of many a poor mother. . . . So many of our men think we should not go out until the children are grown up. . . It isn't the men are unkind. It is the old idea we should always be at home.[15]

Even in the worst of circumstances, an almost stoic forbearance seems to have prevailed. The testimony of Bermondsey housewives, for instance, whose husbands were as often out of work as in it, revealed little self-pity. The wife of a marginally employed docker concluded, 'I am really quite satisfied with life as it is', although she was moved to add, 'if only I had a nice little house or flat of my own, and my husband's work was a little more certain, as it is very hard for a man with no better prospects, and we have carried on this way for eight years.' Few allowed themselves even such dreams; for most it was the view of how much worse things could be that kept hope alive. As another put it, 'On the whole I don't think life is too bad; bad enough for me, but perhaps worse for some other poor devils who have not got so much. I am very happy in my home, I love my husband and child and I don't think there's much more I can ask but that.' Despite the poverty and ill-health, home life and family relations seem on the whole to have been a source of strength and support in a world where there were limited opportunities for more positive kinds of enjoyment.[16] And the accomplishment, limited as it was, was due largely to the efforts of working-class women to make their families smaller and better-managed and, quite simply, to give them a fuller life.

The working class community

In the accounts of these years, it is difficult to disentangle from one another the influences of family, home, and neighbourhood. It was not only that neighbourhood rivalled family as a locus of sociability, but that the two overlapped and helped to constitute each other. Workers themselves found it difficult to distinguish the home, the family and the locality. A railwayman described his new house in Willesden appreciatively and could not keep clear any distinction between the quality of family life, of his house and of his neighbourhood. His leisure was centred in or near the house, and as for his wife and the youngest he explained that 'their hobby is to keep the place clean and feed us. The children like to paint and make the place untidy; then they are happy.' A railway checker, employed at Ilford but residing in the Becontree estate at Dagenham, waxed eloquent about 'the open air and good garden' at the estate, and conceded that his leisure was his free time at home. Closer in, near King's Cross, yet another worker confessed that, 'I make no friends, I simply leave work, and go home, and amuse myself reading the paper, and sitting at the front-room window watching the children play in the street . . . I may mention that we [my wife and I] tell each other what goes on, thus sharing one another's troubles.'[17]

Home was probably even more important to the unemployed worker, for without spare income the normal spots for socializing – the pub and the club – would be closed off. A laid-off electrical engineer from Greenwich thus expressed the problem in relatively optimistic terms, 'Being out of a job has different effects according to the kind of home you have. It makes me think more of my home because I get to live in it more and it is rather cosy, isn't it?' A sheet-metal worker, also from Greenwich, was equally proud of his home and afraid of possibly losing it, or at least some of its comforts, due to unemployment. As he says,

> Suppose I would have to sell that chair over there, there would be more than that chair go out of this room. . . I'd be selling a part of myself. Do you see how it is? Some of these fellows as grumble ought to think back when they was kids and remember that they'd have had to pawn a lot more then than now. It isn't that unemployment insurance benefit makes it possible to live that's important only. *It helps you to keep yourself together that way.*

Unfortunately, many did lose their favourite chairs, and much more, during the depression. Still, one cannot read the evidence without being struck by the resiliency and stability of working-class communities and families during the interwar years.[18]

The stability was achieved, moreover, despite several trends which were thought at the time to be causing disintegration of community ties. There was, first of all, the lack of work, whose effects upon morale and social life became a subject of repeated inquiry. Second, much of the new housing being built was located on estates some distance away from the old centres of working-class life and culture and poorly equipped with amenities and the physical spaces required for social intercourse. Working-class communities, neighbourhoods and local institutions were buffeted by these two new phenomena, mass unemployment and massive public housing, but nonetheless survived.

The main peculiarities of unemployment were its duration and its concentration. Unemployment came to Britain in the latter part of 1920 and stayed for two decades, creating a substantial group for whom it was a semi-permanent condition. A report on the unemployed on Durham and Tyneside in 1934, for example, showed that of 165,000 out of work, no less than 63,000 had been without a job for over a year, 30,000 of these for more than three years. It was often argued that these 'long-term unemployed' were gradually becoming unfit to work and, presumably, unfit for proper citizenship. Real evidence for these fears was never adduced, however, and it seems that the other major peculiarity of interwar unemployment – its local incidence – worked in the opposite direction.

For the highest rates of unemployment were concentrated in the centres of the old industries. In parts of industrial Scotland, South Wales, the shipbuilding centres on the Tyne, much of Lancashire, unemployment affected not individuals but entire communities. The stigma that could well have attached to being unemployed in a town where the majority continued to find work was thus absent when the bulk of the workers could not secure steady jobs. In addition, the areas worst hit by the slump were regions with the best organized working class, with strong trade union and cooperative movements and other working-class institutions. Unemployment in these districts was experienced collectively and, though painful, it was a shared pain that did not produce the isolation and demoralization so feared by social commentators.[19]

This is best confirmed by the results of the Pilgrim Trust study of the long-term unemployed begun in 1936. Areas where unemployment was chronic, like the Rhondda, Liverpool, Crook in Co. Durham and Blackburn in Lancashire, were compared with places where it was more a matter of casualism, such as Deptford, and with Leicester, where there was little of any sort. In Leicester, it was found, the unemployed were often older men whose jobs had been lost due to technological change or to regional shifts in industry. There, it led to isolation and personal depression. 'We've always tried to keep our troubles to ourselves', explained the wife of a 57-year old skilled 'clicker', but 'sometimes I wonder whether we've kept to ourselves too much, whether things might not have been easier if we'd been able to tell other people about them'. In Blackburn, where a substantial block of long-term unemployment coexisted with a modest overall level, there was also considerable isolation. In more prosperous London, the psychological effect of being without work was even more keenly felt, and men tended to 'regard the public-houses as closed to them . . . and in conversation will admit to being afraid someone will stand them a drink they can't return'.[20]

In most areas, though, families remained stable and the home was treasured as the one possession secure from the ravages of the depression. 'Many couples, young and old', – and in all of the towns – 'had their interests almost exclusively centred on the home . . . it was of extreme importance to keep intact the "front room," hardly ever used, but conferring somehow through its shiny furniture a feeling of independence and status. . . .' Among the memoirs of the unemployed gathered by Beales and Lambert in 1933, there were a few instances of family tension generated by unemployment, but in the majority of cases the resilience of relations is striking. A South Wales miner conceded that 'Unemployment has made me very bitter against society', but it 'has not interfered with or changed my family life, since my wife has always had an optimistic outlook and has tried to tell me not to worry. . . .' A London fitter's wife was reported to have played much the same role; there were, of course, lots of minor irritations – 'Afternoons', a worker recalled, 'I used to lounge about the house and the wife used to get fed up' – and more than a little self-doubt – 'I think', said a millwright, that 'my wife looks on me now as a useless piece of goods' – but overall the impression created by these memoirs and other reports is of a remarkable strength and patience.[21]

Still more impressive was the rich social life that flourished despite unemployment in some of the worse affected localities. In inner Liverpool, the lack of work created a 'compact body of. . .young men' who were gradually able to 'evolve both an individual and communal pattern of life'. There was 'a strong community spirit in the Rhondda' as well, where it enveloped most of the adult population in what the Report labelled 'a hotbed of institutions', ranging from the chapel to the Communist Party, from the co-op to the dancing club and the brass band. In Crook, it was said, there was an even greater 'determination not to give way to unemployment and not to subsist on self-pity than there was [even] in Wales', though it was claimed that 'the foundation of that culture . . . apparent in Crook seemed to be family rather than institutional life'. But whether one emplasized in any particular instance the family or the neighbourhood, it was nonetheless the case that, because of the curious geography of unemployment, its effect was normally not to erode but to reinforce the ties that undergirded working-class community life.[22]

If any section of the populace from the depressed areas experienced serious isolation, it was probably those younger men and women who chose, or were forced, to leave for the south or the Midlands in search of work. The Welsh who went to Oxford, the Scots who moved to the Midlands, the tens of thousands from all over the north who migrated to London, must have felt the loneliness of being uprooted, at least for a while, and a sadness at the knowledge that the neighbourhoods of their youth could offer them no hope of future work. A number of older workers, in fact, expressed deep resentment at the need to send away their children, and had no use for the industries upon which their communities had once been built. Still, the troubles were usually just temporary, for most of the migrants appear to have fitted in without enormous difficulty to the working-class communities of Birmingham, Coventry, London and many smaller cities in the growing regions.

A rather different problem confronted those urban workers who took up residence in the new housing estates. Between the wars, nearly a fifth of British workers were rehoused, most of them on estates located in the outer sections of the large cities, but a small number in the older inner areas. The new estates were a matter for considerable public commentary and debate. It was widely believed that the lack of established institutions meant an impoverished cultural and social life in the new environment. Some wrote ominously and frantically of the dire consequences for religion and family life, but even a sober observer like Margery Spring Rice was moved to argue: 'One of the outstanding disadvantages of the new housing estates, e.g., Dagenham, is that by removing families from tenement buildings they have destroyed that compulsory neighbourliness which was a feature of the old system.[23]

The debate over 'the social need of the housing estates' would appear, however, to have been refracted through the very same class biases that prevented commentators from seeing the variety and richness of working-class life more generally. For what detailed evidence exists suggests a very different picture. Terence Young's early study of the Becontree estate at Dagenham, for example, turned up not a dismal social wasteland but a rapidly developing institutional life.

The estate grew slowly from its beginnings in 1922, with a mere 2,000 residents, to over 100,000 by 1932. Almost immediately residents formed themselves into tenants' associations and established Labour and Conservative party branches and Co-operatives. The pub deficiency was made good by quickly organized clubs, like the New Becontree Club, set up in 1924 and attracting in a short time 2,000 adult men. Between 1926 and 1928, a Dagenham Working Men's Club, a new Labour Club and two Salvation Army Halls were opened, along with seven churches. Pub facilities grew proportionately as well, first off the premises of the estate and then on the estate itself. A review of 1927 turned up, in addition to the neighbourhood pubs within reach, four beerhouses owned by the London County Council, and led to a plan for six more. Three co-operative guild branches were in existence by 1927, and two of the ILP; the Dagenham Trades Council was formed in 1928, a sign of substantial prior union organization and a stimulus to more of it. In the early 1930s, the Barking proportion of the estate began to fill up and, of course, replicated the institutional development of the earlier settled north and south sections. By 1933, 'the previous collection of organisations [had] expanded until at present in Dagenham it is probably larger than, although different from, that of an ordinary town'.[24]

The experience of Dagenham was repeated elsewhere. Ruth Darant's study of Watling, for example, concluded that, 'Today Watling is still distinguished by its successful social activities. It appears that . . . there is more neighbourliness, more corporate life on the Estate than in adjacent suburbs or in the parent town.' Durant proceeded in fact to argue the superiority of the social life in places like Watling to that in older working-class areas. As she put it, the new estates 'expose the loneliness of urban people and the paucity of their institutions'.[25]

She did, however, identify certain problems of the new estates that should not be forgotten. At least in the early stages, they caused a substantial increase in commuting, for most jobs remained elsewhere. Gradually, more of the residents found work locally, but the problems persisted even then for a proportion of the population. Second, rentals for the new houses were often much higher than those previously paid by working people and many, after moving to the estate, got quickly into arrears with their rents and either were forced to skimp on other things – food, clothing, entertainment – or had to leave. Ten per cent turnover per year was not unusual. In addition, the substantial rents led to a *de facto* process of selection such that the population of the new estates tended not to be average working-class families but the 'elite of the working class', with a sprinkling of white-collar and supervisory workers. An LCC survey of council tenants in the late 1930s on five major estates showed that 22.6% were the households of skilled workers, 31.3% semi-skilled, 17.1% transport workers, 10% blackcoated workers, 5% retail traders, and 5.6% postal workers, police or servicemen. In Liverpool, the proportion of non-manual workers rose to 20%. The social character of estates, though overwhelmingly working-class, was thus by no means strictly a reflection of those most in need.[26]

The most comprehensive information on housing and communities was assembled by Mass-Observation for their inquiry resulting in the report *People's Homes* in 1941. Twelve working-class communities were studied and compared to each other and to areas studied by Young, Durant, and others. Of the twelve sites, five were older working-class neighbourhoods located in Birmingham (labelled Midtown), Fulham (designated Metrotown), Ilford (Subtown), Portsmouth (Seatown) & Worcester (Churchtown); three were LCC estates, Becontree (Oak Estate), Roehampton (Elm Estate) and Watling (Ash Estate); two others were blocks of flats in Fulham (Metroflats) and Kentish Town (Newflats); and there were samples from two Garden Cities, Bournville (Modelville) and Letchworth (Gardenville). The main findings of the survey – done primarily with housewives and in the home – are presented in Table 5.3.

Though there were some variations across the four classes of housing, the most pronounced difference was that which marked off the attitudes of those living in the older neighbourhoods from the rest. People living in new housing, whether estates, flats, or garden cities, were extremely satisfied with their homes and neighbourhoods and, presumably, with the family and community life that went on in these settings. Although there were fragmentary bits of evidence suggesting that some people preferred the hustle and bustle and street-corner sociability of older neighbourhoods over the 'sterility' and isolation of the new estates, such sentiments rarely found their way into the overall evaluations of homes and neighbourhoods. An inveterate Cockney displaced to Watling complained, for example, 'I dislike everything. I'd sooner be back in London, I don't like the country.' An elderly woman living in a Kentish Town flat felt the absence of activity even more strongly; as she saw it, 'They're not neighbourly here. My husband's out all day. There's nothing going on. As I say, I like a jolly good fight to watch. Mind you, I don't want to be in it.' Nonetheless, the new estates and flats got consistently higher marks than old areas both as homes and neighbourhoods. Even in the older communities, however, satisfaction was high. It seems reasonable to conclude that working people's communities remained vibrant and healthy throughout the interwar period, resisting equally the disintegrating effects of poverty

Table 5.3 *Main findings from People's Homes, 1941–2*

Percent	OLD DISTRICTS					HOUSING ESTATES			FLATS		NEW TOWNS	
	B'gham.	*Fulham*	*Ilford*	*Ptsmth.*	*Worc.*	*Becontree*	*Roehampt'n*	*Watling*	*Fulham*	*Kentish Twn*	*B'ville*	*Letch.*
Class C (artisan or skilled)	14	52	89	8	13	48	70	46	41	44	77	57
Class D (unskilled)	86	43	11	92	87	51	29	54	59	56	18	37
with children under 14	53	29	50	35	59	68	49	54	61	57	31	60
liked homes	67	66	72	55	48	85	86	70	74	84	85	70
had gardens	73	65	60	100	50	100	100	100	0	0	100	100
had bathrooms	3	36		0	0	99	100	100	100	87	79	68
liked neighbourhoods	63	65	48	62	53	63	96	71	59	78	83	77
owning homes	0	5	42	10	5	0	0	0	0	0	23	2
would like to own homes	7	18	46	28	20	14	29	18	26	17	30	38
Ave. Rent per week	10/-	20/6	21/-	12/6	7/-	16/6	22/6	19/-	17/-	16/6	–	–

Source: *People's Homes*, by Mass-Observation (London, 1943). See also note 36 below.

and unemployment and the centrifugal tendencies stimulated by the provision of new types of housing. As the group of Mass-Observers who studied Bolton a few years earlier had concluded, 'It takes more than a semi-detached house and a small piece of garden to destroy the Worktown [Bolton] worker's feeling for fraternization.'[27]

If there was any change at all, it was perhaps a slight shift away from communal ties and activities and towards a greater focus upon the home and the family. The Mass-Observation survey found a distressing absence of community spirit and civic responsibility among respondents, but considerable interest in mass entertainment, particularly the cinema and, to a lesser extent, in dancing. The trend, it appears, was for working people to take their leisure and to spend their incomes more as individuals or families. Still, it was a slight shift of emphasis rather than any qualitative transformation; for most working people home and community were not alternative foci, but part of a single world of daily life.

Consumption and leisure

To the extent that working people did become oriented rather more towards personal concerns and enjoyments, this was partly due to the fact that the new forms of consumption and entertainment available to workers had to be grasped as individuals or as individuals sitting or standing together in a mass. The cinema and the football pool, as much as the wireless, were not particularly collective forms of leisure, and more time and money came to be expended on these as the interwar decades progressed. From the standpoint of most working people, though, what was most new and important was that greater time and income could be devoted to consumption and leisure, of whatever sort.

Just how much extra time and money did this amount to? First, in terms of time, the norm in British industry during the interwar years was a 48-hour week, with a half-holiday on Saturday, compared to a 54-hour week before the First World War. There were, of course, exceptions: in 1935, the Factories Inspector reported 'many cases' of hours up to 55 or 57½ among women and young persons, and there was a broad tendency for employers to give some workers considerable overtime rather than to take on new men (or women). The miners also, it will be remembered, were forced to work longer hours after 1926, though most of this loss was recouped in 1937. Still, workers had an extra 4–7 hours available every week for their own pursuits.

The expansion of daily and weekly leisure time was complemented by a growth in the number of working people entitled to holidays. Holidays with pay were a rarity before the First World War. In 1911, the Trades Union Congress passed a resolution calling for paid annual holidays but little came of it. In 1925, the Ministry of Labour calculated that only 1½ million workers received holidays as part of a collective bargaining agreement; until 1929, this number remained stable, but jumped to three million in 1937–8. Between 1920 and 1938, a rather larger number of workers had been granted holidays in some form or other by their employers, so that a Departmental Committee could estimate in April 1938 that a total of 7¾ million received paid holidays out of a workforce of 18½ million. Of course, the number who took holidays on their own resources was even greater. The New Survey of London estimated in the early 1930s that one-half of London workers took holidays away from home, and the 'wakes system' in the North affected a similar proportion. This gradual voluntary spread of holidays was extended and made mandatory by the Holidays with Pay Act of 1938, which established paid holidays for no less than 11 million by the outbreak of the war.[28]

The modest growth of leisure time was paralleled by comparably modest advances in wages and incomes. Real wages were about 8% higher in 1920 than in 1914. Between 1920 and 1925, both wages and prices fell by a third, and real incomes thus remained about the same. Prices continued to decline from 1925 through 1934, while wages fell only slightly and, in many cases, stabilized. The 'downward stickiness of wages' thus created a real wage increase of another 15% during the worst years of the slump. Adult male wages held up better than the wages for women and young persons, and with adult males contributing slightly more of the family income (and women and youths somewhat less), the income available to the average working-class family therefore increased by between 30 and 40% between 1914 and 1937–8. Such extra earnings made possible an improvement in the standard of living of nearly 70%, however, due to the decrease in the size of working-class families.

An inquiry into working-class budgets in 1937–8 gives an indication of how this income was used. Before the war, about half was spent on food; by the late 1930s, this was down to just under 40%, and that bought 40% more or better food than did the food portion of the 1914 budget. The proportion of income spent on rent and on clothing remained constant. This allowed, however, a 30% or greater increase in the amount of clothing per person. By 1937–8, slightly more was spent on women's clothing than men's, a quite marked change from the previous pattern, in which men's Sundays suits were probably the main type of clothing purchased by working people. The largest increase was in the percentage of income devoted to 'other' purposes besides food, rent and clothing. Estimates of the amount spent on these items before 1914 vary – some put it as low as 4%, others as high as 18%. If the latter was closer to the norm, as it seems to be, it is nonetheless much less than the 30% of income devoted to such items in the late 1930s. This increase was divided among expenditures on household equipment, furniture and utensils, tobacco and cigarettes, drink, newspapers and entertainment, as well as insurance and pension payments. Few of these were luxuries, but the ability to afford them was new and probably seemed a luxury to many.[29]

The great bulk of the additional income coming into working-class families thus went straight out again in expenditures on what might be called the 'essentials of reproduction'. Food, household furnishing and contributions for medicine, insurance and pensions took up almost all the increase. The proportion devoted to genuinely leisure-time activities – travel not related to work, entertainment, reading matter, drinks, smokes, holidays and licences for dogs and the wireless – remained very small indeed, amounting to no more than 9% of expenditure, and a quarter of that was for tobacco. With more money available, workers first improved their diets and their immediate domestic environment, and only then began to turn their attention toward the new opportunities offered by the emerging 'mass culture'.

This rather conservative use of the slightly increased time and money available to working people was a product of the insecurity of employment and workers' uncertainty about the duration of improvement. Those who had greater incomes could not be sure they would continue, and many were reluctant to invest psychologically in the prospect of increasing consumption. Money came and went quickly, but could not be depended upon; as Jack Common put it, 'When they are making good money, it really is "good" money, that is, money which instantly crystallizes into pianos and football teams and motor-bikes and new boots all round for the family.[30] But just as instantly it might disappear, and it made little sense to save up or even to plan on sustained increases in the future.

The second factor retarding the adoption of a more consumption-oriented lifestyle was the peculiar pattern of industrial variation during the depression. The disparity of employment opportunities worked to narrow differences among working people. The elite of skilled workers had been concentrated before 1914 in the prosperous export trades that were most depressed after 1920. The best jobs after the war were on the railways, which were secure but not highly paid, or in the new industries where organization was weaker and wages lower than one might expect. Also, those working in the more prosperous locations were often forced to pay substantially more for rent and other necessities, whereas social provision was more developed in the older communities. On balance, these trends meant a compression of incomes around the mean, and prevented the emergence of a significantly large group of prosperous workers positioned to take advantage of the full range of new opportunities.[31]

The common standard of working-class life is revealed clearly in the marketing research of the late 1930s. The UK Marketing Survey of 1937 collected information on employment and unemployment, on the diffusion of telephones, electricity and the wireless, and on incomes and social composition for over 135 urban areas. The results revealed that the vast differences in income and employment from one locality to the other were not regularly translated into comparable differences in access to electricity or the wireless. Cardiff had three times the unemployment of Portsmouth, but more wireless sets; Birmingham had a 'purchasing power index' twice that of Liverpool, but no more access to electricity or the wireless. Virtually all working-class families had wireless sets, and whether they had electricity seemed to depend upon the competence and energy of local authorities rather than prosperity. On the other hand, virtually nobody had telephones or motor cars. The conventional contrast between the depressed north and the prosperous south was also shown to be somewhat misleading, for the worst hit areas were the smaller, one-industry towns of the north; small, underdeveloped towns in the south, though better off, were not invariably affluent; and the well-developed and populous industrial towns even in the older regions were apparently not so badly off as unemployment rates would by themselves have implied. Since these latter places housed the bulk of the urban workers, it is clear that their stability imparted a resilience to the institutions and culture of these working people as well.[32]

Daily life for most working men and women thus continued to revolve around the family, the neighbourhood, friendships at the pub, the workingmen's club or one of the myriad other social institutions that flourished in urban communities. To the home, though, were added furnishings and amenities that made it more comfortable and healthier; while to the established recreations were tacked on the diversions of the cinema, dancing, the holiday at Blackpool or Margate, the football pools and dog racing. The spread of such novel pursuits did not amount to a new way of life, but served to enrich the old.

The routines of working people inside their homes were also enriched by better amenities, by access to the wireless and the greater availability of reading matter. By the late 1930s, twice as many newspapers and books came into the house as in 1914, and reading increased steadily as the average school leaving age rose first to 14 and then to 15. Of course, to most working-class children the academic world of the school remained just as alien as it had been before the war. Worse still, what changes there were in curriculum and school organization between the wars – the separation of elementary schools into junior and senior primary schools and the spread of certain forms of 'streaming' – reinforced class distinctions rather than removing them. Still, the long-term consequences of public education were to increase literacy and to enlarge the range of information available to working people. Enrolment in various adult education classes, for example, tripled from 1921 to 1937–8, and though such self-improving activity was confined mostly to young men in skilled manual or clerical jobs, reading for pleasure seems to have been spread widely among women. A wide array of women's magazines came onto the market and between 1924 and 1939 the number of library books borrowed tripled also.[33]

The attractiveness of the home was no doubt enhanced, too, by the upgrading of the domestic environment. Between 1924 and 135, consumers' expenditure on wooden furniture rose by half and the amount spent on electrical appliances, lamps and lighting went from £9 to £24.3 millions. The most treasured new item was the wireless. Even in Liverpool, a third of the workers had radios by the early 1930s, and by 1936, nine families out of ten had one. Together, these various additions and improvements began to transform the working-class home from a place to sleep, eat and toil, to a centre of social activity.[34]

Outside the home, the pub remained the major locus of working-class life. Probably the best description of the role of the pub was the Mass-Observation study, *The Pub and the People*, based upon Bolton. As that report argued, 'Of the social institutions that mould men's lives between home and work in an industrial town . . . the pub has more buildings, holds more people, takes more of their time and money, than church, cinema, dance-hall, and political organisations put together.' The pub was not merely a place to drink but a place to talk, to smoke and spit, to play games such as dominoes, darts, cards and quoits, to bet, to sing, to hold meetings of union branches and secret societies – e.g., Oddfellows and Buffaloes – to organize Christmas clubs, outings, pigeon races, dog shows, bowls, and fishing expeditions, and, on occasion, to find or procure sex. Unique in its flexibility, the pub could be the nexus of very traditional pursuits or of the latest fads. It fitted in with the cinema and even with the dance halls, whose young patrons would stop in for a quick drink before, during and after the dance. 'Of the older institutions . . .' of the urban community, 'the pub was in the strongest position' to bridge the gap between old and new.

The pub's most regular clientele was composed primarily of men over 25, but it seems clear that most working men spent at least some portion of the week in the pub, and quite a large minority of the women. Attendance at pubs leapt up, of course, at the weekend – on Fridays, Saturdays *and* Sundays, which meant that both its demography shifted, as more women and young people came, and its tone was elevated, as the clothing and manners of the work-week gave way to the styles of the weekend.[35]

The pub played much the same role throughout the nation, but the number of pubs available varied across the country and even across the areas of a city. Licensing authorities were hostile in the interwar years, and the overall number of pubs actually declined. In many places, working-men's clubs cropped up to fill the gap – no less than 2,692 of these were affiliated to the Working Men's Club and Institute Union in 1933, 109 in London serving 35,000 members. Clubs were allowed slightly more liberal hours, and sold beer more cheaply than the pubs. Presumably official hostility was aimed at curbing drunkenness, but since convictions for this fell by three-quarters from 1913 to 1929, such efforts would seem to have been unnecessary. There is evidence, too, for an inverse relation between the distribution of pubs and the incidence of drunkenness. Liverpool was poorly provided with pubs, but had two and a half times the national average of drunkenness. Some authorities also limited the games and activities that went on in pubs, the theory being that the less hospitable the drinking place, the less drinking would go on. Thus, although 'even the poor type of public bar' in London had a dart-board and though darts were all the rage in Bolton by 1937, there was virtually no darts played in Liverpool, and in 1939 the Glasgow licensing bench went so far as to prohibit 'dominoes, darts and games of any kind' in the 1100 pubs under its jurisdiction.[36]

For most of industrial Britain, however, pubs continued to serve as 'community-centres, where everyone meets, arranges most of his common activities, lays his personal cares aside, and satisfies some of his social cravings'. What did change, though, was that the range of social activities beyond the pub expanded during the interwar years. Dog racing, for example, spread widely after 1925, and came to rival football and, in certain areas, rugby and cricket matches in its ability to attract followers and to compete with horse racing for workers' gambling expenditure. The most important additions to the old repertoire of social activities, of course, were the dance-hall and the cinema. The young and single of both sexes went to the cinema once or twice a week and probably danced one night a week as well at the local 'Palais'. By the late 1930s, almost 20 million admissions to the cinema were sold each week.[37]

The tendency for young unmarried people to frequent the newer forms of entertainment and for older, married people to dominate the pubs and clubs suggests a division of interest by age that could translate over time into more long-term changes in attitudes and behaviour. The participation of young women in the newer recreations was particularly significant as a barometer of change, for they had not been integrated at all well into the leisure activities of the past. Denied the opportunities for self-expression open to young men and confined to the most routine jobs, working-class girls took passionately to the possibilities – real and imagined – of the cinema and the dance-hall, and became their most devoted patrons.[38]

Still, such a transformation was merely inchoate, for in the normal course of events that led from dating to courtship, marriage and children, most young men and women of the working class would follow paths similar to those taken by their parents and would graduate into the established world of the adult working class, centred on the home, the pub and, of course, the workplace. Opportunities for leisure or consumption were severely limited by the intensity of class division and the saliency of class loyalties, which were about as strong in 1939 as they were at any other time since the industrial revolution. The changes wrought since 1919 had brought many new 'goods' – both material and cultural – within the grasp of working men and women, but the pattern and pace of their diffusion were shaped and limited by the realities of class. Once more, British society had proved itself capable of absorbing substantial material transformations without altering, or even loosening, its class boundaries and social hierarchies.

6

The Impact of Defeat, 1929–39

Victories were scarce for working people between the wars. Simply to maintain the strength of the unions and of Labour was difficult enough; genuine advance was normally out of the question. Still, just as the culture of the workers proved resilient enough to resist the corrosive effects of depression and defeat, so, too, the more visible manifestations of class interest – the party and the unions – were quite successful in sustaining membership and loyalties despite the string of losses suffered in the 1920s and 1931, and, after 1935, in beginning again to grow. This defence was based in large part on the inertia produced by the intensely rooted character of working-class life and by the unique circumstances of those particular defeats. By a curious logic, the series of disasters came to be interpreted, not as failures of the movement, but as outcomes forced upon the workers by hostile external forces or by the treachery of individuals under pressure from such foes.

Of course, both the party and the unions faced challenges from within and without. The calling off of the General Strike in May, 1926, for example, left the miners to fight on their own until November, when they finally acquiesced in their inevitable defeat. The owners sought to capitalize on the triumph by encouraging breakaway unions. Their major achievement was the formation of the so-called Spencer Union, based in Nottingham.[1] George Spencer, MP, was a leader of the Nottingham miners who concluded a deal with the owners for a return to work in September 1926. He was duly expelled from the Federation (MFGB) in the same month and proceeded to set up the Miners' Industrial (non-political) Union, which came to dominate the Nottinghamshire coalfield and spread, with mineowners' support, to parts of Scotland, Durham, Northumberland, Yorkshire, Staffordshire, Derbyshire, and South Wales in 1927–8. Overall the attempt to wean miners away from their union met with little success outside Nottinghamshire, but this local tenacity of Spencer unionism, combined with the refusal of the owners to make a national agreement and the sapping of Federation membership by unemployment, served to weaken the miners as a force within the union movement. Affiliation to the MFGB fell from 950,000 in 1920 to something over 780,000 in 1926, and to approximately 525,000 by 1931, and did not begin to recover until after 1935. The Spencer Union was not defeated until 1937, when a fusion of the 'non-political union' and the Nottingham-shire Miners' Association was accomplished and the new organization brought back into the Federation.[2]

The coal owners were not the only employers tempted by the defeat of the General Strike into a more staunchly anti-union stance. Representatives of several employers' groups sought unsuccessfully in 1926 and 1927 to enlist the government in a broad attack on collective bargaining, and when government hesitated, they took the lead themselves in 'victimizing' militants, especially on the railways. But the government was chastened by the solidarity of the General Strike and gave little support. Rather they began to encourage collaboration between organized business and the unions in order to foster more amicable industrial relations and improved productivity. Many employers held back, but others, like Alfred Mond of Imperial Chemicals, did not. Responding to public calls for cooperation from Baldwin and from Hicks of the Trades Union Congress, Mond managed to set up a series of meetings in 1928 between TUC leaders and 'progressive' industrialists. By July an 'Interim Joint Report' was issued, calling for employers to deal with and recognize unions and to refrain from 'victimization', for the establishment of a permanent National Industrial Council, and for joint efforts towards rationalization and productivity.

This essentially 'corporatist' plan was rejected by the employers. Particularly opposed was the National Conference of Employers' Organizations, which in this case meant particularly the engineering and shipping employers. The Mond proposals were viewed, in fact, as a dire threat by the bulk of the business community. Mond's group represented the most prosperous and modern industries rather than the average run of technologically backward small firms, to whom the employers' associations were committed. These firms feared that the Mond proposals would sap their authority and impose conditions they could not afford.

The unions, by contrast, were more favourably disposed. The leaders of the TUC seemed to feel that collaboration would give them an aura of legitimacy sorely lacking after 1926. If they could extract as well a promise of recognition and no-victimization, so much the better. There was also a genuine desire to cooperate in the modernizing of industry. It was becoming clear to many industrialists and union leaders alike that the main obstacles to prosperity were the backwardness of industry and the political dominance of finance, and that both shared interests in pursuing certain kinds of tariff and monetary policies and in accelerating concentration in many industries. Indeed, the only genuine efforts at cooperation came in these areas: e.g., with coordinated testimony to the Macmillan Committee in 1931, and in talks on imperial preference and on breaking the control of the Treasury.

Within the unions, of course, militants attacked Mondism as the betrayal of the class struggle. There was an obvious truth to the charge, but the alternative was neither clear nor attractive at the time. Moreover, the left did not reckon with the sheer obstinacy of the employers who were, as a body, too reactionary even to collaborate effectively. Despite the TUC's endorsement, therefore, the talks ultimately failed, due to employer hostility. The failure signalled a deep-rooted inability within industry to solve its own problems and allowed the initiative in industrial policy to pass into other hands. By not agreeing on a unified policy of industrial relations and economic development, the organizations of British business effectively forfeited the claim to industrial leadership.[3]

The unions and the Labour party were also challenged from within and from the left, but again the effect was minimal. By 1926, the mantle of left leadership had passed from the ILP to the Communists, whose roots in the postwar shop stewards' movement gave them a modest industrial base upon which to build. But at the moment of its greatest opportunity, the party turned away and adopted a highly sectarian stance. The new policy was derived from the Comintern analysis of the so-called Third Period, in which the main task was to attack the 'social fascists' who dominated the labour and social democratic parties of the west. In consequence, the party became increasingly virulent in its attacks upon trade union leaders and members of the Labour party with whom they had differences, and in the process grew more and more isolated from activists, officials and many of the rank-and-file.

Instead of reversing the rightward drift in the TUC, therefore, the ineffectiveness of the Communists probably helped to consolidate the position of the leaders. Unable to influence the direction of policy, moreover, the party began instead to focus its attention on the margins of the movement, where they performed feats of endurance and organization which others were unable or reluctant to undertake. Driven out of the factories, CP members organized the unemployed all over the country and rooted themselves in the communities, where they founded tenants' organizations, local Labour parties and whatever else they could. The CP sent men into Ford at Dagenham, for instance, almost as soon as it opened, and into the main centres of Spencer unionism, such as the Harworth colliery in Nottingham and Bedwas in Wales. Marginalized politically and organizationally, the Communists worked the margins with zeal and effectiveness, and served as recruiting agents for the unions and the Labour party whose leaders they so vehemently denounced.[4]

The party's major success was in the National Unemployed Workers' Movement, led by the CP veteran, Wal Hannington. The movement was founded in 1920, based upon a local London District Council of the Unemployed, but became a truly popular movement only after 1929. When the National Government came to power in August 1931 on a programme of reducing benefits, the NUWM was able to lead substantial resistance among the unemployed. A hunger march was organized from Wales to the TUC meeting in Bristol in September, and a bitter clash with police resulted. In the next month, demonstrations took place in Cardiff, Nottingham, Manchester, Derby and numerous other industrial towns. An estimated 150,000 protested in Glasgow on October 9th, the day when benefits were reduced. By the end of 1931 the NUWM could claim 37,000 members. With growth went continued agitation, and from November 1931 through February 1932, demonstrations spread to Yorkshire, the Northeast, Merseyside and the potteries. Some 40,000 signed petitions in Birmingham, while 100,000 marched on Tyneside in the spring of 1932. In the autumn there were riots in Birkenhead and a national hunger march to London, met by a crowd of nearly 100,000 in Hyde Park on 27th October. The government reacted by beating and arresting demonstrators, and thus provoked an even larger outpouring of support in Trafalgar Square on the 30th. It is difficult to gauge the impact, especially on national policy, but implementation of cuts varied a great deal locally, and by and large they were less severe than the authorities in London had intended. Perhaps more important, the NUWM managed to dramatize the issue and to forge a link, however weak, between the unemployed and the labour movement as a whole. There is, in addition, abundant personal testimony about the movement's positive effect upon the morale of the unemployed who joined it.[5]

The Communists were also involved in attempting to sustain industrial militancy during the slump. Success was elusive, however, until the party managed to shed both its organizing tool left over from the 1920s, the National Minority Movement, and the sectarianism with which it had become identified after 1926. This began to occur in 1931–2, when the party ditched the Minority Movement and began cultivating several rank-and-file movements that had grown up outside its sphere of influence. But it was not particularly effective until 1935–6. Meanwhile, the activities of the left combined with those of the opponents of the unions to reinforce the inertia and stasis which sustained the movement in the unpropitious years of defeat and depression. Neither the employers nor their 'non-political' union allies on the one hand, nor the Communists on the other, could offer a viable and appealing alternative to continued loyalty to the established unions; in the absence of an alternative, the strong roots of the unions in working-class life held firm and the unions, despite inevitable losses, held their own.[6]

Much the same sort of process aided the Labour party as well. Despite a run of failures, the lack of an alternative prevented electoral defeats from becoming occasions for sustained political decline. Again, there was dissension and there were splits, but the sense of loyalty so central to 'the ethos of the Labour party' ultimately prevailed and was perhaps even strengthened in the process.

The best example of this pattern was the reaction to the collapse of the Second Labour Government. Though stronger and more experienced than the government which fell in 1924, that of 1929–31 not only failed in its objectives but destroyed itself during the crisis of August 1931. The party had fought the 1929 election on a militant programme of opposition, and sought to make the vote a 'verdict on the present government' and its lack of a policy to deal with unemployment. Labour offered to the electors 'an unqualified pledge to deal immediately and practically with this question', and on assuming office, MacDonald did proceed to appoint Jimmy Thomas to head a special committee to deal with unemployment. But the effort petered out quickly. Labour in 1929–31 may have been thoroughly 'parliamentarist', but its inability to evolve an economic policy showed that it was far from being a 'reformist' party.[7] It had no strategy for economic growth, but instead wavered between three mutually contradictory policies. Most basic was the belief that unemployment could only be cured by socialism. Short of socialism, all that could be offered were palliatives – mostly better provision for the unemployed – which were admittedly inadequate and unfortunate. Third, the party was committed at the same time to the principles of sound finance. These three ideas were not always explicit, nor were they shared by everyone in the party, but each was held by enough people to prevent the emergence of a new consensus.[8]

Inside the Cabinet, the principle exponent of fiscal conservatism was Philip Snowden. Snowden was preoccupied with government deficits: in 1924, he attacked the Lloyd George government for its failure to raise taxes to pay for the war, and asserted that 'the Labour party puts in the very front of its financial programme a scheme for reducing the interest upon our National Debt'. In 1930–31, he was the strongest supporter of the Treasury's position and managed to defeat all proposals for 'reflation'. In the event, there was no clearly articulated counter-proposal around which dissidents in the Cabinet could rally, for the unemployment committee of Thomas, together with Oswald Mosley and George Lansbury, was itself unable to agree. Thomas, as committed to orthodoxy as Snowden, settled upon rationalization. As he argued, 'It is no use merely spending money on a job of work which when finished does not enable the country to provide more employment than it provided before . . . therefore, my object is to lay out money which will show a clear economic return to the country by increasing its productive efficiency.'[9]

A more attractive set of proposals was drawn up by Mosley and supported by Lansbury. Its inspiration was Keynesian; its aim to expand purchasing power by controlling imports, by a liberal credit policy, and by expanding social benefits. The Mosley Memorandum, as it came to be called, received short shrift in Cabinet but got a good hearing outside. The Labour party conference of October 1930 came very near to adopting it, and Mosley's personal stature rose accordingly. But Mosley's leadership and personality were more of a drawback than an advantage. When he failed to carry the conference, Mosley proceeded to produce in December 1930 a 'Mosley Manifesto' and then to launch his breakaway organization, the so-called 'New Party', which rapidly moved towards the right.

Victorious over Mosley, the adherents of financial orthodoxy were soon to triumph over even the more timid souls who felt that, if Labour could not cure the depression, it could at least minister to its victims. When Labour took office in June 1929, there were 1,164,000 unemployed; by December 1930 the total reached 2½ million. The strain of providing out-of-work benefits increased, and Liberals joined Conservatives in a mounting chorus of dismay about the solvency of the state. Snowden responded by appointing a Committee on National Expenditure, whose report in July, 1931 pronounced Britain to be on the verge of bankruptcy and urged drastic economies to maintain the value of the currency. Rather than wait for the actual deficit to materialize, foreign investors took the occasion of its prophecy to start a run on the pound, to which the Bank of England responded by borrowing from France and the United States. The Federal Reserve of New York demanded that the government demonstrate its good faith by instituting cuts – specifically the 20% cut in unemployment benefits recommended by the Committee. In the ensuing crisis, most of the Cabinet were won over to cuts of up to 10%, but a substantial minority were not. MacDonald resolved the impasse on 24th August by forming a new 'National Government' composed of a minority of himself, Snowden, and Thomas from Labour, a couple of Liberals and a slightly larger number of Conservatives. Ostensibly, the National Government was set up to avert financial disaster. Within a month, the convertibility of gold was suspended and a general election called. Snowden labelled Labour's programme 'fantastic and impractical', verily '. . . Bolshevism run mad', and claimed it would 'plunge the country into irretrievable ruin'. The Second Labour Government ended in a massive, *de facto* Conservative victory.[10]

Labour had assumed office with a pledge to tackle unemployment; it left it with more than double the number out of work. Worse still, it left office minus its three most prominent leaders. Its few minor successes – in foreign affairs, in the reorganization of the mines and of agriculture – were dwarfed by the enormity of these two great failures. Yet somehow, such failures of policy and of leadership did not destroy the party and did not break the link that had by that time emerged between Labour and its working-class supporters, particularly in the unions. The Labour party endured, it seems, because it shared so thoroughly both the strengths and the weaknesses of the class and the movement from which it had sprung. Its great virtue was loyalty, its great weakness lack of theory – the same could as easily be said of the working class as a whole. It cherished few illusions about successful reform, and felt most comfortable in opposition. It had little use for doctrine and for programme, and so nurtured few hopes of implementing what little programme was on the books. It treasured loyalty to the class in its leaders, and could interpret defections only in terms of disloyalty.

More precisely, the Labour party was not a party of social and economic reform. It was a socialist party whose socialism may have often seemed pallid and distant, but whose sense of reform was even more attenuated. Leaders and followers alike clung to an almost utopian vision of socialism and were positively disdainful of the sorts of tinkering with capitalism that Keynes and others found appealing. The first reaction to the debacle of 1931 was thus to fall back upon apocalyptic notions of capitalist collapse. As the manifesto of that year put it, 'the decisive opportunity is given to the nation to reconstruct the foundations of its life . . . the Capitalist system has broken down even in those countries where its authority was thought to be most secure'. In this context, Labour's incoherence in face of unemployment was thoroughly in keeping with the party's lack of faith in reform. What was not in keeping with tradition was the desertion to the side of the 'bankers' of MacDonald, Snowden and Thomas. But their apostasy was seen as merely that – a matter of personal betrayal, 'the greatest betrayal in British political history', according to Attlee, caused by a 'fondness of Duchesses' and a taste for the good life.[11]

The internal politics of Labour after 1931 followed logically upon this lack of programme and surfeit of solid loyalty. First, as soon as the dimensions of the setback were known, the party reaffirmed its moderate roots by getting the unions, via the National Council of Labour, to oversee the party's rebuilding. They saw to it that Labour resisted the urgings of the Independent Labour Party, the Socialist League and, needless to say, the Communists that Labour move left to meet the current crisis.

The major organization to offer an alternative to Labour was the ILP. Before the War, it had served as the individual members' section of the party, but it lost its role in 1918, and in consequence, much of its *raison d'être*. During the 1920s, it functioned as a repository of left-wing ideas. Its most notable product was a set of proposals published in 1926 as *The Living Wage*, and embodying many of J.A. Hobson's ideas about the underconsumptionist origins of depressions and urging a policy of boosting consumption by redistributing wealth. The ILP programme was probably the only genuine alternative to the official line on offer, and as the futility of the latter was revealed in the course of the 1929–31 government, the ILP felt justified in stepping up its criticism of the party's course and leadership. In June 1932, the ILP decided to disaffiliate, hoping the debacle of 1931 would push workers left. That hope proved illusory, and the ILP rapidly declined into insignificance.[12]

A substantial minority knew immediately that disaffiliation meant disaster, and formed a National ILP Affiliation Committee which soon linked up with the Coles' Society for Socialist Inquiry and Propaganda (SSIP) to found the Socialist League. The League was formally established in September 1932, and quickly became the major focus of opposition within the Labour party. At the 1932 party conference, for example, the League led the successful floor revolt against the proposals of the executive. The NEC had in December 1931 commissioned a series of policy reports so that the next Labour government would be properly prepared. The mood of the delegates was much further to the left than that of the leaders, however, and the conference proceeded to amend the reports in that spirit. Sir Charles Trevelyan proposed that immediately upon taking office the next Labour regime should introduce a packet of socialist measures on which to stand or fall. The proposal was carried without a formal vote. The report on banking was then rewritten to require nationalization of the joint-stock banks in addition to the Bank of England and creation of a national investment board. This proposal, too, was carried against the wishes of the leadership. The left also argued successfully against the exclusion of workers from the management of the public corporation as envisioned by Herbert Morrison. Within a couple of weeks of its founding, the Socialist League had pulled off a genuine coup in matters of party policy.[13]

This programmatic success, however, made organizational success more elusive. The more accommodating the response of the party establishment on policy, the more difficult it was for the Socialist League to distinguish its own programmatic alternative. Moreover, despite vast differences in tone and approach, both the League and Labour's leadership shared a great deal in terms of political philosophy. The most significant similarity was in the common suspicion, held by men like Cripps and Wise of the Socialist League as much as by the trade union leaders, of Keynes and his proposed solutions. The left were not much concerned about financial stability, but they looked with suspicion upon Keynes. Although the League proposed planning as part of the solution to the depression, its spokesmen argued that 'Socialism alone can change compulsory unemployment into remunerated leisure, with . . . effective demand equal to productive capacity.'

In the absence of a distinctive policy for radically reforming capitalism, the League came to distinguish itself from the Labour leadership on grounds of political strategy and foreign policy. The League interpreted the 'bankers' ramp' of 1931 as proof not of the weakness of Labour's programme but of capitalism's willingness to sabotage parliamentary progress towards socialism. Cripps, Wise and others in the League called therefore for specific commitments to effect the transition to socialism within the span of a five-year government and urged the proclamation by the next Labour government of Emergency Powers to fend off capitalist efforts at destabilization. Cripps went so far as to attack the Crown in a famous speech in January 1934: 'When the Labour Party comes to power, we must act rapidly and it will be necessary to deal with the House of Lords and the influence of the City of London. There is no doubt that we shall have to overcome opposition from Buckingham Palace and other places as well.' Capitalist power, not Labour's programme, preoccupied the Socialist League in the aftermath of 1931.[14]

There were more substantial differences on issues of foreign policy – on the proper response to the fascists, on Spain, and on the popular front.[15] Nevertheless, they were not sufficiently clear and coherent to provide a firm basis for rallying the rank-and-file to a thorough-going alternative programme. Without such a programme, however, the League could only re-emphasize its distinctive strategic orientation. This was largely self-defeating, however, for the timidity and caution of the party and the unions accurately reflected the underlying weakness of Labour's position. Defeat and depression sapped the basis for local militancy and reinforced the moderate predisposition of Transport House. Exhortations towards doctrinal purity and full-blooded socialism might meet with sentimental agreement, but they could not generate a sustained opposition to the policies and practices of the leaders. The success of the Socialist League at the conference of 1932 was thus never repeated, and over the next two years the Executive managed to secure overwhelming support for the advanced, but less radical, positions of its programme, *For Socialism and Peace*. With its adoption in 1934, the party demonstrated its fundamental, centrist solidity and its reluctance to support novel strategies or leaders.[16]

By 1935, therefore, the Labour party had fended off challenges from the ILP and the Socialist League and had prevented any serious erosion of support to the right or left. Instead, Labour had moved resolutely to the centre and fallen back, in its time of distress, upon its critical allies in the trade union movement. It had managed as well to develop substantially its policies and its programmatic thinking. In this odd fashion, it managed to emerge in 1935 as more resolute, practical and united.

This stabilization was confirmed at the General Election in 1935.

Labour's vote rebounded to the position of 1929 and produced 154 seats in Parliament. The results disappointed those who hoped for an outright Labour victory, but the voting did at least ratify Labour's claim to be the second party in the land, and more important, to speak authoritatively on behalf of the industrial working class. Its minority status, moreover, was an accurate reflection of the workers' much weakened position. That would change only after 1935, when conditions altered to permit a new industrial aggressiveness and an increased capacity to organize. These conditions did come, but only after 1935, and even then only quite gradually and in quite specific locations.

1935–9: The beginnings of the new militancy

The labour movement resumed the offensive after 1935, but with great difficulty and indifferent success. When breakthroughs in organization were achieved, they did not come by any simple extension of organization from the old to the new industries or from the skilled to the less skilled, but required the mobilization of resources beyond a mere revival of trade. Unfortunately, the resources available to working people between the wars were limited and severely strained. They might well have possessed a vital cultural and institutional life, but that was extremely local in character and not easily transferred to new communities in the prosperous regions. The unions conserved their strength, but were thoroughly on the defensive, and only the general unions, particularly the TGWU, were aggressively exploring opportunities for growth.[17]

In such a context, the revival of organization depended heavily on local combinations of three types of resource: the consolidation of working-class communities, the presence of politically committed organizers and the residual strength of skilled workers' unions. It depended also, of course, on a prosperous local firm or group of firms. When two or more of these preconditions obtained, progress was possible; otherwise not. The combination of favourable local circumstances proved crucial in the beginnings of organization among car and aircraft workers, and in the upsurge of activity among engineering apprentices.

As the most buoyant industry in the interwar decades, the car industry afforded steady employment and high wages. By coupling these conditions with paternalistic styles of management and a reduced dependence on skilled labour, car producers sought to stave off attempts at organization. Ford at Dagenham and Vauxhall at Luton were able to keep the unions at bay until the Second World War or later. Elsewhere, however, organization came earlier, and even at places like Dagenham there were some notable efforts before the war.

A typical case was the Austin Company, with its main plant at Longbridge. Austin grew rapidly in the 1920s, using both skilled and semi-skilled labour, with increasing reliance on the latter. A strike by skilled body makers in 1924 won a temporary victory, but after 1926 management attitudes hardened and the reorganization of work was pushed still further. This produced yet another strike in 1929 against the adoption of flow production and new payment schedules. Five thousand went on strike and briefly occupied the factory. Skilled and unskilled both participated. The agitation was led, it seems, by an ex-miner named Bowen recently arrived from Wales, and its most forceful supporters were among the lower-paid men and women. The Communists were also active. Prospects for union growth seemed good in 1929, but with the depression they were pushed back again to 1936, when about 5000 workers struck over new piece rates. A non-union strike committee took the lead, including a number of Communists, and the unions registered more lasting gains.[18]

Located close to Birmingham, the Longbridge plant recruited from that city's stable working-class communities. No bastion of union strength, it nonetheless offered a better atmosphere than that which prevailed in places like Luton. Still, it took the presence of politically-minded activists to implant the spirit of organization among the less skilled. A similar combination of community strength and politics was required before gains could be registered in the Oxford area. Cowley in Oxford was the site of both Morris Motors and Pressed Steel; success came at the latter, the American firm, first, at Morris considerably later. The key moment was the Pressed Steel strike of 1934, the first major victory in the struggle to organize the car firms. The workforce in the Oxford car plants was concentrated in the south-east, where housing estates were constructed and where most of the car workers came to live. The small size of the local working population meant that a large number of migrants were needed. Such men more commonly found work at Pressed Steel than at Morris, and the former also employed somewhat more skilled workers. There seems to have been a relatively rapid development of community life near Cowley in the 1920s and '30s: a number of Welsh choirs and sports clubs were founded, a working-men's club was formed in 1929, and tenants' groups were very strong.

There had been small strikes at Morris and Pressed Steel in the late '20s and early '30s, but nothing that led to permanent gains for the unions. In 1934, the entire Oxford district of the AEU had only 68 members. The power of the skilled workers was therefore very slight, and the initiative passed to other workers in July 1934. Appropriately, the strike of that summer broke out first in the press shop, where the workforce was young and unskilled and included many women. In a matter of days, the strike had spread to over 2500 workers and a strike committee, dominated by workers from Wales and the north and by Communists, was set up. The T&GWU succeeded ultimately in enrolling the strikers and got thereby a genuine base within the industry. The strike sparked a more general growth of unionism and Labour politics in the town, and by 1938 a number of shop stewards had been appointed even at Morris Motors.[19]

Success was also hard to come by in Coventry. There, the prior history of unionization, followed by utter catastrophe in the 1920s, left a residue of disillusion which retarded revival even after 1935. The growth of car firms imparted a dynamism to Coventry comparable to that of Birmingham or Oxford, but its long history of engineering meant that local industry was not forced to recruit from outside; hence, that particular leaven to working-class activity was missing. The revival of organization in Coventry was thus somewhat later, though, in the end, more diffuse and effective than in Oxford or Birmingham. In 1933, the AEU had 2415 members scattered throughout the city's shops, but very few were in the car factories; by 1939, the general total had reached 11,000. This modest growth came primarily in 1936–7 and was aided by the engineering apprentices' movement and the activities of the aircraft shop stewards.[20]

The difficulties in Coventry were as nothing compared with those at Ford in Dagenham. Though the Becontree Housing Estate and the Ford and Briggs car factories grew up at roughly the same time, the connections remained weak for at least a decade. Only very slowly did residence and workplace at Dagenham come to overlap; not until 1943 was the Ford factory organized. There were strikes in the early 1930s, and tenants' groups and the Labour party flourished on the estate, but they did not merge or even reinforce one another. Organization languished despite major efforts. The most dramatic came in 1933. Almost as soon as Ford began producing at Daghenham, the Communist Party and the AEU targeted the plant, but neither of these had any noticeable effect until the strike of March 1933. The immediate cause of that dispute was a reduction in wages connected, it was claimed, with the application of the Bedaux system to the factory. The night shift in the toolroom took the lead, and Jack Tanner for the AEU and others from the CP became quickly involved in spreading the strike to the dayshift and to the bulk of the workforce. A mass picket was thrown across the road and created a virtual state of siege at the factory. A local journalist reported the prominence of Lancashire and Irish accents on the picket line, and by the second day the stoppage was 95% effective. Within a week, work was resumed with the strikers having won substantial wage gains and flushed with victory.

Militancy broke out at nearby Briggs the day after it ended at Ford's. The demand raised there – for equal pay for women, for a minimum for young workers, a 47-hour week and union rates for overtime – suggest the substantial presence and role of the semi-skilled, of women and young workers. The skilled at Briggs advanced no demands of their own, and were among the first to return to work; the young workers were the keenest and did not return in large numbers until increases were won for both male and female.

The two strikes met with immediate success because they took the management by surprise and allowed the workers to press their tactical advantage to the fullest. But the underlying base of support was not available either in the community or on the shop floor, and when Ford counter-attacked, there was little ability to resist. By 1934, organization was back to its previous low levels, and only gradually did the workers at Dagenham win the right to bargain collectively. When union recognition did come in 1944, it was through the efforts of those outside the Dagenham site itself – that is, the TUC and top Ford management. In the meantime, activists turned to work in the community and to building up a core of unionists among the skilled toolroom workers at Briggs. This was not much of an advance, in view of the concerted efforts aimed at the problem.[21]

Rather more progress was recorded among aircraft workers and engineering apprentices. In both instances, the traditional solidarity of the skilled was supplemented by political commitment. The aircraft industry represented the Achilles' heel of management in the 1930s, for by its very nature it encouraged strong trade union organization. The leading firms – Vickers, Armstrong-Whitworth, Hawker, A. V. Roe, de Havilland – had been nurtured through the depression by contracts from the government, anxious to ensure a core of arms-producing capacity. Such a sheltered position made it possible to preserve union organization in the older firms during the 1920s and 1930s and to implant it quickly in the new. This was further aided by the skilled

THE IMPACT OF DEFEAT, 1929-39

character of the work. Only with the setting up of 'shadow factories' after 1937, usually by car firms copying the methods used by established aircraft producers, was there even a hint of rationalization and deskilling. The enormous influx of workers into aircraft production from late 1936 to August 1939, when employment went from 79,000 to 290,000, thus consisted mostly of skilled men or their helpers.

These conditions were extremely favourable for an upsurge of militancy. The craft basis of production, in combination with the leadership given by the Communist Party, guaranteed that the form this growth would take would be a revived shop stewards' movement. The result was the Aircraft Shop Stewards' National Committee, first formed in 1934 and increasingly visible from 1935. The committee began publication of a paper, the *New Propeller*, which soon became the most effective rank-and-file publication of the 1930s, with a circulation of 27,000 in 1939. Initially, *New Propeller* and the ASSNC fought for a separate aircraft agreement within the national engineering agreement. Though popular with the aircraft workers, resonating well with their craft sensibilities and their understanding of the economics of the industry, it threatened to pit the new movement against the established leadership of the AEU and the T&GWU. The issue came to a head in 1937 when the *New Propeller* and the stewards launched a campaign for a separate agreement and set a strike deadline of May 25, 1937. When the campaign failed to produce an agreement, they backed down, and from this point on, the group around *New Propeller* focused on 100% trade unionism and the deepening of shop steward organization. Clearly, the Communists' new emphasis upon the popular front had something to do with the turn towards cooperation; but whatever the reason, the effect was to ensure that most of the shadow factories were soon unionized.

The major limitation, of course, of the movement within aircraft was that it began as, and for a long time remained, an expression of craft militancy. Aircraft shop stewards consistently fought against rationalization and dilution. There was a skirmish at Glosters in 1937 over the use of semi-skilled men in the machine shop and at Rolls Royce Derby in 1938 over a time and motion study, both of which were won by the men. Similar strikes occurred at Fairey Hayes in Stockport, at Short and Harlands in Belfast and at several factories in Coventry and in west London. The movement's craft orientation was revealed also by its rhetoric. The local factory paper, *Fairey Battle*, for example, took to lecturing the non-skilled in February 1938 on their duties to the trade: 'Our colleagues in the semi- and unskilled work in the trade must be wary of the temptation placed before them', the paper said, especially 'the intriguing bribes of equal pay'.[22]

On the other hand, the political orientation of the stewards tempered the exclusivity of their organization. Many gave encouragement to the organization of the less skilled, particularly to the quite remarkable movement of apprentices and young workers that swept most of engineering in 1937. Once again, there is substantial evidence of Communist involvement, especially by the Young Communists' League, but two other factors were also critical: first, the strikes of apprentices were started in older areas, where the youths could draw upon community tradition and resources, as in Glasgow, Manchester, Newcastle and Coventry; and second, there were important linkages with the stewards and activists among adult engineers.

The decay of apprenticeship was a common complaint of the interwar years. Boys would be taken on for their seven years' training and then let go by employers. When the engineering industry began to prosper after 1935 the fate of apprenticeship seemed very much in doubt. The employers hoped to resist its revival and instead to use more semi-skilled workers on new machines. The expanded intake of apprentices *and* unapprenticed trainees in 1935–7 signalled such a hope, and a leader in *The Aeroplane* confirmed it: 'As union men have to be paid union rates, the only solution is to take on trainees.' The situation created a momentary convergence of interest for the skilled engineers, who wanted to protect their positions, the apprentices, who sought future access to these positions, and even the trainees, who could not fail to benefit from any improvement in wages and conditions. The issues were crystallized in 1936–7 by the stagnation of apprentice rates of pay in comparison with the increases recently won by the adults. The result was two waves of strikes in the spring and autumn of 1937.

The first began in Glasgow in March and April. A few hundred came out in one shop, then made the rounds to other workplaces, hammering on doors and developing a kind of moving picket. In two weeks, 3700 were out; the next week John Brown's came out and then the Greenock shipyards. By 8 April, 11,000 apprentices and trainees were on strike and a strike committee, chaired by a member of the YCL, had been selected. On 16 April, the local AEU called a general stoppage, and over 100,000 men ceased work. The strike ended with an agreement to open national negotiations.

The negotiations dragged on inconclusively into the autumn, when the lack of results produced another wave of militancy. This broke out in September in Manchester; it spread farther than the spring strikes and involved girls as well as boys. Starting at a small shop in Salford, the strikes quickly affected some of the largest works in Manchester – Gardners' Peel Green factory, A.V. Roe's Crossley Motors and Mather and Platt's. Strikes broke out as well in Leeds, Halifax and Hebden Bridge and, on 30 September, in Coventry. At Coventry, several Armstrong-Whitworth factories were affected, and the unrest also drew out 8000 women and girls at Courtauld's rayon factory. In October, they spread to London. By December, the AEU had secured the right to bargain on behalf of non-indentured young workers and an agreement to tie their wages to those of adults. Most important, the experience had by then schooled a new generation in industrial struggle and furthered organization among the less skilled more broadly.[23]

None of these efforts, of car workers, aircraft workers or young engineers, were of sufficient breadth to spark an offensive among the working class as a whole, but they did reverse the trend in union membership. From 1934 to 1939 the ranks increased from just over 4½ million to almost 6.3 million. Some of that was no doubt due to unemployed trade unionists returning to work, but a second factor was the beginning of organization in the new industries made possible by the advances of car workers, aircraft workers and the youths in engineering. It was not merely a matter of keeping alive the spirit of militancy in the depressed years – the miners did that, and so, too, did the London busmen and builders – but of establishing a route into the expanding sector of the economy and thus widening the frontiers of the labour movement.

Still, the gains of 1935–9 were limited. Most new firms remained unorganized, and would only be brought within the ambit of trade unionism by the exigencies of war. Moreover, at least at first, the renewal of industrial militancy did not translate easily into political activity. The Labour party's electoral incapacity was acute even in 1939. The Gallup Polls of 1939 and 1940, for example, showed Labour as weak as in 1935. It was reported that, if a General Election were to be held in January, 1939, 54% would vote for Chamberlain, only 30% for the opposition. The results were no better for Labour a year later. Politically, the Labour party could not break out of the 'ghetto' of solidly working-class support, which it held even in 1931 and 1935, and offer itself as a genuine alternative for the bulk of the electorate.

This prolonged weakness helps to explain the surprising support received by Cripps and other advocates of the Popular Front during

1937–9. Whatever else it may have represented, the Popular Front was offered as a means of overcoming Labour's electoral failures. Conversely, the desire not to stray from their working-class roots was at least one reason why the proposal for a Popular Front met with such a negative response from the leaders of the party and the unions, who remembered only too well the desertion of the class by MacDonald, Snowden and Thomas in 1931.

The one sign of life inside the party in the late 1930s was itself a reflection of the limited possibilities open to Labour. It came from the constituency parties anxious for a greater role in policy-making and eager to throw off, as much as possible, the stifling moderation of the trade union leaders. The so-called 'Constituency Parties Movement' had its origins in the growth throughout the 1920s and 1930s of local parties whose impressive membership – over 400,000 by 1935 – had little or no effective voice in party affairs. It reflected, too, the fact that Labour's electoral fortunes revived sooner on the municipal than the national level after 1931. During the 1920s, the Labour vote in local elections lagged behind that in general elections; after 1931, it pulled even and, given the national stalemate, made for greater intensity and interest in Labour's work in the localities. Labour's most important experience of office, moreover, came from its base of power in London after 1934.[24]

The 'Constituency Parties Movement' made something of a splash at the 1936 annual conference, and in 1937 succeeded in winning representation for local parties on the Executive. Its effects were no more than that, but its brief flourishing was a sign of where, within the labour movement, there was vitality and where there was not.[25] The union leaders had been put entirely on the defensive by the slump while the party was battered and beaten down by the enormity of its political task. The base of the unions was beginning by 1935–9 to regain a sense of competence, but the job of building up organization was extremely difficult and produced only modest returns. The only source of insurgency was in local parties, where militants could mobilize strong working-class communities behind those local candidates with a chance of winning; these, if they won, could use their offices to mitigate the effects of those terrible years. It was not a very grandiose prospect, but it was something.

7

The Triumph of
Social Democracy, 1940–48

The coming of war in the autumn of 1939 did nothing to revolutionize British society or politics; indeed, its first effect was to rally the country behind Neville Chamberlain. As the war progressed, however, and as the dimensions of the conflict and of the measures needed to wage it expanded, so too did the sense of what was possible and necessary in home affairs. Gradually, the fatalism of the interwar years dissipated and was replaced by a resolve never to return to that kind of world. That resolution was registered politically in the election of 1945, and was subsequently embodied in the institutions of 'the welfare state'. Whatever the shortcomings of that new institutional structure, it represented a qualitative transformation in the relationship of classes in British society.

The victory of social democracy required several key prerequisites for its achievement. The first was organization. Before Labour could grow again, the unions had to enroll the many thousands of workers in the so-called new industries that had risen up between the wars. Second, strength at the workplace had to be linked up with political support for the Labour party and its programme. Labour had somehow to position itself during the war so as to take some credit for its winning, but avoid appearing merely as an appendage of the state or of the Conservative-dominated coalition. Potential conflicts between Labour's rank-and-file and its leaders had also to be muted. If this were done, Labour could count on the solid support of a revitalized working-class movement at the end of the war.

The victory of 1945 was based as well on the electoral support of sections of the middle class. Equally important was the post-election cooperation of Britain's administrative and business elites. These were not won easily, but seem to have come about through the politics of war. Before the war, Labour had a list of specific reforms to which it was committed, but little sense of how these fitted together and even less faith in capitalism's reforming potential. The war replaced such pessimism with an emerging vision of full employment based on government intervention.

The experience of war not only changed attitudes within the labour movement, but also created a broader public consensus on the shape of postwar society. It nudged political discourse to the left, and made Keynesian economics and state intervention acceptable to 'middle opinion' and to the bulk of the electorate. Labour's programme thus came to be seen and defended both as a set of desirable reforms and as a plan for national reconstruction. This allowed for the working-class interest to be 'universalized' as the public interest. To some extent this meant a toning down of socialist commitment, but during the 1940s Labour's programme was never reduced to a mere reforming Keynesianism. It retained a distinctive class appeal and a thrust towards structural reform. Labour benefited from the Keynesian consensus but was not submerged in it.[1]

This new, implicitly social-democratic, consensus became the banner behind which large numbers of voters who had never before supported socialism rallied in the summer of 1945. As early as the mid-1930s, the more perceptive political commentators had begun to point out the potential for socialist support among the middle classes, particularly among those who drew their incomes from the public sector. During the war, these middle-class voters became increasingly disenchanted with the Conservatives and by 1945 were ready to opt for a programme of reconstruction that provided a much greater positive role for the government and for the civil servants who staffed it. Labour became the party of the planners and bureaucrats, the teachers, social workers and 'progressive intelligentsia', all predisposed to be Keynesians, as well as being the historic party of the workers.

The Labour victory of 1945 was thus a product of long-term processes of class formation and organization, which had brought Labour into being as the mass party of the working class, and of the political conjuncture of 1945. The combination translated a narrow working-class majority into a broader mandate for structural reform, and generated a rhetoric that facilitated the implementation of Labour's programme.

Manpower and organization in wartime

When J.T. Murphy, the veteran socialist and engineer, reentered the trade at a large London works in late July 1940 after an absence of two decades, he felt surprisingly at home. His lathe was of the same type as used twenty years before, and he 'was soon to find that much besides the machinery belonged to yesteryear'. Even in this relatively 'modern' and 'well-planned factory', the pace of work was slow and union control of the shop floor pervasive; there was 'no piece-work system, no overtime, no nightwork and no "chasers"' . . . and no evidence at all of the 'Dunkirk atmosphere'. Work proceeded as usual, management remained aloof from workers and the workers suspicious in return. The war seemed distant, and its consequences for the home front seemed barely to be glimpsed, let along understood.[2]

Whether or not Murphy's experience was typical is difficult to say. What is clear is that the prosecution of the war in its first nine months was phlegmatic and uninspired, as was war mobilization, and that this experience had a profound effect on the politics of wartime. It served to discredit Chamberlain and the Tories far more effectively than did the dismal economic record of the 1930s or even the foreign policy failures leading up to Munich, and it guaranteed that when Britain did finally mobilize to win, credit would go elsewhere. It would be seen as a victory of the nation achieved despite its leaders. Orwell grasped the implications immediately, arguing as early as 1941 that, 'One of the dominant facts in English life during the past three-quarters of a century has been the decay of ability in the ruling class'. Tom Wintringham, the left-wing expert on military affairs, likewise declared that 'obviously the first thing to do is to get rid of the men at the top'.[3]

Nowhere was the failure of the old rulers more obvious than in the organization of manpower during the first year of the war. Employment increased by only a million persons, despite the demand for armaments. Half a million men remained registered as unemployed, and the potential for mobilizing women was almost totally untapped. By late spring 1940, according to Margaret Gowing, 'the Government's economic advisers concluded that the war programmes [for armaments production] were probably unattainable'. Those who were absorbed into war production, moreover, often met with conditions in the shops like those described by Murphy. The organization of work was outdated and inefficient, with management less inclined to break with tradition than the union. Since profits were assured by the backlog of government orders, there was no incentive to solve production problems. Nor did employers rush to join the unions in a cooperative effort aimed at increasing production. Union membership did grow during 1939 and 1940, but by much less than the increase in employment. No real breakthrough in unionization was possible until later in the war.[4]

The absence of change in the factories paralleled the lacklustre leadership of established authorities in the government and the armed services, and helped to convince many workers – and a goodly number of others – of the need for broad social changes after the war. It resonated well, too, with that more specifically working-class critique of management and its refusal to adopt the latest technology that had been expressed after the First World War and repeated so often during the depression. It reinforced the perception that the employers could not be trusted to run their own shops efficiently – let alone to run society.

With the fall of Chamberlain in May 1940, and the formation of the wartime coalition headed by Churchill and staffed by Attlee, Morrison, Bevin and other Labour leaders, the period of 'phoney war' ended, and slowly Britain became geared up to fight a 'people's war'. Changes were soon registered in 'morale', in the temper of politics, and in the daily lives of workers. Almost immediately, Attlee introduced an Emergency Powers Act, which commanded all citizens to place 'themselves, their services and their property' at the disposal of the Government while Bevin, as Minister of Labour, moved decisively to make mobilization effective. As a trusted and sincere union leader, Bevin had the respect of labour and proved extremely successful at extracting cooperation from workers for the war effort.[5]

Bevin quickly got control of the whole of labour policy; by August 1940, he had in hand estimates showing that 3.2 million workers would be for the services and munitions. He and his staff recognized an impending 'famine of men' that would in turn 'breed a hunger for women'. Though these estimates were later revised, they made clear the need for mechanisms that would virtually eliminate the free market for labour. It was the measure of Bevin's commitment to his working-class roots that in devising these mechanisms, he sought to minimize their negative impact upon the unions and that, as the price for the unions' cooperation, he used his position to pry concessions from the employers.

The mechanisms for mobilization were several. The centrepiece was Regulation 58A, which gave to local National Service Officers the power to direct workers to jobs, and to Inspectors of Labour Supply the authority to compel employers to improve working conditions and wages. All men, and later women, were soon required to register for national service, either military or civilian. Registration was backed up by the Essential Works Order, which prevented employees from switching jobs in key industries and employers from enticing them to do so. These devices gave government the capacity to expand the numbers available for employment and, somewhat less efficiently, to allocate them to the most critical sectors. Problems remained, of course, and forced strict controls on the location of industry from 1942. Also in 1942, efforts were undertaken to build up the workforce in the mines. Sterner measures still were needed in 1943, and conscripts were given the option of joining the forces or working in the mines. This array of controls was integrated in a coherent policy by means of the manpower budget, from 1941 the core of national economic planning, 'determining every part of the war effort from the number of RAF heavy bombers raiding Germany to the size of the clothing ration'. Much has been made of the first successful use of Keynesian estimates of national income and war finance during mobilization, but the main burden of organizing the nation's resources was borne by those who sought to distribute its manpower – an appropriate symbol of the requirements of a 'people's war'.[6]

If it took something like a revolution in administration to move workers from the dole queues into industry to win the war, it would require a similar upheaval inside the workshops to make sure that their presence resulted in increased production. For his part, Bevin guaranteed that mobilization would lead to improvements in working conditions and in unionization. Between 1940 and 1943, over a million and a half workers entered industry, and almost exactly that number were added to the ranks of the unions. The motor car companies were brought within the orbit of trade unionism, and more than ever before the unions opened their ranks to the unskilled and to women. Membership reached 8.2 million at the end of 1943, representing a density of 45.5% among men and 29.5% among women. Conditions improved enormously – canteens and washrooms and nurses and welfare workers appeared all over industry – shop steward organization spread widely, and management was forced to rule by consultation rather than by decree. Joint Production Committees, conferring co-equal status on the representatives of the employers and of the workers, were set up in all firms engaged in war production. What years of painful organizing had failed to achieve occurred almost inevitably under the impact of war.

Inevitably perhaps, but not effortlessly, for organization was resisted by management even during wartime, and required the assistance of the state. But the requirements of mobilization forced government to incur a heavy debt to labour, and organization was the price. Put simply, Bevin called upon the unions to drop their restrictions on production in return for increased membership. In 1940, a woman organizer remembered, he called in representatives of the employers, of the AEU, still essentially a male preserve, and of the TGWU and NUGMW, the two unions most active in recruiting women in munitions work, and forced them to hammer out an 'Extended Employment of Women Agreement' governing the terms on which women recruits were to be hired and ensuring them trade union rights. Such pressure led ultimately to the AEU's decision in 1943 to open membership to women and to an overall wartime increase of 600,000 in permanent female union membership.[7] The engineers were further appeased by a guarantee, embodied in the Coventry Toolroom Agreement of 1941, that their wages would not be surpassed by those on piece rates, skilled or unskilled. Bevin sought as well the compliance of the unions with Order 1305, which imposed compulsory arbitration and banned strikes, and this, too, led him in turn to extract concessions from the employers.

A classic example of how war mobilization aided organization was at Ford. All the efforts of the 1930s had failed to win recognition from the complex of motor companies at Dagenham – Ford, Briggs Motors and Kelsey-Hayes – and prospects for recognition seemed almost as remote in 1939 as when the Ford plant opened a decade before. But the war tipped the scales in the workers' favour, and with the sympathetic intervention of the Ministry of Labour, organization was quickly established at Briggs. Agitation began in mid-1940, and a network of stewards was firmly in place by December. In early 1941, a brief strike resulted in the recognition of the unions at the Ford factory in Manchester, and in April 1941, a disputed sacking at Briggs led to a Court of Inquiry, which recommended 'the recognition of those Unions who fairly and largely represent [the] workpeople'. These steps forward stimulated further action by Feather, Deakin and Citrine of the TUC. They pressed for action at both Manchester and Briggs and, with help from the Ministry of Aircraft Production, won recognition at Manchester and *de facto* bargaining rights at Briggs.

The main Ford plant at Dagenham resisted organization for another two and a half years. Two factors, in addition to employer intransigence, delayed unionization. First, many of the militants at Ford were CP members and the CP had shifted its stance on shop-floor militancy with the Soviet entry into the war in June 1941. They strove for all-out production and, although they also sought to extend the frontiers of organization, were reluctant to provoke strikes. The hope was that pressure from the TUC and the government would do in war what might have been done by strike action in peacetime. On the other hand, the Communist presence inside Ford made the TUC hesitant about pushing for a settlement that would institutionalize the power of the left-wing stewards. Victor Feather and Sir Walter Citrine thus engaged with the local activists in a constant jockeying for position, each side hoping to bring about organization in such a way as to claim victory.

The impasse was resolved in 1943–4. At the urging of the local unions the TUC approached the companies and the government together and urged recognition. Briggs came round immediately, Ford very slowly. A meeting with Ford was finally scheduled for December, but just before it was to be convened management posted notices disclaiming any intention of recognizing the unions. A disaffected and impatient group of stewards took the opportunity to 'sit-in' until the company agreed to talk in earnest. The Ministry of Labour was called in first; they brought in Feather; this joint intervention finally persuaded management to reach a deal. Details were worked out in the spring of 1944, an agreement signed in the summer. In the end, Ford and the TUC concluded an agreement with virtually no role for shop stewards, ensuring that the battle for the shopfloor would carry over into the postwar period.[8]

The struggle at Ford was paralleled in factories throughout the country, and in most cases the outcome was comparable. The smaller British car firms in the Coventry area were most easily brought into line; the larger British firms near Birmingham and Oxford gave ground more slowly. By the end of the war unionization had reached 80–90% at Standard, but only about 30% at Morris and 50% at Austin. Vauxhall was able to avoid even this degree of union implantation and, like Ford, probably had less than 25% unionized. Even there, however, the war allowed for the development of informal organization and recruitment; and virtually all firms were forced to treat labour in a more civil and humane fashion. With the state exercizing close control over production and the conditions of work, it was possible for local activists to utilize the need for war production to gain management concessions. With Bevin formulating state policy, moreover, the unions were accorded a status and a dignity scarcely imaginable before 1939.[9]

Probably the clearest symbol of this altered status was the official role granted to trade unions in organizing production. It was recognized early on that consultation was required in certain industries, and by 1941 Pit Production Committees and Yard Committees were common in mining and shipbuilding. But Bevin's call in December 1940 for the wide adoption of the principle was greeted with little enthusiasm, and managers remained aloof and the workers wary throughout the munitions industries. In the summer of 1941, however, attitudes began to soften; engineering shop stewards began to advocate joint committees, as did employers such as Lord McGowan of Imperial Chemical Industries (ICI). The Engineering Employers' Federation continued to oppose the idea until January, 1942, but under pressure from the government signed an agreement with the AEU establishing Joint Production Committees (JPCs) in all plants of 150 or more.

By June 1944, over 4500 had been set up and they were a focal point for union activity. They dealt primarily with questions of production, but they necessarily touched on working conditions, welfare, and discipline. Their very existence signified a distinct loss of managerial control and, predictably, most managements remained unenthusiastic. But this very reluctance of management to share control of the shops through JPCs enhanced their political impact. The critique of capitalist inefficiency and employer conservatism was confirmed once more by what appeared to be an absence of cooperation in the battle for production.

An example from the Midlands will suffice. A Mass-Observer happened to record the proceedings of a stewards' meeting in Coventry in January 1942 at which the workers' rage at management's incompetence exploded. It seems that a group of workers at the firm of Cornercroft, Ltd. had been sacked for having taken time off for Christmas shopping, and then reinstated. Upon their return, they found that management had removed critical tools and fixtures and they were laid off as redundant. The men labelled this a 'scorched-earth policy' by the firm and its owner Captain Strickland, Tory MP for Coventry, and convened a meeting on 8 January in the lounge of a local pub. Ostensibly the aim of the meeting was 'to find a method of dealing with the underproduction and unemployment of skilled men'. Quickly, though, the discussion spilled over into 'talk about the workers understanding the meaning of the fight against Fascism whereas the managements didn't mind so very much who won. There were Municheers still in the Government and there were Municheers still running business'. The meeting resolved to send a delegation to

London demanding an inquiry and, in the meantime, to distribute a leaflet entitled 'Points for a policy for the Shop Stewards' Movement'. The leaflet began by stressing 'that increased production is the key to victory' and proclaiming the workers' readiness to 'accept whatever sacrifices are necessary' to that goal. To do so, however, would require the 'total mobilization of the man and woman power resources of the country' and 'the immediate establishment of Production Committees in all factories representative of Managements and men ... with plenary powers to operate recommendations directed to securing improved output'.[10]

Clearly, 'plenary powers' for joint committees were inimical to any notion of managerial prerogatives. But in the context of 1941–2, when the war was going poorly and all were being called upon to sacrifice for the common good, the cry for cooperative endeavours in industry became powerful enough to force the setting up of such committees. That they had to be fought for by the men and that the employers appeared hesitant or worse was especially important, for by such dilatory behaviour management lost considerable moral credibility and helped to burn into the minds of workers an image which would remain in 1945 and after. Conversely, by skilfully linking notions of worker rights with the national interest, union activists helped to fix an image that attached the fate of the nation to the cause of labour. That connection would also stick, at least for a time.

Activity in support of greater production and more union organization also served to bridge the gap between the rank-and-file and labour's industrial and political leadership. During the First World War, the shop stewards had defined themselves in opposition to the government and, quite often, to the officials of the unions. There was potential for a similar deterioration during the Second World War, but it did not materialize. Even during the period of 'phoney war', there was little overt opposition, and when Labour entered the government, the chances of a major rupture became still more remote. The closest it came was in January 1941 when the Communist Party called the 'People's Convention' to plan for a 'people's peace', and surprised even themselves by attracting almost 2500 'delegates'. The CP was still at the time formally opposed to the war as an 'imperialist' venture, but their practical work focused on the horrors of the blitz and the ineptness of the government's precautions. The argument struck a responsive chord and the meeting generated a good deal of excitement. But the 'People's Convention' passed and was soon forgotten; moreover, the Communists changed their line shortly after and became the keenest advocates of prosecuting the war. They went so far in the later stages of the war as to disband their industrial sections, probably losing the greatest opportunity ever to expand their influence in the unions. The decision deprived any incipient shop-floor discontent of one possible source of articulate leadership, and the relatively few strikes that did occur outside the mines in 1943–4 came, therefore, to be led by a strange and shifting coalition of Catholics and Trotskyists.[11]

The alignment of political forces within the trade union movement ensured that no thorough-going antagonism, comparable to that which characterized 1917–20, would emerge in 1942–5. Instead, the left and the more moderate elements cooperated to their mutual advantage. Organization increased massively, employer resistance was brushed aside as unpatriotic and self-interested; inside the shops, the stewards had greater freedom and authority, and conditions improved visibly. Bevin and the other Labour ministers proved their competence and the rank-and-file their loyalty. Both emerged from the war stronger and more self-confident.

The battle for political advantage

There was no simple transition, however, from industrial organization to political strength. Indeed, working-class power in the workshop could, and for a time did, co-exist with apathy and pessimism towards political matters.

Cynicism ran high among working-class men and women, in and out of uniform. In the forces, for example, discontent was mingled with a distrust of all politics and a generalized lack of morale. The problem led the War Office in June 1941 to undertake a massive campaign of Army education through the Army Bureau of Current Affairs (ABCA). Its programme was epitomized by a set of booklets on the 'British Way and Purpose', designed to remove 'apathy and complacency' by stressing notions of citizenship. Despite such efforts, the men were unconvinced and remained much less sanguine about the prospects for postwar than the bulk of the civilian population.[12]

Scepticism was also difficult to dislodge at home. Despite all efforts to the contrary, skilled engineers continued to resist dilution by women workers and, as the war wore on, fears of postwar displacement increased. Similar concerns touched the less skilled as well. A Gallup Poll of July 1943 found that only 31% of the population felt there would be 'jobs for all who want to work' after the war, and that of those only 40% were confident 'that full employment will last'. Mobilization had peaked by 1943, and some munitions firms began laying off in 1944; predictably, shop stewards in Coventry, the best-organized section of engineering, began a campaign to prevent redundancies after the war. This was not the sort of thing to make workers complacent or optimistic about their prospects.[13]

This would seem to have been equally the case for the tens of thousands of women workers who played such a critical role in munitions production. Though the documentation is scant, it appears that fatalism and lack of interest was widespread, and Mass-Observation's detailed study of women workers, published as *War Factory* in 1943, reported a *'dangerous decline in positive citizenship'* that threatened 'the health of all democracy'. The reason, it was argued, was 'not that the girls do not realise that their work is important to the war, but that the majority of them are so little *interested in the war that they do not care whether their work is important to it or not.'* Somewhat later in the war (1944), the Industrial Health Research Board undertook a similar study in four different factories, and also found that a 'comparative lack of interest in the war effort seemed to exist when work was monotonous or meaningless, and when the women were overtired. . . .' Since those conditions were anything but rare, such attitudes were common. Much like the women studied before the war, they found more satisfaction in companionship than in the job itself. No wonder some women were found to be more interested in returning to the home than staying at work, and that they were at least as interested in the provision of family allowances as in the campaign for equal pay.[14]

Despite such lingering pessimism, by 1945 working people were sufficiently aroused to believe that their votes mattered and should be cast for Labour. Somehow, the experience of war gradually dampened cynicism and allowed workers' increased organizational strength to be transferred into victory for Labour at the polls. Though the precise mechanisms remain obscure, certain key features and moments of the transformation are relatively clear. The most important fact was the least visible: because of either good sense of good fortune, the Labour party did little to alienate or disappoint its potential supporters. Bevin, though charged with getting the most out of the workers, did so in a manner that probably gained rather than lost support for the party. Other Labour ministers also gave credible performances in government, and the party as a whole appeared eminently 'responsible' throughout the war. This image was enhanced by Labour's ability to maintain unity throughout the life of the coalition. Dissent in the Parliamentary party was confined to a very small group, mostly around

Aneurin Bevan, and relations between the leaders and the party conference amicable. The control of both the National Executive Committee and conference was in the reliable hands of the union leaders and, except in rare instances, their loyalty could be guaranteed. There were difficulties over the government's inept handling of the Beveridge Report in the winter of 1942–3, over strikes in the mines and intervention in Greece in 1944 and, in the same year, a successful conference rebellion over the inclusion of specific demands for nationalization in the party's programme, but seldom was the unity of the Labour party terribly disturbed.[15]

By remaining relatively united and by not having to take primary responsibility for the problems associated with war, Labour positioned itself to take maximum advantage of the largely independent upsurge of popular radicalism. The party also managed to distance itself from the Conservatives despite participation in the coalition. Even under Churchill, the Tories could not shed their identification with the recent, dismal past. Beyond this, the Conservatives refused to commit themselves wholeheartedly to postwar reconstruction. By contrast, Labour needed only to re-affirm its long-standing programmatic commitments in order to place itself at the forefront of popular feelings on the future. It managed to reap the benefits of wartime radicalism without having to instigate it.

That radicalism began as a critique of the old society and its failure to avoid or, when it could no longer be avoided, effectively to prosecute, the war. Its slogan was 'the war to win the war', and its aim was effective mobilization. The movement climaxed in the crisis of the summer and autumn of 1942. From late 1942 to 1945, it turned its attention to 'the war to win the peace' and, despite the association with the Common Wealth Party in 1942–3, came ultimately to pin its hopes upon a Labour victory in 1945. From 1939 to late 1942, popular radicalism spoke a language of criticism and pessimism; from early 1943 until June 1945 it spoke a language of reform and possibility. In both phases, it was closely in touch with the mood of the people.[16]

Popular revulsion against the 'old gang' of 'Guilty Men' was reflected in the speeches of Priestley, in the campaign for mobilization led by the *Mirror*, and in the mass reaction to Dunkirk. J.B. Priestley's Sunday night 'postscripts' to the news attracted 30% of the population during the summer of 1940. He argued forcefully that 'this war, whether those at present in authority like it or not, has to be fought as a citizens' war'. By October, Priestley was kept off the air, largely in response to those 'Stupid persons [who] have frequently accused me in public of . . . taking advantage of my position to bring party politics into my talks . . . .' The same themes, though, were continually sounded by the *Mirror*, which established itself as the paper most preferred by the forces, by women and by working people overall. Tom Wintringham's series on the 'war to win the war', published in early 1940, called for a 'clean sweep' of the old elite. The leader column of 12 June was even more pointed in its demand for new men: 'In these critical times dead wood isn't even of use for the coffins of those martyred through muddle'. William Connor, under his byline of 'Cassandra', was still more blunt. Just after Dunkirk, he pilloried those responsible for defeat and accused them of wanting 'an Anglicised Reichstag egged on by organised cheerleaders'. But 'Cassandra' was only expressing the core beliefs of the paper, and the editor of the letters column urged 'any sacrifice that will rid us of slothful politicians, of old-fashioned soldiers and of parasitic communities, both rich and poor, who are indifferent to our cause'.[17]

The efforts of the *Mirror*, of *Picture Post*, of writers and publicists like Priestley, Wintringham, Orwell and others in the 'war to win the war' were probably less important in changing government policy than in shaping public opinion. By casting the argument in terms of the people versus the classes, the *Mirror*, Priestley and the rest fixed responsibility for previous failures on the party of Churchill and on the class from which it sprang. They guaranteed that the positive political advantage that would ultimately accrue from victory would go elsewhere – or at least be shared out in a fashion unfavourable to the Conservatives. They did not, by themselves, coax working people out of their cynicism, but they did chart the direction their subsequent enthusiasms would take.

That happy moment, when wartime critique would merge with an upsurge of mass activism, was still some way off in 1940–1, and seemed to recede even further into the future during 1942. Despite two years of massive efforts to mobilize the nation's resources, victory remained elusive. The Axis powers continued their advances, and there was increasing criticism of Churchill, the Cabinet and the military commanders. In the spring a series of by-elections returned independents critical of the government, and in July Priestley's '1941 Committee' and Sir Richard Acland's Forward March Movement joined to form the new Common Wealth Party.[18]

Discontent threatened to engulf both partners in the coalition, and Labour suffered along with the Conservatives. Mass-Observation claimed in January 1942 that many of its panel members were extremely disappointed with the Labour party. 'Apparently Socialism has merged with the government for the duration', was how one observer saw it; another explained more fully that 'I have always considered that a socialist principle of government is the only really good type of government; but the application of that principle by the Labour Party in England is muddling, near-sighted, and probably more bound by conservative principles of "old school tieism" than any other party programme in the country'. Many local activists eagerly joined in the campaigns fought by Common Wealth after 1942, and others joined the Communist Party, which experienced the most extensive growth in its history from 1941 to 1943.[19]

The crisis broke in November 1942; by February, 1943 a dramatic transformation had ensued. With the Germans advancing to the outskirts of Stalingrad during the late summer, all hopes turned to the campaign in North Africa. On 2 November, 1942, the Germans were broken at El Alamein. Churchill modestly claimed victory and public optimism returned. As Orwell recorded in his diary on 15 November, 'Church bells rang this morning – in celebration of the victory in Egypt – the first time that I have heard them in over two years'. Military success was followed up quickly by hopes for a better Britain. Early in December, the Beveridge Report on the social services was published. It had a sensational effect. Written in the staid prose of the senior civil servant, it became a best-seller overnight. Whether one regarded the contents of the report as revolutionary and, as Beveridge allegedly put it, designed to 'take the country half way to Moscow', or, as Orwell saw it, as a very 'modest measure of reform' was largely beside the point; what mattered was its reception and political impact.[20]

The Beveridge Report, timed to take advantage of the optimism over North Africa, turned the public's attention to reconstruction and forced the hand of those who wanted to refrain from explicit commitments about the shape of the postwar world. It also began to revive the stature and prospects of the Labour party in several critical ways. First, it was well-known that the Report stemmed from an initiative taken by the Labour leader Arthur Greenwood in 1941. Second, its proposals were highly compatible with Labour's own programme. Third, and most important, was the controversy sparked by the report. Churchill and the Conservatives reacted negatively and were seen to do so publicly. With a short space of time, there emerged a distinctly 'hostile minority', linked to the Conservatives, whose opposition led many to worry that it would not be implemented. As if wanting to fuel such fears, the government first published, and then withdrew, a summary of the report written up by Beveridge for the forces. When the plan was debated in Commons in February, the government would not endorse it fully, much to the embarrassment of the Labour ministers. The Gallup Poll found in March that far more people were dissatisfied than approved of the Government's response to the report (47%–29%). However, the National Council of Labour had approved it back in December, and in Commons itself the party voted overwhelmingly against the government. The temporary discomfiture of Attlee, Bevin and Morrison was as nothing compared to the long-term positive effect, which was to reinforce once again, and at a particularly critical juncture, the characterization of the Tories as the party of reaction and to dissociate Labour from the negative consequences of participation in the Coalition.[21]

The response to Beveridge also revealed a substantial shift in attitude among the middle classes away from Conservatism towards a qualified support for a kind of radical reconstruction. The Gallup Poll found that the report was viewed favourably by all classes, even by professionals and employers, and that nine in ten professionals and civil servants supported its proposals. Somehow, between 1935 and 1943, Conservatism had lost some of its loyal following among the middle classes.[22]

In fact, the loss was long in the making. Civil servants, for example, bore a large share of the economies forced on the government in 1931, and teachers and other public employees were extremely poorly paid throughout the 1930s. A description of London teachers in the mid-1930s depicted the men as suffering from abnormally high death rates, the women subject to unusually heavy rates of 'breakdown'; and all teachers labouring for extremely meagre rates of pay. Walter Greenwood's depiction of 'the clerk' in 1939 was similarly depressing, and few would quarrel with Orwell's dismal characterization of lower-middle class life in *Coming Up For Air* (1939).[23]

Before 1940, however, the middle class had no means of expressing this dissatisfaction politically. Labour, keen to re-affirm its working-class roots after 1931, seemed unable to offer a reasonable alternative; and the Liberals were an even more ineffective opposition. The result was disengagement and a measure of resignation comparable to, if less intense then, that felt by most working people. A minority moved sharply to the left and became the social base of the Left Book Club and the like, but before a significant section would move left, it was necessary for them to begin to perceive Labour as the best hope for the future. Astute observers recognized even before the war the need to link socialism to the middle classes, but they had little to propose. Lancelot Hogben argued in 1939 that the trend of social change was to expand the middle classes and to create among manual workers conditions of life more closely resembling those of the middle classes. The Labour party's approach failed to recognize this and had failed, in particular, 'to furnish a broad basis of agreement for constructive social innovations'. According to Hogben, this was not due to Labour's ignoring the problem of the middle class, but to their misunderstanding of it. Labour, he explained, 'has wept copiously at royal funerals . . .', but, unmoved by such sycophancy, 'the middle classes have not mourned when it went out of office'. A more realistic view would distinguish two main groupings among the middle class. One, composed of technicians, teachers and administrative workers, 'must be a bulwark of any progressive movement which can hope to gain and retain office. The other', Hogben continued, 'is made up of individuals whose activities would be quite unnecessary in a rationally planned society'. It was a mistake to think that 'a united front of wage earners and salaried employees. . .' could be constructed by trying to 'allay the fear that a Labour Government will undertake drastic innovations and daring social experiments'. The way to win the allegiance of white-collar workers was to offer a 'bold and challenging programme of technical expansion based on the socialization of industries'.[24]

Whether Labour, left to its own devices, could ever have fashioned such an appeal is doubtful, but in the end it did not have to. The war made full employment and government intervention appear reasonable, possible and morally desirable not just to the working class but to large sections of the middle class. A poll taken in June, 1945 showed that the middle classes disagreed with the notion that the best way to get jobs was through private enterprise by as wide a margin as the working class. That sentiment would, of course, be registered even more decisively in the general election, but it surfaced first in the reaction to the Beveridge Report.

The government's handling of the Beveridge Report stimulated concern that the insurance companies, the doctors and the Tories would get together to block its implementation. But the despair of 1942 did not return; instead, opinion moved further to the left and swung increasingly behind Labour. The key factor seems to have been the course of the war itself, for the victory in North Africa was followed by further advances on several fronts. Most important of all was the Russian victory at Stalingrad. News of the Nazi defeat at the hands of the Red Army reached Britain in January, 1943, and the British began several weeks of celebration. Town halls were draped in red flags while local councillors and justices of the peace joined in singing the Internationale in massive parades staged on 20 February, designated officially as 'Red Army Day'.

Coming as it did so close on the heels of El Alamein and the Beveridge Report and at the peak of mobilization, Stalingrad marked a decisive turning point in the political, as well as the military, history of the war. It signalled the ultimate victory over fascism and lifted the mood of even the most dire pessimist. It also shifted political attention to postwar and served to boost the stock of Labour and the left. From that moment, the Labour victory of 1945 became not merely possible but likely, and the outburst of popular enthusiasm produced by the events of November 1942–Feburary 1943 fuelled a political revival of massive dimensions. Almost immediately, Labour's fortunes revived: the 'movement away from party' of 1942 was reversed, and individual membership in the Labour party rose dramatically from under 250,000 in 1943 to almost half a million in 1945. By July, 1943 polls gave Labour a 38%–31% lead over the Conservatives. That margin had improved to 40%–27% by December and remained at that level into 1945. As the election approached, the Conservatives regrouped and pulled up to near 40%, but Labour's support solidified. The result was an impressive victory in which Labour won 48.2% of the votes and 394 seats, the Conservatives 39.7% of the votes but less than two hundred seats.

The margin of victory showed how much Labour had gained from the upsurge of popular radicalism. This is revealed also in the impact of Common Wealth. Formed primarily out of frustration with both major parties, Common Wealth had put the case for socialism and reconstruction to increasing numbers of people while Labour was still hamstrung by participation in the coalition. It carried its vaguely millenarian message of 'Common Ownership', 'Vital Democracy', and 'Morality in Politics' largely to the middle class, and achieved notable success in by-elections. Since few of Common Wealth's 15,000 members were of working-class origins, however, and since its major appeal was to the middle classes, its separate existence undoubtedly did Labour more good than harm during 1943–4. It served more as a surrogate for Labour than as its rival, propagating socialist politics without seriously compromising Labour's hegemonic role as the main opposition to Conservatism. Nor did the Communists pose any threat to Labour. In most areas the party's apparatus was turned to Labour's support and members worked to dampen rather than to encourage industrial militancy, helping to prevent the outbreak of disputes that might have embarrassed Labour prior to the election.[25]

Agitation within the armed forces also worked to Labour's advantage. Political discussion was rampant in the services, particularly after Beveridge, and reached a crescendo in the 'mock parliaments' and 'mock elections' held in North Africa. Edward Thompson has described how the debate over reconstruction swept the troops in other theatres also: 'everywhere across Italy, on wall newspapers, in bivvies around our tanks, in supply depots, the argument was going on'. The trend of opinion was decidedly left. A major recalled how a discussion on the Russian campaign ended with the singing of the Red Flag. Listening, he turned to a fellow officer: 'My goodness', he said, 'I seem to have got the Bolshie squadron in this battalion'. The other officer replied, 'Sir, the whole of the eighth army thinks the same way'. Fittingly, the Forces vote was overwhelmingly Labour in 1945. So, too, were the votes of soldiers' wives who were encouraged by the *Mirror* and by Labour to 'vote for him'.[26]

The social geography of Labour's triumph reflected all these developments. The major gains were in the urban areas. From the large majorities totalled in such areas, it is clear that working-class women voted Labour in larger numbers than ever before. The Labour majority in the Forces was also overwhelming, reaching as high as 90% for some constituencies. Labour won 79 seats for the first time, finally carrying 10 of 13 seats in Birmingham, 48 of 62 in London and 9 of 10 in Manchester. Gains were registered, too, in white-collar suburbs around London and the major cities; in general, more than a fifth of the middle-class vote went to Labour. The biggest plus on the Labour side was the number of young, new voters who, though not staunchly loyal or overly enthusiastic about the party, voted for it nonetheless. They may have known the traumas and deprivations of the interwar decades only dimly, as children, but their rejection of that past was the most decisive.[27]

The progress of reform, 1945–8

The victory of July 1945 was in itself no adequate guarantee that the weight of the past would not overwhelm the optimism of the present. There were real doubts in 1945 about all parties, all party nostrums and visions of the future. If the experience of war demonstrated the expanding possibilities of government action, the last peace had shown how quickly the expectations generated during war could be dissipated. Labour, moreover, may well have come to power armed with a programme of reform, but it was as yet untested and its plans were in many cases vague and incomplete.

The implementation of Labour's vision during 1945–51 was hampered by two other liabilities. The first was the country's severe economic plight. Britain had exhausted reserves accumulated over two centuries in just six years of war, and ended the conflict with a shortage of raw materials, of foodstuffs, and of the cash to pay for them. Lord Keynes spent the better part of his last year negotiating a loan from the United States, but the Americans drove a hard bargain. The loan was spent faster than expected, and when sterling was made convertible in summer 1947 – one of the conditions of the loan – the outflow of currency became critical. The Marshall Plan eased the problem temporarily, but balance of payments crises hit again in 1949 and 1951, each time with devastating effects on policy. Controls had to be maintained after the war and shortages of some items were worse; the economy of peace was almost as hard to administer as that of war.

The second factor circumscribing Labour's freedom of action was the fragility of the consensus inherited from the war. Both the Conservatives and Labour shared a belief that government would play a greater role after the war, but agreement did not extend much beyond that. Throughout the war, the Conservatives had sought to limit commitments about the shape of reconstruction. The coalition's White Paper on Employment of 1944, for instance, committed the government to 'the maintenance of a high and stable level of employment after the war', but refused to contemplate deficit financing: 'None of the main proposals contained in this paper involves deliberate planning for a deficit in the National Budget in years of subnormal activity'. Official policy lagged well behind public discourse in coming to terms with Keynes, and there were a striking contrast between the limited scope of the official policy and the more ambitious proposals contained in Beveridge's *Full Employment in a Free Society*, to which the White Paper was itself a response.[28]

The distance separating the two partners in the coalition was revealed dramatically in the bitter election campaign of 1945. The Tories in particular sought to distinguish their plans sharply from those of Labour. The Conservatives identified the private sector as the key to economic revival, and were eager to free it after the war. Labour was attacked for its commitment to controls for their own sake, and Churchill gave every indication that life would be different under a Conservative government than under Labour. There seems little reason to doubt that he meant it.

Even on matters where there was general agreement, substantial differences remained between what Labour and the Conservatives actually planned to do. Perhaps the firmest consensus existed on education. Labour and the Conservatives concurred with teachers, administrators and the public on the need to provide better educational opportunities for ordinary people after the war. Nevertheless, one of the reasons why Butler and the Conservatives pushed for passage of the Education Act in 1944 was the fear that, if Labour undertook the restructuring of education, it would be done with much less regard for private interests.[29]

On matters of social policy the limits of consensus were narrower still. In health there was agreement on the necessity of reforming the old system, but visions of what to put in its place diverged at critical points. The 1943 White Paper on health services was appropriately ambiguous on the future balance between private practice and public health centres. As the prospect of reform came nearer after 1943, the suspicions of the doctors hardened into firm opposition to Labour's proposals. Bevan's commitment ultimately ensured that it would be overcome, but he was forced to make compromises. The consensus was equally tenuous on social security, family allowances and child care, though perhaps more genuine in these areas than on matters of economic policy *per se*. On balance, the consensus for reform was real, but hardly strong enough to ensure Labour's success. The best measure of that success was that the shape of the postwar world came to approximate so closely to Labour's version of the consensus and to be accepted as the starting point for policy by all parties. That acceptance came, however, not in 1944–7, when the 'welfare state' was put in place, but during 1947–51, after the Conservative alternative had been decisively repudiated and Labour's vigorously implemented.[30]

The carrying out of Labour's programme was therefore critical in restructuring social relations and in making the electoral triumph of 1945 into a more or less permanent political realignment. That the Labour government did so under such adverse conditions was a major achievement. Immediately upon assuming office, Attlee, Bevin, Cripps, Bevan, Dalton, Morrison and other key ministers set about putting into law the main planks of the party's programme. Among their very first actions was the nationalization of the Bank of England. Then came coal, civil aviation and telecommunications, all within the first year. The Trade Disputes Act of 1927 was repealed at the same time. The government also sought as soon as possible to make the proposals of the Beveridge Report a reality. The National Insurance Act was passed in 1946, along with the National Health Service Act; the means test was abolished, workmen's compensation improved, family allowances extended and rent controls stiffened.

Labour continued its reforms into 1947 and 1948, but with less dramatic results. The railways and ports were nationalized along the lines developed by Herbert Morrison for London Transport, as was electricity. Both measures attracted opposition from the Conservatives, now beginning to recover from the debacle of 1945. Equally antipathetic to the Tories was the Town and Country Planning Act of 1947, which asserted state control over building. An Agriculture Act became law as well, and helped to produce a sustained boom in farming. Also in 1947 the section of the 1944 Education Act raising the school-leaving age to 15 was made effective.

The impulse for change was still not exhausted; 1948 witnessed the conclusion of the battle between Bevan and the doctors over National Health. It saw, too, the enactment of the Children's Act and the Criminal Justice Act, each completing long-needed reforms, and the further progress of nationalization, with the state taking over the provision of gas. The efforts of 1949–50 were less successful: the 1949 Housing Act was well-intentioned but had little effect, and the long-drawn-out battle over iron and steel did little but afford the Conservatives an issue with which to beat the government.[31]

The combined record of 1945–8 probably represented the most successful effort to restructure British society ever attempted. Taken separately, each measure was a distinct improvement over the past; taken as a body, they added up to a great deal more. Much like the Beveridge Report, whose appeal derived not from the specifics of its proposals for the social services but from its integrated vision of a better future, so also the sum of Labour's programme was much more than the cumulative merits of its parts. Combined with the effort to institute a planned prosperity, which may or may not have been essential to the achievement of full employment, the reforms of 1945–8 ushered in a new era in British social and political history. It was an achievement so solid and so successful that the Conservatives accepted its main contours as the basis of the postwar consensus. After all, they did not adopt the Industrial Charter of 1947 out of benevolence, nor did they decide, after 1951, not to tamper with the institutions of the welfare state because they loved the poor. They did so because the British people would not tolerate otherwise. Of such an imperative was the postwar consensus built.

There was, to be sure, another side to the successful 'climax of labourism'. That was the impasse which Labour confronted when, its vision only partly realized, it lost first its parliamentary majority and then, more gradually, its claim to represent the party of progress battling against the party of reaction. As the reforms of 1945–8 were made practical, new, unforeseen problems would arise to call into question much of the earlier wisdom. The nationalized industries, it turned out, did not always flourish under public ownership, and the workers who staffed them discovered that the state could be almost as distant and unresponsive as many of the old managers. Most important, the changes in British society wrought by a decade of war and reform unleashed a wave of economic expansion that made the critique of capitalism less trenchant and the lure of socialism less appealing. To all this must be added the overriding impact of the Cold War, whose outbreak in the late 1940s nearly derailed the progress of that era and whose long-term effects upon socialist commitments would prove dangerously corrosive.

These difficulties, howeever, were still to come, and in 1948 it was reasonable for ordinary working people to feel proud of the new world that their efforts, their votes, their organizations and their party had created. That they did indeed feel this way was demonstrated with great force by the surge of loyalty with which workers responded to the mounting crisis of the Labour government during 1949–51. The unions gave up potential gains on the shop floor and suffered losses in real wage rates. Yet the members remained loyal. In 1950 the engineers actually voted down by 3–1 a recommendation from their executive for a national strike over wages. By 1950–51, moreover, when many of the middle-class voters who had opted for Labour in 1945 had drifted away, the working class rallied to it. This was no mere reflex action, no instinctive class allegiance, but a conscious decision based upon an appreciation of Labour's strengths as well as its limitations. As Raymond Williams has argued, 'The huge vote of 1951, still in conditions of post-war austerity and planning, was the most conscious working-class determination ever recorded in Britain, to reject the conditions of pre-war society and go on with the new system'.[32] It is difficult to disagree.

PART THREE

Class Relations and the Political Consensus

8

Class and Party, 1945–51

Labour's electoral victory in 1945 and its subsequent achievements in government occupy a unique place in the history and mythology of the party. In the lore of the labour movement, it was a time when a new breed of men came to power and moved to fashion a future of social justice and prosperity. If the reality was somewhat less heroic, the record was nevertheless impressive and, in many ways, highly exceptional. A proper appreciation of it requires a recognition of just how exceptional that era of success was in the history of the party and of the working class. It was special, first of all, when measured against the long years of electoral disappointment and industrial defeats experienced by working people from 1920 to the early 1940s. It was also peculiar in that the link between the party and the class would never again be so close or so effective, nor would the combined strength of working-class institutions ever again be so formidable as in these years.

Probably nothing epitomizes the uniqueness of the moment better than the curious unfolding of events while Labour was in office. For, unlike so many reforming governments that have held power only long enough to discredit themselves and to undermine their bases of support, Labour had a stronger tie with the workers in 1950–51 than in 1945. The difficulties which marred the last three years of Labour's rule did not weaken, but strengthened, the connections between the party and the class.

The tightening of the linkage between the class and the party was accompanied by an intensification of class identities that would have potent consequences for the entire postwar era. It would mean that the starting point for the evolution of society and politics after the war would be marked by the solidity of the social formation and of political allegiances. Grasping this point of departure is especially critical when trying to understand the direction and dimensions of subsequent development, for the greatest single difficulty in assessing the extent and impact of social change is in settling upon a base against which to measure it. The 1940s were, in fact, atypical in two essential ways. Not only was it the time when the link between class and the party, the workers and Labour, was closer and more all-encompassing than ever before or since. In addition, the 1940s, though a time of considerable political reform, witnessed little social structural change. The working class that gave its votes to Labour in such massive numbers was firmly rooted in the economic development of the previous century. Neither the war nor the changes of 1945-51 did much to spark off a social transformation within the class itself.

The working class that came to be represented by the Labour party in 1945-51 was thus a mature social formation, and the party, with its cautious demeanour and pragmatic outlook, was its thoroughly apposite political vehicle. This rather neat, if temporary, fit was a source of strength as well as weakness. Labour would continue to profit from the inertia of political loyalties for years to come, but its very rootedness in the institutions of the working class would make it less adaptable than might otherwise have been desirable.

A brief look at the working class and its link to Labour in the late 1940s will highlight both of these characteristics. The occupational composition of the class, as always, depended upon the technical and industrial organization of the economy, and these changed rather little from 1939 to 1950. Several studies of industrial concentration, for example, have shown that the share of output produced by the largest firms either declined or, at best, stayed stable. Other measures, such as the ratio of supervisory to manual employees or the size of establishments, also changed very little. The combination of depression and war served to favour the growth of middle-sized firms at the expense of both the small firm and the corporate giant. Several aspects of government policy in the 1930s – the encouragement of industrial cartels and of consolidation of small firms into more compact, efficient ones in cotton, mining, shipbuilding and steel, for example – reinforced that pattern, as did the system of wartime planning. The modernization of British industry was thus modest and halting, the transformation of work and of the working class equally so. The social fluidity of wartime was not correlated with any fluidity of industrial or technical structure.[1]

Data on industrial and occupational distribution confirm this view. The number of workers engaged in mining stood at 849,000 in 1938, at

839,000 in 1948. In textiles, employment was equally steady: 861,000 in 1938, 835,000 in 1948. The numbers involved in construction increased slightly, those in clothing registered a slight decrease. Yet these were all old, backward and inefficient industries which would have to shed many workers in order for employment in more dynamic, new industries to have significantly increased. They did not, which meant that the growth of the new industries was attenuated. Metal and engineering, for example, occupied large numbers of workers during the boom in war production but then reverted to a level just 15% higher than in 1939. Employment in chemicals likewise stabilized in the late 1940s at a level only slightly above prewar. Whatever the achievements of mobilization during the war, the economic machine it left behind was scarcely more developed than before. There were reasons for this relative stagnation, but that it happened was extremely significant for the evolution of the working class.

In 1951 the occupational structure of Britain was not markedly different from two decades before. The rate of labour force participation for women stood at 34.7%, not much of an increase over the 34.2% of 1931. It is true that the higher rates of participation by women aged 35–54 in 1951 showed the long-term effects of increased opportunities during the interwar years and, in a sense, prefigured later changes of a more substantial nature, but in view of the massive mobilization of women during the war and the campaign to entice women back into industry during the late 1940s, the stability and the low overall rate are quite remarkable. Some increases had occurred in the number of clerical workers, who grew from 7% to 10.7% of the workforce, but it is likely that much of that shift had probably occurred before the war. The percentage of the workforce involved in sales actually decreased slightly; professionals and employers remained stable; while the combined ranks of the skilled and semi-skilled also remained about the same. Only the unskilled decreased substantially, and a large portion of that change was no doubt due to the decline in numbers of farm labourers and domestic servants. The latter dropped from almost 1.3 million in 1931 to under 350,000 in 1951. The jobs lost in domestic service, mostly women's jobs, were almost exactly matched by the gains in clerical work, leaving the general participation rate unaffected.

For men, gains in white-collar work were fewer, and most of the shifts in male employment involved a movement from old to new industries. Still, the extent of change overall was surprisingly small, and the composition of the working class in the late 1940s and early 1950s was heavily weighted towards those older industries and occupations that had shaped the structure of the class in the early part of the century. No wonder management, the state and even the unions became preoccupied in the late 1940s with Britain's lagging productivity and that the Labour government took it upon itself to send over 50 teams of managers and workers to visit and report back on the practices of American firms. The transformation of British industry, which was slowly gathering momentum between the wars, was somehow suspended in 1939, and did not begin again until several years after the ending of hostilities.[2]

This relative backwardness in the industrial underpinnings of the working class was matched by the persistence of styles of life inherited from before the war, and together these made for a certain hardening of class identities and allegiances. The political triumph of Labour was in the first instance accompanied by a consolidation of working-class culture and ways of life. The war, such a powerful solvent of political allegiances, disturbed merely the surface of social relations and allowed the enduring structures of society to re-assert themselves powerfully after the war.

Family life was seen as especially quick to revert to past ways. The marriage rate jumped dramatically at the end of the war, for obvious reasons, and with it the birth rate. The number of births in England during 1945-50 was nearly 20% above the level of the late 1930s, despite a markedly older population. The women who bore these children were not, to be sure, leading a return to some Victorian pattern of marriage and the family. Even working-class couples went on to have the same, small families as middle-class couples married between the wars normally had, but they did participate temporarily in the movement out of employment and back into the home. Only later, their children sent off to school or work, would these women re-emerge from the home to take the growing number of service jobs produced by the economic growth of the 1950s.[3]

It is extremely difficult, of course, to determine just what transpired within this increasing number of small, working-class families. Most likely some significant improvements were registered. Judging from the available accounts, the standards of behaviour of men and women towards each other and towards their children between the wars left considerable room for improvement. Slater and Woodside, for example, found in their wartime interviews that neither men nor women were particularly happy with the way things had been and were determined to do better. Not surprisingly, people began to approach marriage more pragmatically: 'At this social level', they argued, 'practical advantages were given a higher rating than temperamental compatibilities'. Young men and women increasingly combined a firm desire to marry with a determination to make life more bearable than it had been before the war, and tempered fanciful notions of love with a keen understanding that happiness depended largely upon material circumstances. A 'new realism' concerning married life, coupled with a novel sense of possibility and seriousness, seems to have caught on among women and men, but it was most obvious among women, and most reflected in the dramatically changed content and tone of women's popular magazines, in their dress, and in their behaviour.[4]

The intention both to marry and to improve the marriage bargain was particularly evident among the young women – all of marriage age – interviewed by Pearl Jephcott just after the war. She found that a common consequence of living in the overcrowded homes of their parents was a determination to avoid such conditions themselves: 'They have seen and shared these burdens [of their mothers] for all their eighteen years and they do not intend, if they can avoid it, to have a similar life for themselves'. Equally universal was a revulsion against the absence of work that the girls' fathers had so often experienced and, perhaps more interestingly, at the kind of work their mothers were forced to do. Though many of the mothers had done domestic service, 'None of the girls likes the idea that her mother does, or ever did such work even though the mother herself may be rather proud of the fact that she was in service "in the big house" when she was a girl'. For their part, the mothers concurred with their daughters' desires to do something different, even if that something merely involved securing a more amenable married life at home. For good or ill, both generations of women placed (or displaced, if one prefers) their hopes for a better life upon an improved marriage and a better domestic environment. More ambitious hopes, comprising visions of career *and* marriage, were not likely to be fulfilled, and were in consequence very rare.

The 'dominant interest' of these young women was courting – i.e. finding a marriage partner. If this focus narrowed their options, it also led them to think very seriously about the sorts of marriages and homes they sought. Most had clear ideas about men or boys, and standards were often quite practical and hard-headed. In addition, they were absolutely clear about wanting a small family – 'Two, a boy and a girl' was the stock answer about children – and they clearly connected family size with the quality of life. As one girl put it, 'If you have a big family like next door you can't give them the education and the clothes you want'; or another, 'you can't go biking with the kids'. Jephcott's findings were made even more explicit in a Mass-Observation study done at the end of the war. Not only were working people found to want small families, but that desire was bound up with a resolve to exert greater control of one's life and to upgrade oneself after the war. Thus, Mass-Observation discovered that large families were considered by many not merely as a burden, but as somehow immoral and indecent, a cause for embarrassment or contempt. Similarly, though couples could multiply their reasons for wanting a small family, they had 'great difficulty in imagining circumstances in which they might want a bigger one'.[5]

It seems unlikely that these women would have allowed a return to the pattern of family life of the 1930s, or that they would have accepted such a fate if their husbands had sought to impose it. And the evidence on completed family size for this generation indicates decisively that they did not. Rather, working-class women and men seem to have carved out a more comfortable space for their domestic affairs and seem to have begun to build more egalitarian relations in the process.

Unfortunately, the scope for improvements in the comforts of home was very limited in the straitened circumstances of postwar. By all accounts, however, income was more evenly distributed after the war than before, and the living standards of working people improved substantially. Price increases were modest during the 1940s and earnings kept pace well enough. The expansion of social provision under the Labour government also added noticeably to the welfare of working people. Family allowances and free health care were particularly important. Rowntree found on his visit to York in 1950 that so-called 'primary poverty' had diminished from 31% in 1936 to just 2.8%. But the measure of the depth of prewar deprivation was how little such improvements did to advance working people towards any kind of genuine affluence. Survey data from as late as 1953–4 showed that working people spent about as much for necessities then as they had in 1937–8, between 30% and 40% going just for food. Only about 7% of family income was available for the purchase of durable household goods, another 8% for 'other goods and miscellaneous'. To the extent that additional income was available, it went towards a very primitive kind of accumulation, mostly the acquisition of better clothing or domestic amenities. Overall, the proportions of consumer expenditures spent on food (29.1%), drink and tobacco (16.5%), and clothing (11.5%) remained extremely high in the early 1950s, while that devoted to household goods, furniture, electrical goods and appliances, motor cars and fuel together came to less than a tenth (8.8%). The change since prewar was minimal, both for the country as a whole and, as the postwar marketing surveys indicated, for the various regions in Britain.[6]

The lack of change in the class structure, coupled with the inability of workers to translate their greater share of national income into increased personal consumption, meant that, for all the differences in political matters, everyday life remained remarkably similar to what it had been before 1939. The levelling up of incomes, it is true, gave near universal access to those aspects of working-class leisure – the pub, cinema, the dance-hall, the wireless at home – that had begun to be widely diffused between the wars, but it brought nothing particularly new into working class life. The postwar years witnessed peaks of attendance at football matches and of betting, and probably the fullest flowering of almost all those, by now 'traditional', working-class pastimes. Rowntree and Lavers's 1947–8 study, *English Life and Leisure*, gave evidence of very few innovations in the use of free time, but they provided overwhelming documentation of the vitality of the clubs, brass bands and similar self-activities organized by working people. Dancing, drinking and the cinema continued to draw more powerfully than the churches and adult education, reading and repertory still lagged far behind darts and gambling. The cynicism and secularism that characterized earlier attitudes were much in evidence and were, if anything, stronger. On religion, for example, the following quote from a working-class housewife was offered as typical: 'A working-class family that is religious is working against its own interest. Everyone knows religion isn't true, but the nobs try to make working folk believe it is, so that they won't kick up a fuss'. It appears that the distinct working-class culture, based upon the institutional networks of local communities and workplaces, and nurtured by decades of common want, was as strong in the late 1940s as it had been in 1939 or earlier.[7]

Just how strong is indicated by the results of two major studies done in the late 1940s. The first was a 1948 survey by Mass-Observation of the attitudes towards class held by the members of M-O's national panel. Like the earlier questionnaire of 1939, it asked panelists to assign themselves to a class, though it also gave them an opportunity to say whether they felt they belonged to a class or not. Curiously, and despite the supposed 'classlessness' of the times, very few took the opportunity to place themselves outside the class system. The overall results were in fact extremely similar to those obtained in 1939; if anything, antagonisms were sharper. A number of men, for example, coupled their claim to membership in the working-class with comments about middle class snobbishness and exclusivity. As one young man from a long line of workers put it, 'I belong to this class because I was born in it, and because I want to be in it. I am proud to be in it because of its forthrightness, honesty, and capacity for hard work, and because I despise the English middle class.'[8]

Such feelings were reciprocated by the middle class respondents, and together suggest the strength of class sentiments just after the war. In part these were surely a carry over from the heightened sensitivities of wartime, but there was more involved than a simple intensification of feelings, and a later question in the M-O survey hints at this second factor. Panelists were urged, after giving their own class identity, to provide a list of ten typical middle-class occupations and ten working-class ones. The answers showed the sharply divergent images of society and class structure held by members of different classes in the 1940s.

To begin, there was virtually no overlap between the lists of jobs considered middle-class or working-class by respondents of different social backgrounds. Typically, middle-class panelists could name only a handful of working-class jobs, and most of these involved servicing the needs of the middle class. Most commonly mentioned were labourers, servants, handymen, dustmen, bus conductors or construction workers. Despite occasional reference to a miner, the lists prepared by middle-class respondents missed the entire world of industrial production. Naturally, their picture of the middle class was richer, subtler and more specific. For workers, just the opposite held: their listings conjured up the infinite complexity of the world of work; they could tick off a wide variety of productive jobs. On the other hand, their notions of the middle class were as imprecise as the middle-class concept of the working class. Two types predominated on the lists prepared by working-class respondents: either the stereotyped professional occupations of doctors, lawyers, dentists or parsons, or the ubiquitous shopkeepers, who turned up as publicans, greengrocers or chemists.

What was obvious from these lists was not just the social differences and the lack of understanding that they betokened between classes, but the sense they conveyed of the distinct worlds inhabited by the working and middle classes. Each followed a separate way of life, based upon comparably intricate sets of associations and institutions. Their different views of society corresponded to discrete social locations between which there was hardly any intercourse.

The second study, which rather neatly dovetails with the Mass-Observation data, was the well-known LSE inquiry of 1949 into social mobility. That study confirms the impression of sharp class differences derived from other sources, in three ways. First, the investigation revealed that social mobility over the previous several decades had been slight. Sons tended to have jobs in the same class category as fathers, and when they did move up or down the distance traversed was minimal. Nor was there any tendency for mobility to increase over time: those born during 1920–29 had no more opportunities than those born before 1900. Second, the survey revealed substantial differences in the social grading of occupations by those in different classes. Upper-class subjects had a clear idea of the social hierarchy and of where each group fitted; those in the lower grades responded in a much more varied and inconsistent fashion. Workers seemed not even to share with the upper class a common notion of what was and what was not a better job to have.

Thirdly, this disjuncture in the ranking of occupations carried over into broad differences in other 'subjective aspects of stratification'. Just as in the Mass-Observation results, workers themselves had a much richer, more variegated, view of the composition of their own class. 'The least skilled and least esteemed kinds of work are scarcely ever mentioned by the self-rated working class itself; on the other hand, descriptions of the working class as consisting of "dustmen", "road-sweepers", "navvies" and so on – a description which may be said to maximize social distance – are given quite often by subjects who regard themselves as middle class. . . .' Workers, in addition, had a more expansive notion of the boundaries of their class, extending them to include clerks, shop assistants and others. The principle informing their mental class maps was inclusion based upon some productivist notion of social worth, rather than the mapping by exclusion more common among the middle classes. The different mental worlds of the working and middle classes were also reflected in patterns of aspiration. Though large numbers of both groups thought it might be nice to have one's own business, less than one worker in four thought it feasible. Similarly, although most working people wished for their children to stay at school longer than they themselves had, most had no desire to keep them at school beyond 16–17 years of age. And while working people wished their children to advance in occupational terms, they hoped mainly to see them secure a stable, skilled job; far fewer aimed at crossing the mental-manual divide into the routine grades of white-collar work. Finally, despite all the disadvantages and discontents of working-class jobs, seven out of ten workers were happy with their positions. In short, the British working class of the late 1940s held to a distinctive set of values and perceptions that not only distinguished it from the classes above, but which also served as a reasonably coherent and self-contained view of the world and of the worker's place in it.[9]

Popular attitudes and styles of life thus reinforced industrial stagnation and the stability of consumption standards so as to solidify class awareness and class relations. But all of these were further reinforced by the rhetoric and politics of class during the period of the Labour government. Labour was an avowedly class party, however moderate its behaviour, and its coming to power brought an escalation of class antipathies. Sir Hartley Shawcross's oft-quoted statement – 'We are the masters now' – may well have exaggerated the spirit of *resentment* among the workers, but it certainly captured one aspect of Labour's triumph. Inevitably, such notions produced an equally class-conscious response from the upper and middle class. The '"plight of the middle class" . . . was rarely out of newspapers in the postwar Forties', it was said, and that plight was seen to be a rapidly deteriorating one. It was commonly accepted that the middle classes had lost out in the political and economic changes of 1939–48, and their losses were taken to symbolize all the evils let loose by the election of 1945.

The strength of these arguments is perhaps best exemplified by how seriously they were taken by staid and otherwise level-headed academics. The introduction to the LSE social mobility study, for example, admitted that this was its initial preoccupation: 'As a starting-point it was proposed to focus upon the formation and structure of the "middle classes". Much has been said in recent years about the changing circumstances of this section of the community.' Fortunately, the inquiry asked other, more interesting, questions, but others did not. Rather, the tendency was to praise the English middle classes who, according to one study 'provide most of their nation's brains, leadership and organizing ability. . . .' and yet 'are being squeezed economically. . . .'; their 'incentives . . . rapidly reduced, and their living standards progressively impaired. . .'[10]

It was easy enough to demonstrate the fallacy of such arguments and to show that, as G. D. H. Cole explained, 'the development of the Welfare State . . . has not . . . thrown down the professional and managerial groups into the ranks of the proletariat. . . .' What counted, though, were not the facts of privilege and inequality, but the

143

perception, and in the late 1940s the perception was that the middle classes were suffering at the hands of Labour. Moreover, the association of suffering, rather than complacency and comfort, with middle-class status may well have served to expand the frontiers of the class. Indeed, Mass-Observation claimed to have found in its surveys a growing consciousness of being middle-class. As one woman explained, 'I never thought of myself as belonging to any particular social class until recently – other people say I am "middle-class". . . .'[11]

This waxing sense of middle-class identity, bound up with the corresponding belief in its threatened quality, guaranteed that the political consequences were highly conservative. The heightening of middle-class concerns was a key factor in the revival of Conservative fortunes after 1945, and made Conservatism even more of a class phenomenon than it had been between the wars. As the *New Statesman* put it in November, 1947, 'Austerity has awakened the middle classes and made them politically active. . . .' The logic of politics between 1945 and 1951 made both the major parties more class-oriented. The Labour victory of 1945 had been built of solid working-class support and some votes from the middle classes. Very quickly after 1945 middle-class electors began drifting away from Labour, while the working-class moved in the opposite direction. In 1945, it was claimed that the workers 'expect disappointment and are on the look-out for it', but with the implementation of Labour's programme such detachment diminished. The workers were much impressed with the government's actions and so, when things became politically rougher after 1947, rallied to the support of their party.

The first evidence of this increasing political loyalty was the willingness of the unions and the workers to accept a *de facto* wage freeze from March 1948 through the 1950 election. This they did solely out of political loyalty, for it brought no real other benefits. The second came in the dramatic increase in local affiliations. Individual membership jumped from a little over 600,000 in 1947 to over a million in 1952. However unreliable these data, the dimensions of the rise are notable. More important, it was these local members who provided the backbone of Bevanite support. Conversely, one might well see Bevanism as a logical outgrowth of this general revival of socialist support against the mounting Conservative challenge.[12]

The third and most striking manifestation was in the election results of 1950 and 1951. Labour raised the spectre of pre-war Conservatism and urged consolidation of the gains of 1945–50; the Conservatives harped on the issues of controls, of bureaucratic interference and of nationalization, and promised a return to freedom and prosperity. Each was effective in mobilizing solid support from the party's 'natural' class base, and the results reflected the ossification of class political loyalties. The returns in 1950 and 1951 together showed that Labour had the firm backing of nearly two-thirds of the working class, and that the Conservatives had secured the allegiance of just about the same proportion of middle-class votes. Between 1945 and 1951 Labour lost a quarter of its already small middle-class base; while the Conservatives picked up most of these Labour losses plus some defections from the Liberals. In sum, class polarization in politics peaked in 1950—51, as did Labour's share of the vote. If this was also the moment of consensus, it was probably due less to the convergence of party programmes or to shared values than to the firmness of opposing loyalties and to the delicate balance between the parties, aptly symbolized by the fact that the Conservatives came to power in 1951 with fewer votes than Labour.[13] Consensus and compromise are always more attractive options when outright victory is elusive.

9

The Pattern of Social Change, 1950–65

The firm social identities and political allegiances that emerged from the war and postwar experiences would persist through the fifties and beyond. But the reforms of 1945–51 combined with the prosperity of the 1950s to set in motion economic and social changes that would gradually alter their meaning and effect. Working people had achieved a new status after the war, a new kind of citizenship. At first, this involved mostly the lifting of those deprivations so long associated with working-class membership. Over time, it would grow to include also access to more and more of the goods and benefits generated by economic growth.

Class alignments were resilient, however, and the coming of this novel form of social participation – this citizenship by consumption – redefined, but by no means removed or dampened, working people's sense of inequity or class antipathy. Class came to be understood more in terms of inequality and wealth, rather than as different cultures and ways of feeling, and social conflict came to revolve more around distribution than around power. Class was no less salient, workers no more 'bourgeois' or individualistic than before, but their aspirations were grander and more focused upon improvement than upon security, and their demeanour was less tolerant of privilege, hierarchy or deference. This transformation had its roots in the economic and social structure, but was reflected also in changing customs and opinions. Let us begin with the structure.

Class and Occupation after 1950

The retardation of industrial development from 1939 to 1950 meant that the British economy had a great deal of catching up to do and that much of the growth in the 1950s would be concentrated in those industries and occupations that had matured elsewhere before the war. Movement into the next generation of products and technologies had to wait until still later. Change in Britain had to contend with a more complex institutional structure which cushioned the impact of growth and slowed it down. Despite all this, structural transformation did inevitably occur, ensured above all by the unprecedented expansion of the world economy. Industrial output rose at a rate of 3.7% per annum during the 1950s, and investment consumed nearly 15% of GNP. The implications for the composition of the working class were quite serious. The most visible effects had to do with the shifting occupational balance within the class, i.e., with the altered mix of white-collar and manual jobs. Less visible, but also important, was the transfer of large numbers of workers from old, backward industries to newer, more technically advanced ones.[1]

The growth in white-collar workers was the easiest to spot and the most widely commented upon. Between 1950 and 1966 total employment grew by 10%, but the number of manual workers remained constant, declining as a percentage of the workforce from 64.2% to only 58.3%. Correspondingly, white-collar workers increased from 30.9% to 38.3%. The number of clerks expanded by over 900,000 during 1951–66, from 10.4% to 13.2% of the occupied population. 'Higher professionals' grew from 435,000 in 1951 to 829,000 in 1966; 'lower professionals and technicians' from 1,059,000 to 1,604,000. Many of these jobs were in services, although surprisingly few were employed directly by the government. The distributive trades also added almost a million new jobs between 1948 and 1965, insurance and banking another 220,000. Local government employment grew by about 100,000, but this was offset by a more than equal drop at the national level.

The redistribution of workers within manufacturing and mining was perhaps less spectacular, but nonetheless very significant in terms of productivity and work. To take the most obvious case, there were 880,000 employees in mining and quarrying in 1948, but only 629,000 in 1965. A quarter of a million jobs had disappeared, mostly from coal. Other industries followed the same path. Nearly half a million jobs were lost in textiles and clothing between 1951 and 1965, and over the same period the output of British shipbuilding declined by two-thirds and employment was reduced to a mere 200,000.

Counterbalancing these losses were substantial gains in what had been labelled between the wars as 'the new industries'. Overall manufacturing employment grew by over 800,000, and continued to employ slightly more than a third of the working population. This was made possible by substantial growth in such industries as electrical goods, whose labour force went from 524,000 in 1948 to 894,000 in 1965, mechanical engineering, which probably grew by about the same amount, and vehicles, which gave jobs to approximately 690,000 in 1948 and to 930,000 in 1960 before stabilizing at about 875,000 in the mid-1960s. Other industries – food processing, chemicals, printing and publishing, iron and steel – also expanded employment, though altogether they probably added no more than 350,000 workers.

These shifts in the structure of the working class were accompanied by changes in its sexual and its ethnic and racial composition as well. The participation rate for females rose from about 35% in 1951, to over 42% in 1966. The increase was almost entirely in routine clerical or sales positions or in manual jobs. Six out of ten clerks were women in 1951, seven out of ten in 1966. Among manual workers, the female percentage grew by 3% – but this total masked a decline in skilled, a modest gain (4.5%) in semi-skilled, and an increase of 7.2% in unskilled jobs held by women. Of the nearly two million women added to the paid labour force between 1951 and 1966, therefore, most entered at the bottom rung of manual or non-manual work.

The ethnic character of the working class changed somewhat less. Just after the war, there was an influx of Jewish refugees and of emigrés from eastern Europe, especially Poland and Russia. In 1950, for example, there were approximately 150,000 Poles in the UK. Together with the Irish, Commonwealth immigrants and others not born in England and Wales, these made up about 6% of the population. By 1966, this had grown to 7.8%. Until 1961, the largest single group were the Irish, but by 1966 they were outnumbered by those from the Commonwealth. Immigrants from the West Indies, India and Pakistan constituted a distinct, if hardly homogeneous, coloured immigration numbering some 210,000 in 1958. Immediately they arrived in Britain, they became the objects of discrimination and antagonism, their migrations a matter of political controversy. Attempts to regulate the flow only led to a panic of immigration in the early 1960s, so that by 1966 they and their children had increased to almost a million. The concentration of immigrants in major urban areas and their high rates of economic activity made their presence within the working class of these cities even more noticeable.

Overall, these data suggest a complicated pattern of change in the backbone of the class structure. The industrial reorganization of Britain, so long delayed, finally began to gather momentum. And yet the pace of the transformation was sufficiently controlled and modest as to make the achievement a relatively smooth and, for most, painless process. The restructuring of the economy that occurred before 1939 had been done by the ruthless imperative of unemployment, and its human toll was everywhere evident. After 1948, the reshaping of the working class was accomplished without leaving entire areas devastated, without wrenching adult workers from their homes and neighbours and impelling them to seek work in totally alien environs.

The consequences of these changes for working-class life, attitudes and behaviour were many and varied. In general, it seems that working people were able to profit from the various changes without having to undergo the trauma of broken communities or vanished jobs and that they were able to compensate for what trials they did endure with increased incomes and a greater degree of security. It is easy to exaggerate the gains in living standards in the 1950s, but their cumulative effect did allow ever-increasing numbers of working people to evolve a style of life substantially better in material terms than what their parents had enjoyed.

If this was caused ultimately by economic growth it was ensured in practice by the new distribution of political and industrial power. The return of the Conservatives to office with the slimmest of parliamentary support predisposed them to moderation during 1951–55, and the taste for office made for a continuance of that pattern after that. With no lead from the government, employers were unable to mount a successful attack on the unions and so acquiesced in the latter's enhanced bargaining position. Union membership held steady through the 1950s, and served to prevent any industry from reverting to the anti-union stance of an earlier era; the institutionalized power of the unions restrained the freedom of employers on the shop floor and mitigated the effects of technological change.

Of course, these trends were mediated, at times distorted, by the continuing diversity within the working class. Men and women, skilled and less skilled, white-collar and manual workers did not fare equally well. The basic thrust may have been in a moderately egalitarian direction, but there were exceptions. By 1950, the less skilled in building, shipbuilding, engineering and on the railways were making an average 80% of the skilled rate, but there was no further progress for a decade and a half. Likewise, women's pay advanced from 55% of men's in 1935–6 to 58% in the mid-1950s, but remained at that level until the late 1960s. Moreover, the apparent stability of the relationship between men's and women's pay actually understates the impact of sexual inequality in different occupational groups. The biggest gains for women in terms of both employment and pay happened in clerical work, but this was due entirely to the fact that, as women entered this sphere of white-collar work, it came to be paid less and less well. On the other hand, the bulk of the women in manual jobs were located in the semi-skilled category, where their relative earnings have dropped from 75% of men's in 1935–6 to 58% in 1960 and a mere 50% in 1970.[2]

These exceptions and qualifications to the aggregate trends suggest the need to differentiate carefully between various sections of the class, between what has happened to men and to women, to white-collar and to manual workers and, within the latter, to the skilled and those without recognized skills. For if it is true that 'After 1945 ... the working class presents a homogeneous appearance', it is nonetheless obvious that beneath the appearance of homogeneity lurked historic distinctions of considerable import.[3] It may well be, in fact, that the critical question for historians is how the persistence of divisions within the working class coexisted with a popular image of a solidary class.

Probably one reason for the perception was that the strong link between the workers and the Labour party inherited from the 1940s persisted long after. It was, however, the changing reality of life at work that lent genuine substance to the image.[4] A useful starting point is the work of Ferdynand Zweig, who published several studies in the early '50s which, if deficient on specific points, ring true in general. Zweig saw workers as being at a peak of class awareness, as irreligious, impervious to middle-class values, and proud: 'The working class is the backbone of the country, the most hard-working and useful class', was how they apparently put it to him. The most interesting findings concerned the world of work. Despite the long-term influence of technical change and the short-term levelling of wages, craft workers were numerous, well-organized and secure. Skilled men in construction, engineering, in spinning and printing, for example, had maintained their organization, their roles in the production process and their pride and identity as craftsmen. Even in engineering, the most advanced of British industries, the status of the skilled was not seriously threatened, and the 'Upgrading of semi-skilled men to skilled jobs' was resisted by the men and hence 'not much practised, apart from the war period. . . .'

The ability of the skilled to maintain their positions did not mean the degradation of the rest. Indeed, Zweig uncovered a surprising ability among the semi-skilled to exert some control at the workplace and a considerable occupational solidarity and sense of personal worth. Full employment apparently tilted the balance of tactical advantage away from employers and towards all grades of labour (or at least male labour). The non-skilled workers in construction could turn their backs upon jobs they disliked: 'I don't care, I can go around the corner and get another job', Zweig quoted them as saying, and the effect was to force an upgrading of the conditions, if not the terms, of their work. Likewise in cotton, the collective power of the skilled spinners was nearly matched by that of the less skilled weavers, and 75% of the looms were still run on the old, 4-loom system. In the absence of major innovations the workers in both sections had managed to erect 'protective walls of Unionism' and to resist the imposition of managerial control. As one employer put it, (no doubt exaggerating somewhat), 'A weaver felt like a queen on her looms, or anyway a mistress of her own fate'. In iron and steel, by contrast, the discretion and autonomy of the men were necessarily less, but here, too, the unions had succeeded in establishing distinct procedures and the recognition of workers' rights by management. In this case, the workers were protected by a sort of 'workplace rule of law', rather than by informal or customary controls, but it was quite effective nonetheless.[5]

It appears that the upgrading of semi-skilled work had proceeded considerably since between the wars. The clearest examples were those industries which, for different reasons, were considered to offer the least attractive work situations before 1939 – mining, dockwork and motor car manufacturing. However strong the proud traditions of the miners had been before 1926, it was obvious that defeat and depression had made life difficult, and the literature of the 1930s abounded with examples of derelict communities of miners huddled around idle pits. The dockers also suffered greatly during the slump and all the schemes from earlier in the century for controlling casualism foundered on the persistence of unemployment during 1920–39. The motor industry, of course, offered reasonably secure employment and good pay, but the introduction of mass production and strict discipline made the work unattractive for many. By 1950, however, each of these occupations was transformed.

One may begin again with Zweig, who explained how those who laboured in the mines shared a common culture: 'They all live in closely-knit communities where there is a strong projection of the group on the individual.' This communal sentiment involved an intense class solidarity, a 'proneness to grievances' and a 'suspicion against men on the top'. Among dockers much the same type of occupational community prevailed. At Manchester docks it was found that the disorganization of dockers in the labour market was compensated for by an intensive solidarity at work and during industrial conflicts. Moreover, steady work and the National Dock Labour Scheme, put in operation in 1947, had begun finally to limit the competition for jobs, and the more solid aspect of the group was further accentuated. By the early 1950s dockers and miners were being grouped together as the two occupations most noted for their strong loyalties, the overlap of work and community, and for their high propensity to strike. In part, this reflected the persistence of highly visible disputes in these industries after the war, but it also reflected real and positive changes at the workplace.[6]

Work itself probably changed less in motor vehicles than it did in mining or dockwork. The car firms were weakly organized at the end of the war, and remained so through the mid-fifties. At Ford, for example, management strongly resisted an attempt by supervisors to unionize in the late '40s, seeing it as an opening wedge for the shop stewards. Formal organization languished, and workers' positions on the shop floor remained vulnerable. On the other hand, the tight labour market and the acknowledged need to fend off the unions kept management from resorting to the kinds of direct control of men by machines and intensive pacing which might otherwise have occurred. The alternative to dealing with the unions and the stewards was paternalism, which itself placed limits on management. Moreover, this was surely the worst case and applied with full force only to Ford and Vauxhall. The more typical case afforded workers more union protection and at least comparable conditions in the shop. More favourable still was the situation at the Coventry firms, particularly Standard's, run on the so-called 'gang system', in which workers themselves controlled many of the details of work. This pattern may have been exceptional, but it became the ideal towards which industry shop stewards strove throughout the 1950s.[7]

At least two qualifications need to be entered in this general account of changes at work. First, there is little evidence of any increase of workers' intrinsic interest in work. Rather, their greater complacency about the job derived primarily from the fact that it was regular and paid a modest salary and, secondarily, from factors only incidental to the job itself – like the companionship of workmates and the overlap between work and community. Well into the mid-fifties, most workers judged their jobs by very low standards, and only among craftsmen was work valued for itself and for the opportunities it offered for the practice of skill. In this sense, 'instrumental' attitudes towards work were prevalent much earlier and in much more 'traditional' occupations than later arguments would suggest.[8]

The second qualification is much more serious. Most of the jobs where workers exercised control or autonomy were held by men. With the exception of weaving, which would decline seriously after 1950, women held jobs that were far less stable and allowed for far less autonomy and discretion than did men. Unfortunately, the sex blindness of social science led to very few studies of women's work. Even so, Zweig's rather superficial study, *Women's Life and Labour*, of 1952, makes the difference between the male and female experience clear enough. His analysis was very similar to descriptions penned before the war, suggesting how little had changed. Women continued to work in boring and repetitive jobs, assembling small parts, packaging, and so on; they were paid, far more often than men, on piece-work; and their prospects were correspondingly darker. Overt dissatisfaction was apparently lower than men's, but mainly because expectations were also lower. The most common complaints had to do with the difficulty of making piece-work quotas and the dependability of earnings. Once these conditions were fulfilled, attention turned to other aspects of the job environment, but ordinarily it was the lightness of the work, the quality of the supervision or the social relations of the factory that elicited the most favourable responses. In consequence, the women workers studied by Zweig held to rather different images of society than did working-class men. There was among them 'a close link between working-class consciousness and the problem of the cost of living'. They were less proud of being working class, more aware of its deprivations. The result was a different form of class awareness – less aggressive and self-satisfied, more bitter and, in a sense, more 'pecuniary'. As Zweig himself concluded, 'It is fair to say that class consciousness, *as we understand the term*, is primarily a masculine conception' (my emphasis).[9]

Granted these two important qualifications, it nevertheless does appear that the world of work had become marginally less oppressive for many types of workers by 1950. The less skilled jobs in transport had been organized and made tolerable, the worst driving tendencies of mass-production employers had been checked by unionization or the threat of it, and groups like the miners had won a new status. Better still, none of these improvements seem to have been eroded by developments after 1950. Rather, throughout the 1950s and early '60s social scientists kept replicating the findings of the 1948–52 period and fleshing out their depth and meaning. Studies of miners and dockers, of redundant manufacturing workers, of shipbuilders, printers, fishermen, tin workers and others confirmed the broad outlines of this picture from the late 1940s and early 1950s. It was, indeed, the gradual accumulation of such results that led social scientists to conclude that most manual workers could be grouped together and their images of society considered as a composite. David Lockwood, in a seminal article in 1966, labelled these workers 'traditional proletarian', and proceeded to describe them in terms derived from this growing body of literature. They were said to possess 'a high degree of job involvement and strong attachments to primary work groups that possess a considerable autonomy from technical and supervisory constraints', to live 'in solidary communities' where the bonds of work and kin and sociability overlapped and, as a consequence, to view the world as a power struggle between 'them' and 'us'.[10]

It is easy to criticize such a view, with its papering over of long-standing divisions and its sloppy use of the notions of 'traditional' and 'proletarian', but it does serve to indicate the underlying direction of change at work. Lockwood seems to have grasped that structural change after 1950 produced substantial redistribution between industries and the use of more technically advanced methods and machinery, but did not revolutionize the factory or enhance management control of the production process.[11] The evidence for this can be found in several places. To begin, the structure of industry itself evolved only gradually. Although the top 100 firms continued to increase their share of output from 26% in 1953 to 42% in 1968, they did not radically restructure industry. The pace of mergers increased over the level of the 1930s and 1940s but fell far short of the 1920s rate. Mergers that did occur, moreover, in many cases did not alter management structure or policies. The consolidation of Austin and Morris into BMC in 1952, for example, did not increase managerial efficiency, and Ford's subsequent absorption of Briggs caused them only trouble. The rise of Leyland, which took over Standard Triumph in 1961, likewise did not transform conditions at plant level, however effective it might have been as a matter of pure business.[12]

The modest nature of change at factory level was evident in surprising places. Joan Woodward's 1953–4 survey of industrial organization in South Essex, one of the more advanced and prosperous regions, showed how few firms employed truly 'mass' or even 'large batch' production methods. Data on plant size show, too, that the trend towards larger units of production was steady, but not disruptive in its extent. By 1961, more than half the manufacturing workers still laboured in firms employing fewer than 500 workers. The evidence on skill levels and payments systems tell much the same story. Skilled workers grew absolutely and as a percentage of the workforce between 1951 and 1961, despite the decline of strongholds like mining, textiles, and shipbuilding. After 1961, the fate of the skilled became more tenuous, but only slightly so. The evidence on payments systems is consistent with that on skill. Payment by results encompassed 38% of workers in manufacturing in the late 1940s, and an even higher percentage among women. From 1950 to 1961 that percentage increased by another third, which meant that the pattern was extended throughout industry and that many of the newer processes were being operated on that basis. Confronted with a choice between adapting an old established payment scheme to new work or using the innovation as an opportunity to rationalize pay structures and increase control, managements seem to have opted more often than not for the former, the path that offered the least resistance.[13]

The evolution of the work situation of white-collar workers is somewhat less easy to gauge. A critical problem is that the rapid growth of the sector during 1950–65 was accomplished largely by an influx of female labour, particularly in the routine jobs that normally can be considered within the orbit of the working class. By 1965 most of the lower-paid clerical jobs in the larger offices were held by women. Male clerks continued to find work in banks, as insurance agents and in government service, but these jobs differed substantially from those held by female white-collar workers. Thus in banking it was found that 'careers are for men; the routine work such as machine-operating is for women'.[14]

The changing sex composition of white-collar workers therefore makes it difficult to generalize. Much of the literature has been focused either upon the so-called 'proletarianization' of office work or upon how changes in the character of the work affected levels of unionization. The issues are separable, however, and need separate study. It appears that the feminization of the office did not lead to an intensification of work. 'Mechanization', presumably a necessary precondition of any such process, was found in the mid-1950s to be 'affecting the social relations of office work to a much smaller extent than is often imagined'. That judgement was based in part upon the fact that statistically just 3.4% of clerks were classed as 'machine operators' in 1951, only 9% of women listed as 'typists'. Most had less precise descriptions and apparently worked on a greater variety of less specialized jobs. Even by 1971, machine operators still amounted to just 5% of clerks, while the ranks of the typists and shorthand typists only grew proportionately. To the extend that the term 'proletarianization' can be applied at all, it is to the situation of those male white-collar workers who entered their positions with expectations of mobility that were later closed off and disappointed. A study of male clerks in a Glasgow steel firm, for example, showed that it was the decision of the company to institute a management training scheme that drove them to unionize. But such cases were exceptional, for the overall reduction of men in clerical jobs tended to mean that most held those jobs only temporarily while on the way to some better paid and more responsible job higher up the managerial hierarchy.[15]

Overall, then, the growth of white-collar jobs did not imply any significant degradation in the work done by men or women. The men probably profited from the trend, and the women most likely continued to experience rather similar conditions of work. If anything, the gradual shift from 'the personal and particular relationships of the counting-house work environment' to a more formal bureaucratic setting surely benefited many women, who have always known the harsher side of paternalism in the form of sexual harrassment. This may not have compensated for the continued discrimination visited upon women in the labour market – in terms of pay and promotion – but it did mean that some of the more unpleasant aspects of work were mitigated.[16]

The lack of truly dramatic change in the work situation of white-collar employees, of course, meant that the stimulus which 'proletarianization' was supposed to give to unionization was also lacking during these years. Without it, the advance of white-collar unions came to depend upon fortuitous combinations of other factors. The most important was the role of the government, which encouraged bargaining among its workers through Whitley Councils and through a quite sympathetic attitude towards recognition. When employment was highly concentrated in large firms and when, for other reasons, employers were predisposed to grant recognition, white-collar unions also took root. But such conditions did not obtain throughout industry, and white-collar unionization, though increasing from just under 2.1 million in 1950 to over 2.8 million in 1966, actually declined slightly as a share of its total potential membership.[17]

In both manual and non-manual work, then, the industrial growth and reshuffling and the significant advances in technology throughout the economy did not lead to a visible deterioration of work. Control of the workplace in industry remained balanced between workers and employers. Among the men, the time-served craftsmen maintained their position, while many with merely job-specific skills or with strategic positions in the production process increased their leverage. Of course, women workers in industry did not exert such control and seldom enjoyed the prerogatives of their male counterparts, but it seems reasonable to assume that their situation was better. Much the same was surely true for the increasing numbers of female white-collar workers. In sum, British management failed to refashion relations at the workplace despite growth and development. Conversely, though, neither full employment nor the institutional power of the unions succeeded in bringing about a major shift in control towards the workers or a substantial 'humanizing' of work.[18]

Social Change and Working-Class Culture

The great boom of the 1950s and early 1960s may have left conditions at work largley intact, but it did bring about major changes in living standards. Prosperity slowly lifted virtually the whole of the working class to a higher standard of comfort and well-being and, with some lag, workers' expectations about what constituted a reasonable standard also rose. The limited horizons forced upon the class by a generation of depression and insecurity began to widen, and a style of life filled with all sorts of new possessions came dimly into view.

The precise extent of the new prosperity can be debated, and qualifications again need to be entered, but in the end there is no disputing the trend. Real wages grew by more than a quarter between 1950 and 1965, earnings by over 40%. The first use to which such increases were put was the better provision of food and the upgrading of the domestic environment. Food expenditure remained a key item in the family budget throughout the 1950s, eating up (so to speak) close to a third of household spending. But the constant proportion of spending devoted to food procured a steadily improving diet: by 1962, the average worker consumed 5% more milk, 40% more meat, 25% more eggs, more than double the butter and over 20% more vegetables and fruit than at the end of the war. About this time, workers finally began as a class to turn towards the satisfaction of other needs. The figures of 1960–2 show the first significant decrease in the relative size of the food budget, and the share of food kept falling from then on. Income began to be spent on other things – consumer durables, entertainment and alcohol, cars, and, especially important, a better quality of housing. Consumer spending on furniture and household goods increased 42% between 1950 and 1965, on housing 37%, on radios and electrical appliances 180% and on motor vehicles and fuel by nearly seven times.

Just how much of this new consumption went to the working class is not entirely clear, but several surveys suggest a rapid diffusion of items like television sets, and a slower spread of more expensive and sturdy items like refrigerators and cars. A national survey of housewives done in 1956 revealed that among the manual working class 35% had televisions and 40% vacuum cleaners, with 23% possessing electric kettles, only 13% washing machines and a mere 4% refrigerators. Two years later over 60% had TVs and 28% washing machines. Car ownership also lagged, but began to spread after 1957–8. By 1959, a survey of the top half of manual workers showed 44% owning a washing machine, 32% a car and 16% a refrigerator. When Goldthorpe *et al* studied a large sample of 'affluent workers' in Luton in 1962–3, they discovered that nearly 6 in 10 had refrigerators and fully 45% motor cars. By 1967, a national survey revealed how widespread such advances were: a majority of working-class families had washing machines and more than a third refrigerators.

Rather similar patterns took hold a bit quicker among white-collar workers. The 1956 national survey claimed to show that the percentage of clerical households owning washing machines and refrigerators was more than double that of manual workers; by that early date half owned TVs and three-quarters vacuum cleaners. In the 1960s, however, the gap began to narrow appreciably. In Luton in 1962–3, the ownership of refrigerators and cars was just marginally higher among white-collar than among manual workers, and by 1967 the difference between clerical and manual levels was minimal.

The rapid advance of material consumption also had the effect of creating a distinct youth market in the 1960s, although only then. When the American ad-man genius Eugene Gilbert, who made his fortune identifying and catering to the teenage market, visited Britain in 1954 and 1956, he was forced to conclude that the potential for a permanent office there simply did not exist. By 1959, however, Mark Abrams estimated the spending power of the young at £330 million per year. There was no youth market cutting across class lines in place by 1959, but there was an enhanced market for the things young workers had always bought – clothes, cosmetics, drinks, cinemas and records. And the potential was developing for a truly distinct youth market, which would be realized in the mid- and late-sixties.

It appears, then, that there was a sustained, long-term improvement in standards of consumption and that the pace of the advance quickened over time. The exhaustion of the economy and the depletion of reserves during the war guaranteed a lengthy period of readjustment, lasting almost a full decade, but after 1959 there emerged something that could honestly be labelled mass consumption. Inevitably, some workers could afford televisions and cars sooner than others, but what is most striking in retrospect is how collective the progress of the workers was. Large sections of the workers seem to have achieved the wherewithal to buy this or that major item at more or less the same time. It is unlikely that this happened by design, but it did impart a kind of rhythmic, marching pattern to the workers' material advance and may well have helped to dampen notions of individual movement.[19]

It was this visible material progress that lay beneath the widespread public discussion of the fate of the postwar working class. That discourse produced an array of concepts designed to capture the meaning of the change. None was particularly successful, however, for neither social scientists nor commentators nor activists had developed a vocabulary that could adequately convey the compatibility of dramatic material improvement and persistent class identity. This was particularly evident in the notion of 'embourgeoisement', which linked together a variety of specific ideas about changing incomes, life-styles and politics into a comprehensive theory of the direction of social development.

The most critical theoretical flaw in the 'embourgeoisement' argument was its assumption that structure, attitudes and behaviour were all neatly correlated. But from a historical perspective, its great weakness was the extremely narrow vision of class structure upon which it was premised. The very term 'embourgeoisement' – and 'the affluent worker' carried the same connotation – implied two basic and opposing classes, so that the transformation of the working class could only be interpreted as its becoming more like the middle, or bourgeois, class.

What was missing from this argument, and from most other attempts to come to grips with the 1950s and 1960s, was a recognition of the possibility of substantial material progress occurring within the existing class structure or, to put the matter more positively, of the fact that working people could take advantage of the new opportunities for consumption and make use of their new-found prosperity without

159

losing their sense of class awareness. Some notion related to the expansion of citizenship or to the ending of workers' social disfranchisement would seem most helpful, but whatever the phrase, something other than the concepts used in the 1950s is necessary. This is not to suggest that the descriptions of working-class life from this period do not contain useful information and insights. It is rather that these must be carefully extracted from the theoretical apparatuses in which they were so often encased. When that is done, much can be learned.

Three particular traditions of social investigation are most relevant to the problem of working-class attitudes in the 1950s and 1960s. Each set itself different questions and reached different, if related, answers. The first was what has been called 'cultural studies', and was associated with the work of Richard Hoggart and others focusing upon mass culture. The second was made up of studies of the family and the community, identified most clearly with the Institute of Community Studies in London. Last, there was the rather more diffuse interest in youth, perhaps symbolized best by Colin MacInnes's essays and his novel, *Absolute Beginners*, but increasingly veering off into the study of working-class gangs, violence and sub-cultures. A review of these three bodies of research, proceeding from an analysis of the presuppositions to a resumé of the most important empirical findings, will, it is hoped, afford at least a first approximation to the patterns of change in working-class culture.[20]

The starting point for virtually all this discussion was Hoggart's *The Uses of Literacy*, published in 1957. Its significance derived from three interrelated characteristics of the book and of the moment. The book was based upon Hoggart's thorough immersion in the details of Northern working class life as a youth and, later on, as a university extension lecturer. This immediacy imparted an authenticity which has never seriously been called into question. Second, Hoggart was also positioned well enough within the middle class, as a university graduate and teacher but still something of an outsider, to grasp critically the essence of the new mass culture that had earlier enveloped the middle classes and that was now beginning to affect the working class as well. Third, having experienced the tensions personally, through individual mobility, he was able to discern the contradictions between the values of the new mass culture and those congealed in the institutions of the urban workers.[21]

The effect of the book was immediate, massive and, on the whole, beneficial: it marked a new phase in the postwar discovery, or rediscovery of the working class; and it offered an important stimulus to the study of the emerging mass culture by showing that it was possible to criticize that culture from a populist, rather than an elitist, stance. Hoggart's analysis pointed towards a critical evaluation of contemporary society from within English popular culture, in much the same way that Raymond Williams would locate the native literary sources for a critique of the culture of industrialism and Edward Thompson would identify the indigenous roots of political opposition to early industrial capitalism.[22]

The link with Thompson and Williams also serves to highlight the special character of Hoggart's contribution, for while Thompson charted his course through working-class history and Williams through English literature, drama and the emerging mass media, Hoggart brought high and low together and attempted to show the lack of fit between them. The comparison serves also, though, to show Hoggart's limitations, for it suggests strongly that *The Uses of Literacy* could only have been written when it was and probably only by someone whose personal experience mediated between the two rival cultures. It could come only after the consolidation of a distinct urban, working-class culture, which could be described relatively intact, but before the new mass culture had seriously penetrated that life. Indeed, the tensions between the two were not truly described by Hoggart, for by the early 1950s they had yet to engage; rather they were felt, intuited by him personally, as a socially mobile scholarship boy. He anticipated the clash as the likely result of the further spread of prosperity and the advance of working-class purchasing power. Hoggart's book therefore succeeds brilliantly in evoking the texture of working-class life as it was lived in the 1930s and 1940s, and adequately as a prologue to the critique of mass culture, but much less well as a study of the transformation of working-class culture after 1950.

What one can take from Hoggart, in short, is a confirmation of the trends of working-class life up to 1950, and a first attempt to define the meaning of the newer forms of mass culture embodied in the popular arts. Indeed in many ways the most important legacy of Hoggart is those studies of the media and advertising which have sought to document, qualify and elaborate the criticism of mass culture made so poignantly by Hoggart. In most cases, however, later findings have tended to replace Hoggart's dichotomy between mass culture and working-class culture with more complex notions. More detailed analysis of the mass circulation dailies, for example, has shown that only by tailoring their ideas, language and format to conform roughly to the daily rounds of ordinary people were the *Express* and the *Mirror*, among others, able to get and hold their share of the readership. Thus the *Mirror* quite consciously aped the 'us-them' rhetoric of certain sections of the working class and filled its pages with homely advice that spoke directly to the domestic experiences of working-class women. There was no simple imposition of individualistic values onto the workers, but a conjuring up of familiar routines and rituals, a pandering to established tastes and a fitting of the advertising in particular to the world of the workers.

A still broader analysis of the growth of the 'popular arts', by scholars following Hoggart's lead, concluded even more strongly that popular art did not overwhelm 'folk art', or 'working-class culture', but actually grew out of it. The television and the cinema, it was shown, had much in common with the music-hall – a sense of the personal, an immediacy, a preoccupation with 'misunderstandings, disguises, anger at imaginary hurts, pursuits', a recurring use of shared language and other conventions. Other new cultural forms were equally close to old patterns. Rather than counterposing the one against the other as Hoggart had, these later writers stressed the fundamental link 'between folk art and popular art'. The main result of Hoggart's analysis of the clash between working-class culture and the emerging mass culture was therefore to challenge others to discover their underlying continuity and compatibility.[23]

The second tradition in the analysis of working-class life focused upon the roots of workers' culture in the community and family and upon changes occurring there. Two early studies – one based upon the Yorkshire mining community of Ashton, the other upon extensive interviews with twenty 'ordinary families' in London, set the tone for this research, though its full flowering came later at the hands of Michael Young and Peter Willmott at the Institute of Community Studies.

The premier case study was that of Ashton, where 6 in 10 men worked in the pits, and where workers were found to possess an exceptionally strong sense of community. The men worked together and shared the dangers and troubles of the industry. They also pursued a collective kind of leisure organized through a network of clubs that boasted nearly 7,000 members between them, drawn from an adult population of less than 5,000. Other institutions – the pub, regular attendance at rugby matches, gambling – also flourished. The women, however, were shut up performing separate duties in the home, going out occasionally to church or some social gathering, more regularly to the cinema but, in general, participating in a segregated and restricted community of women. The study of London families by Elizabeth Bott told a similar story. Working-class families tended to be more extended than those in the middle class, to exhibit more separation in the roles of women and men, and to bind both sexes tightly to their respective communities of male workers or housewives.[24]

While the Ashton study involved a detailed description of an entire community, the London study was based on the narrowest of intensively-studied samples. Though neither could claim much typicality, their combined effect was to reinforce the image, set out by Hoggart amongst others, of the traditional working-class as composed overwhelmingly of a series of self-contained communities spread across the map of urban Britain. These quasi-anthropological renditions of working-class community life were further amplified by the results of several simultaneous investigations undertaken by the Institute of Community Studies. The aim of the Institute was explicitly reformist: Michael Young in particular was a social democrat interested in humanizing the welfare state. It was obvious to him and his co-investigators that planning, nationalization, re-housing schemes and the like, while bringing substantial gains to working people, were often carried out with insufficient regard for personal or community relations. The work of the Institute focused in particular upon the unintended social consequences of the movement of working people from settled, inner cities to more suburban housing estates. By the mid-1960s, some three and a half million British workers and their families lived on such council-built housing estates. Before 1939, the spread of this new form of housing had come in for considerable criticism for allegedly bringing about a decline in the spirit of community and associational life. The Committee on the Appearance of Housing Estates acknowledged these criticisms in 1948 and attempted to address the problem by changes in design. But the idea that housing estates encouraged only a barren form of social life continued to have force into the 1950s and, indeed, merged with the more general conservative critique of the welfare state.[25]

In part responding to this view, and in part seeking to extend the reforming zeal of social democracy into the realm of personal relations, the Institute of Community Studies produced reports describing what happened to working people when they moved from 'traditional' working-class areas, such as Bethnal Green, to new housing on the fringes of London.[26] The argument was that as people moved from the old to the new communities, something vital was lost. Families tended to drift apart, particularly those linked by the extended kinship networks that had overlapped with the ties of residence. Mothers and their married daughters were most adversely affected, but relations atrophied amongst others as well. Families in the old neighbourhoods had opened outwards and merged with the community; families in the new areas turned inwards and became isolated. The problem was especially acute for old people and for those with young children, but it was said to touch the majority of those in the new, suburban environments. Typical of the general phenomenon was the case of Mrs Harper, which supposedly showed 'how great can be the change for a woman who moves from a place where the family is linked to relatives, neighbours, and friends in a web of intimate relationships to a place where she may talk to no one, apart from the children, from the moment her husband leaves for work in the morning until he comes home again, tired out by the journey, at seven or eight at night'.[27]

The impact of the Bethnal Green studies was nearly as great as that of Hoggart's evocation of working-class life, and the two traditions fed upon one another. Their particular significance lay in imposing an analytical framework upon a plethora of often diverse findings on the character of community and family relations. Young and Willmott's descriptions of Bethnal Green were placed alongside studies of Swansea, Oxford, Liverpool, Ashton and elsewhere and assimilated to a common pattern; while the apparently contrasting cases of various housing estates in Bristol, Sheffield, Coventry, Oxford, Liverpool, etc., were arrayed together with those for Dagenham or 'Greenleigh' into a stark, opposing pattern. The process was further codified by a tendency to compress and summarize these results in several standard works produced in the mid-1960s. These synthetic accounts smoothed over the ambiguous details buried in these individual studies, and presented in the clearest terms the argument about the break-up of traditional communities and family patterns among the newly affluent workers living on the new housing estates.[28]

It is clearly not possible to undertake yet another re-compilation of these many separate studies. Nor, fortunately, is it necessary, for with the continued advance in sociological understanding, researchers have themselves generally come to abandon the oversimplified dichotomies enshrined in these premature formulations. Three types of revision have occurred.[29] First, it has become increasingly clear that kinship ties remain strong among working people even in the face of substantial geographical mobility. Daily, direct interchange necessarily becomes rarer as distances become greater, but the role of kin remains central. Second, investigators have replaced notions about the desolation of social life on the new estates with a more refined focus on the problems and stages of community formation in such locales. The impetus for such a rethinking came from the Institute of Community Studies itself, specifically from Willmott's follow-up study of Dagenham, which pronounced the new area not the antithesis of Bethnal Green but, rather, 'the East End reborn'. The rebirth took about a generation, but it did happen, and the coming to light of such cases has suggested to many that housing estates, like other communities, develop over time. Initially, it appears, the inhabitants respond to their move with mixed feelings, and often either throw themselves furiously into the affairs of the new area or retreat totally. Gradually, however, both the early enthusiasms and stresses diminish. With the growing up of children and the coming together of parents around the needs of their families, a community life comparable to that in older working-class districts begins to emerge. Minor differences may remain, but they rarely amount to much more than that.[30]

The third line of revision has emphasized change between generations and variation over the life cycle. One of the major weaknesses in the early studies was that they often mistook changes experienced by individuals as they moved from one place to another and, upon the move, entered a new phase of their lives, for broad-based changes in the character of the working class. The new housing estates ordinarily attracted young couples in which the husband was at the peak of his earning power and the wife at the onset of child-bearing. Since people with small children seldom have the time or funds for extensive socializing, social life on the estates often has taken on an attenuated cast. No doubt going through that stage of life at some remove from one's parents and one's childhood community may establish patterns that persist; nevertheless, in the short run at least, the shift in relations is entirely an artifact of demography. So while changes may well occur from one generation to the next, the experience of moving to a new housing estate is but one of the many factors that operate over the long term, and it is unlikely to be determinant.

What are likely to be important, however, are the desires and opportunities men and women have to control their fertility, to fashion a domestic environment to their liking and to select not only their friends but which of their kin they want to associate with. These more general considerations, moreover, do seem to have guaranteed a gradual, but decisive, shift in the behaviour and attitudes of working people in their relations with husbands and wives, kin and friends during the 1950s and 1960s. Indeed, the main finding from the postwar community studies that has held up subsequently is that concerning the shifting relationship between husbands and wives. Most of the studies of older working-class districts showed a rigid division of labour between men and women. Men's work and women's work were different, as were the networks of association which men and women entered into as part of these distinct roles.

Even in the 1940s it was found that young people had a different future in mind for themselves. The determination to have small families was widespread and, judging from the statistics, governed behaviour throughout the 1950s. As working-class women had fewer children, they more often re-entered the workforce; even when they did not, domestic life became more comfortable and secure and, in response, more central to workers' non-working lives. The home became 'an easier, more welcoming place'; and in the late '50s and early '60s more and more studies showed increases in the domesticity of men and their willingness to share the tasks of childrearing. Zweig, for example, claimed to have found in 1958 a general 'feminization' of the working class, whatever that might imply. There were increases, too, in the amount of leisure time spent at home and in the value placed upon the home and the goods that filled it. Probably the strongest evidence of this alteration in family life came from the final study of London done by Willmott and Young. A decade and a half after they first framed the discussion in terms of the old, close-knit communities versus the new, less sociable ones, the two authors reinterpreted their entire corpus under a new rubric: 'the rise of symmetrical family'. In spite of the ambiguities and elisions contained in that notion, it was a clear advance over the previous vision of decline and disarray in the communities of the urban workers. In short, students of community and family life gradually realized that working people could remake their relations without necesarily giving up their personal or class identities. As Brian Jackson's subtle treatment concluded, life for 'the working class is undoubtedly far, far better than it was. But in essence it *feels* the same, offers the same kind of *experience*'.[31]

The persistence of class identities amidst changes in patterns of daily life was equally evident from the rather different progress of studies of youth culture. By the early 1950s, the average young worker, male or female, had half as much again spending money as his or her counterpart in 1939. At the same time, the numbers of young people who had yet to enter the adult world of work was increased by the raising of the school-leaving age and the spread of secondary education. Together, these factors made youth, or working-class youth, a more distinctive and visible group than ever before. Very quickly, the visibility was magnified by the emergence of new styles of dress – the Edwardian costume of the Teddy-boys, for instance, who appeared in South London in 1953–4 – and new tastes in music and leisure. Pop singers got younger by the year until by 1956 Tommy Steele, a working-class kid from Bermondsey, became an overnight success at 19. In the fall of that year, Bill Hailey's film, *Rock Around the Clock*, opened to packed cinemas and led to riots. Hailey's tour of Britain later that winter proceeded more peacefully, but it nonetheless marked a turning point in the emergence of a distinct youth culture. Through the mid-1960s, this was overwhelmingly a working class phenomenon; only then did it filter up to lower middle and middle class youth.[32]

Almost from the beginning the new youth culture became identified with violence. Many of the early reports of the 'Teddy-boy' phenomenon were in accounts of beatings and stabbings; and the term first attained wide usage and recognition in April, 1954 after a fight between two groups of young men spilled over from a local dance hall to the platform of a railway station in Kent. There were large-scale fights in 1956 in the London suburb of Tooting, and a nasty incident in Fife in Scotland, both involving Teds. In 1957, the veteran Mass-Observer Tom Harrison, back from his field trips to Borneo, wrote ominously of 'this new terror that stalks the land, the Teddy-boy. The first time I went out in Hampstead', he added, 'I was so frightened that I nearly took off again for Borneo and the comparative security of head hunting'. If such descriptions were largely rhetoric, they seemed nevertheless to be confirmed by the behaviour of the young people themselves. The very next year, 1958, for instance, small groups of alleged Teds were involved in two dance-hall killings and, most important symbolically, in the Notting Hill race riots.

The public debate over the new youth culture seized upon its penchant for violence and hooliganism and guaranteed as well that the first scholars to scrutinize the experience of youth would be those concerned with crime and deviancy. Almost immediately they had focused on the problem, however, it began to disappear, for the new youth culture was scarcely more criminal than the adult world from which it was distinguished. More important, it soon became evident that what had happened was that the novel styles of dress and

167

comportment made possible by young people's new consuming power and visible by their increased mobility, were labelled deviant by those with the power to so stigmatize. That power largely resided with the mass media which tended to emphasize instances of crime, violence and popular disturbance. One fascinating case study showed how a minor scuffle between police and apprentices on a Saturday night in Huddersfield became in the press 'the night the town went mad', and how, a week hence, the rhetoric of the press and the over-reactions of the police provoked yet another incident, which in turn sparked three more over the next 14 days. Much the same kind of thing happened with the Mods and Rockers battles at the sea-side resorts between 1963 and 1966; as one researcher rather cautiously put it, 'the development of this behaviour was not independent of the reaction it provoked'.[33]

If this type of analysis did not of itself reveal much about the character of working-class youth culture, it did suggest that it was perhaps better understood in terms which could explain, not its deviant aspects, but its heightened visibility. Although detailed ethnographic studies of working-class youth groups did not emerge until the 1970s, it nevertheless became obvious to investigators that young male workers had always gone around in packs, that their social worlds ordinarily had less to do with the family and more to do with their peers than those of middle-class youth, and that such a pattern was not marginal but central to working-class life.[34] Jack Common had described the way boys had the run of the streets between the wars, and would regularly engage in sparring matches, petty thefts and fights with the police. Others have shown that cliques of young men, or gangs in extreme cases, had been common for many years.[35]

These patterns persisted into postwar, but were slowly transformed. In the 1950s, a study of a group of young workers in London showed how their lives were enmeshed in those of their peers, and how their group 'became a powerful influence. . . during the period between their leaving school and becoming engaged to marry: home became a "hotel", and all spare time was spent with their "mates", with whom they went to cinemas, joined clubs, took up and dropped recreational activities'. If formal gangs were rare, informal groups were thus the norm. What was new was their ability to purchase consumer goods and to evolve styles that marked them off from one another ar d from their elders. But young people in the old, traditional communities were affected as much as those on new husing estates or in better-paying jobs. Even in Bethnal Green, a majority of boys interviewed in 1965 were found to want more rewarding work and improved housing, a fuller family life and higher incomes than their parents had dared to hope for. Hence Willmott argued that, 'If one chose to define "middle-class" in terms of aspiration to higher consumption standards, together with some limited aspirations at work. . ., then many. . . could indeed be described as "middle-class" in outlook, and more so than earlier generations of East Enders'.[36]

A New 'Affluent' Working Class?

The burden of all these diverse studies, of course, is that it would be a profound mistake to define 'middle class' in this way or to interpret the postwar transformation of the working class as having made them more 'middle class'. The most convincing proof of this comes from two studies of class from the early 1960s. The first to appear was Runciman's national survey on issues concerning class and equality, *Relative Deprivation and Social Justice* (1966); the second was *The Affluent Worker*, based on Luton. The field work for both studies was completed in 1962–3, so the results should fit together well, as they in fact do. To make proper historical sense of them, however, it is necessary once more to place these two projects in context and recast their initial terms of reference into a language more useful for historical analysis.[37]

The context, of course, was the intense debate over *embourgeoisement* stimulated by the economic changes of the late 1950s, but made more urgent by the third successive Conservative general election victory in 1959. The 'relative deprivation' and the 'affluent worker' studies were both conceived and executed in the shadow of Labour's defeat. In this they shared a common concern with the studies of working-class conservatism undertaken at about the same moment, the difference being that the latter aimed at uncovering the roots of apparently aberrant voting patterns, while the former sought the sources of working-class defeat in the decline of class identity and political allegiance among the workers as a whole. This political purpose imparted a pessimistic tone and mode of interpretation to all of these studies.[38]

Given these circumstances, it was inevitable that the arguments of both studies would be seen as adding substance to the prevalent notions of working-class decline.[39] Thus, the 'relative deprivation' study came to be associated almost single-mindedly with the argument that the secret to working-class political quiescence, whether that be evidenced by Conservative voting or by a weak attachment to Labour, was the narrowness of workers' views of the social world. Their 'orbits of comparison', as measured by their choice of comparative reference groups, were said to be extremely limited. When questioned about their incomes, for example, a surprisingly large number of manual workers thought they were paid well, and felt that there were not many people paid appreciably better. Of those who did feel deprived the choice of a comparison group was from a nearby social location, suggesting very limited horizons. Few workers compared themselves to managers, employers or well-paid professionals, and most seemed to have markedly working-class notions of a proper standard of living.

The 'affluent worker' studies, by contrast, emphasized the changed orientation to work and community of the Luton sample as the key to political apathy. Work, it was claimed, ceased to have any intrinsic worth except for the small number of craftsmen, but was valued only for the money. There was little sense, too, of occupational community, for not only was the workplace not congenial to such sentiments but the neighbourhoods were also lacking in communal warmth or even simple connectedness. Most spent their spare time at home, in front of the television or in the garden, and combined their desire to acquire more goods with a wish to enjoy their possessions alone, or as part of the nuclear family. The supposed result was a 'privatized' ethos which emphasized personal advantage. Since most Luton workers were sensible enough to recognize that their economic progress would depend upon collective rather than individual efforts, they eschewed political individualism and espoused instead a kind of 'instrumental collectivism'. 'Instrumental collectivism' led to membership in trade unions and votes for Labour, but the attachments were weak and without emotional force.

The compatibility between these themes and the pervasive sense of working-class political moderation is obvious. However, quite different inferences could be drawn from these very same findings. Take Runciman's point about the allegedly narrow reference groups among workers. Would it not have been just as reasonable to read that as a sign that workers' distinctive social world was still very much intact, rather than to take it as a measure of their limited sensibilities? The fact that working people compared themselves to their own kind would seem to suggest a finely developed sense of their place in the class structure, the options open to them and the range of rewards likely to come their way. Surely it would have been taken as an indication of wild and wishful thinking, would it not, if workers were found routinely to complain that their pay rises did not match those of doctors and stockbrokers?

Similarly, the findings of the 'affluent worker' studies, to the effect that workers' attachment to the job was largely pecuniary and that their allegiance to the unions and the Labour party was mixed with a measure of scepticism, would hardly seem to have been news. The stalemate in workplace relations in the 1950s and early '60s surely ought to have caused at least some workers to have turned their efforts towards realizing a better life in other directions. And the rediscovery of cynicism towards the institutions of the class only confirms the historical ambivalence in that relationship which had been obscured somewhat by the apparent tightness of the connection in the late 1940s and early 1950s.

Such findings, which at the time were thought to betoken working class decline, can therefore be fitted into a rather different picture. Other findings, lurking in the two reports, also suggest a different interpretation. In the 'relative deprivation' study, for example, virtually every respondent could assign himself or herself to a definite class category. There had been no decline in this index of class awareness since the 1940s. And, of course, manual workers still overwhelmingly saw themselves as working class, non-manual workers as middle class. However, there were as many white-collar workers who classed themselves as working class as vice versa – a clear increase in white-collar identification with that status – and as many women who considered themselves working class as men, another gain in working-class awareness. Obviously, whatever effects rising prosperity or improved housing or developing technologies may have had, they did nothing to lessen the elementary sense of class among ordinary people.

In Luton, purposely selected as a place likely to exhibit the new attitudes following upon affluence, class feelings also remained distinct and resistant. Manual and white-collar workers seldom mixed, nor did their families; middle-class styles of consumption, entertainment and aspiration remained the property of the white-collar employees only, and not all of them; and working people kept to themselves and wanted it that way. Though Luton's workers expected and aimed at increased incomes, very few saw this in terms of individual advancement; and hardly any had a clear perspective of what changes a large increase in money income would allow.

The two studies, moreover, each demonstrated that while the great bulk of the workers were eager for material progress and higher incomes, they also still gave their votes to Labour and their dues to the unions, even if they did so with little enthusiasm. They mostly followed the familiar patterns of their fathers and mothers, and saw little reason to switch. This, in fact, is probably the critical finding of both of these studies, undertaken as they were after fifteen years of sustained economic expansion. Although there had been a slight decline in the share of the working class vote going to Labour since the high levels of 1950–51, the link between Labour and its working-class base or, conversely, between the workers and their political party, had persisted. Not only was the cumulative effect of so-called affluence not resulting in any 'assimilation into middle-class society', it was also not directly undermining the tie between the workers and their institutions, but rather transforming the manner and saliency of the linkage. Increased expectations did not lead workers to place their hopes in a party other than Labour, or in the typical middle-class routes to prosperity, i.e. small business or promotion. They simply altered slightly the feelings workers had as they gave their loyalties to Labour or the unions and, perhaps, elevated somewhat the standard against which working people judged the performance of each.

'Affluence' would, of course, have long-term effects. Over time, new forms of consumption and leisure would allow working people to by-pass some of the older institutions that had mediated between the class and the party, and help to loosen the links between them. But this happened gradually. This is not to deny the political impasse in which Labour found itself from 1951 to 1964, nor is it to minimize the evident failings of the unions over the same period. It is to suggest that the sources for these were to be located elsewhere than in the shifting structure of the working class or the supposedly corrosive effects of social change. For the failures of Labour and the unions in these years had virtually nothing to do with the weakening of support from their traditional working-class constituents, but with their inability to advance, to build up new bases of support and to attract new adherents. Particularly lacking was any strategy for speeding up the recruitment into the ranks of the unions of the rapidly expanding numbers of white-collar, service-sector workers, especially the women, or for turning their membership in the unions into support for Labour, or socialist, politics. Nor was there any recognition of the potential for mobilizing the increased material expectations and the growing sense of entitlement on the part of ordinary people behind a programme of structural reform. These were failures of omission, missed opportunities, and they were preeminently political failures.

10

The Politics of Stagnation, 1950–70

Opportunities not taken

The balance sheet for social change in the 1950s and early 1960s presents a complicated mix. Old industries shrunk, new ones grew; Britain's workforce became increasingly female and increasingly white-collar. Yet relations at work remained much the same as just after the war – a moratorium in terms of unionization, in the extent of managerial control, and in the quality of work itself. Outside the workplace, workers experienced more expanded opportunities to enjoy the fruits of rising prosperity, and standards rose accordingly. But even in the sphere of consumption inequities prevailed, and attitudes and patterns of social life continued to be infused with a profound sense of class and social location. Expanded citizenship rights for working people had been translated into material progress, but their application to the job, to education and to the processes of government lagged considerably. Still, progress was real and visible and began to transform the outlook and aims of working people.

Unfortunately, there was little reflection of any of these developments in politics or industrial organization. The Labour party stuck firmly to its roots in the past, and the leadership of the unions was cautious and defensive. Labour in opposition developed few new plans, and contented itself with echoing the slogans appropriate to an earlier era. What little notice was taken of social change focused upon the problems it posed to Labour rather than on the opportunities it might afford, and the most characteristic invocation of the trends of social development was as a rationale for doing nothing or for moderating Labour's message and commitments. This was regrettable, for the implications of industrial change for union growth and the mobilization of Labour support were at worst neutral, at best very favourable. Prosperity gave workers bargaining power and made employers less willing to resist wage demands or efforts at unionization; while the nature and pace of employment shifts created opportunities for recruitment to the unions and for winning such recruits to the party. The political configuration within the party and the unions somehow coloured the perception of social change so as to convince the leaders that it represented more of a threat to their strength than a frontier for expanding it. Moreover, this negative estimate of the potential for Labour and the unions affected both the left and the right of the labour movement, Bevan no less than Gaitskell, Crosland and Crossman alike. Briefly, the right saw social change creating a mass base for political moderation and welcomed it, the left saw it much the same way and lamented it.

In retrospect, the arguments of both sides in the debates of the 1950s betray a marked superficiality and indicate the great chasm of misunderstanding that separated party and union leaders from ordinary workers. Thus Gaitskell had been converted to a thoroughly anodyne version of Keynesianism and sought mainly to assure critics of Labour's concern over inflation and its disdain for physical controls over the economy.[1] Similarly, Anthony Crosland maintained in *New Fabian Essays* that 'capitalism is undergoing a metamorphosis into a quite different system, . . . rendering academic most of the traditional social analysis'. More pithily, he wrote that 'capitalism, with no hope of abortion, is forced to give birth to a new society. . . .' That new society would have little reason to fear a return of unemployment and every reason to expect a continually rising standard of living. The result would be a new social structure, whose shape Crosland claimed already to discern: 'The class structure of society is more than ever variegated, and the classic outlines characteristic of early capitalism give way to a baroque confusion of detail.' Logically, such an analysis led to a programme that stressed the social, rather than the economic, that took the solution of material problems as given and urged therefore a move forward towards the creation of a cooperative, just, humane civilization. As Crosland put it, 'It still remains to create the new society of which socialists have always dreamed, a society which is not bedevilled by the consciousness of class.[2]

The notion that economic problems had been left behind, that what remained on the socialist agenda was 'the desire for equality', was widespread in the early 1950s. H. L. Beales, for example, writing in 1953, accepted Crosland's assessment of the dramatic qualitative transformation in the nature of capitalism and argued that the task for the future was 'to establish our civilization at new high levels of diffused culture, material advancement and rational living'.[3] Clearly, these 'revisionists' shared a common belief that the old socialist shibboleths were outmoded and that Labour must base its future appeal on policies of a different sort. In the early 1950s, however, none were forthcoming, and even during the later debate over the attempt to remove Clause Four from the party constitution, the revisionists had little to offer. Their alternative was a kind of progressive managerialism, laced with a dose of concern for issues of equality, liberty and 'rational living'. The most articulate expression of these notions was Crosland's *The Future of Socialism*, which concluded with bromidic calls for more growth and less inflation, for 'democratising' the schools, for taxing gifts, for more fraternal relations between staff and workers in industry, for better welfare provision and for more 'liberty and gaiety in private life'. Crosland recognized that 'this emphasis . . . cannot claim the label socialist', but this to him was a sign of progress, and certainly nothing to be deplored.[4]

What the left offered to oppose this vision was equally uninspired. Crossman, for example, shared with his fellow contributors to *New Fabian Essays* the sense that postwar capitalism really was different from prewar capitalism and that, 'after scarcely four years in office, the [Labour] Government had fulfilled its historic mission' and, in the process, more or less 'exhausted the content of British socialism'. Rather than join in praise of this new system, however, he drew attention to its limitations, questioned its stability, and pointed out that 'the Labour party was in danger of becoming not the party of change, but the defender of the post-war *status quo*'. Crossman urged a return to theory, partly as myth and partly for critical inspiration. His own was very confused. He perceived the twentieth century as a prolonged era of world revolution and somehow wanted to support this revolutionary thrust against both American reaction and Soviet totalitarianism. He wanted Britain to be a third force in world politics that would keep the cold war cold and offer a democratic path to social progress. Since, however, the capitalist path advocated by the United States was destined to lose, the primary need was to make the new, planned society more humane and responsive. By this circuitous reasoning Crossman came to the conclusion that the main danger was the 'Threat of the managerial society'; hence, 'the main task of socialism to-day is to prevent the concentration of power in the hands of either industrial management *or* the state bureaucracy – in brief, to distribute responsibility and so to enlarge freedom of choice'.[5]

This plea for a radically democratic socialism seems to have been genuine enough, but it hardly translated into a programmatic alternative. As a critique of the emerging welfare state it succeeded only poorly, as policy it gave no direction at all. Nor was Aneuran Bevan, for all his oratorical brilliance, capable of articulating a coherent counter to the arguments of the revisionists. Instead, he and the left focused largely on issues of foreign policy and failed to engage the leadership directly on domestic policy. The emphasis on events outside Britain was by no means foolish. The Cold War and the American alliance were crucial factors in post-war politics and the left was right to see that as long as Britain was tied to the American vision of the new world order, the scope for reforms would be circumscribed. Indeed, the most notable product of the Labour left in these years was the *Keep Left* manifesto of 1947, urging the Labour government to steer clear of both the US and the Soviet Union. In addition, the nearest the left came to defeating the leadership was at the 1954 conference on the issue of German rearmament. But this was no substitute for a genuine policy of social reform at home.[6]

The weakness of the left allowed the theories of Crosland and Gaitskell to blossom, especially in the wake of the party's second defeat in 1955. It was decided then to undertake a series of policy reevaluations which led, over the next two years, to a firming up and elaboration of revisionist themes. The culmination was *Industry and Society. Labour's Policy on Future Public Ownership*, adopted by the 1957 Conference. This document replaced the traditional espousal of nationalization with the rather less inspiring prospect of the state taking shares in private industry so as to allow 'the community. . . . the opportunity of participation in the almost automatic capital gains of industry'. Progress was now 'almost automatic', what was left was determining how to distribute it. By the end of the period of rethinking following 1955, the revisionist position was more prevalent than ever.[7]

Curiously it was at this moment that it began to falter. The first setbacks came on defence policy. The Campaign for Nuclear Disarmament was launched in the fall of 1958, and its march the next Easter marked its emergence as a mass movement outside the Labour party. Throughout 1959 and 1960 its presence came to be reflected inside the party as well. A number of unions endorsed its aims and in 1960 the party conference went against Gaitskell in voting for unilateral disarmament. Though the position was reversed the next year, it was a major defeat for Gaitskell and revealed the tenuousness of his hold over the heart of the party. At the same time, the Gaitskellites failed in their attempt to remove Clause Four, which committed the party to securing the common ownership of the means of production, from the party's constitution. Gaitskell himself led the campaign and opened the debate with a plea to recognize 'a significant change in the economic and social background of politics' that required Labour to abandon its old doctrines and slogans, particularly on the matter of public ownership.[8]

Gaitskell's plan ran aground because its thrust was almost solely negative. It would take away a powerful symbol and put nothing in its place. Gaitskell himself could propose only flexibility, empiricism, a case-by-case approach; his followers could come up with little more. Rita Hinden, summarizing the revisionist 'Lessons for Labour' to be learned from Mark Abrams's survey of 1960, did not do much better. Rising prosperity among the workers, she felt, placed a definite limit on 'the old class appeal', even among workers, while the reluctance to give up that appeal restricted Labour's ability to attract others. The sole comfort to be derived from the survey, for Hinden, was that it revealed a certain degree of tolerance and generosity among the working and middle classes, especially among the young. Such sentiments might be developed into a full-scale programme of benevolence aimed at helping society's 'Unfortunates'. Who were they? Not the ordinary workers, for 'in the contemporary environment, when workers are certainly no longer defenceless, a simple class appeal [to them] so easily degenerates into class selfishness'. No, the 'real unfortunates' were 'elsewhere'; they were 'the casualties of the welfare state', the '"minorities" whom our society neglects or despises – the mentally ill . . .; the sexual inverts . . . .; the prisoners . . . .' and, beyond Britain's shores, the 'coloured races generally'. The sentiments in such an argument were indeed noble and the focus on social issues, curiously, anticipated themes that would surface forcefully in the ferment of the 1960s, but it is difficult to see them as the elements from which Labour was to fashion a new programme.[9]

A decade of internal debate and bitter factional rivalry had been in the end remarkably unproductive in terms of programme. In consequence, both sides moved after 1960 towards a compromise based more on torpor than on genuine agreement, and it was out of this exhaustion that the new emphasis on Labour as the party of the scientific revolution emerged. The claim that Labour would get the economy moving by harnessing science surfaced as a major theme in 1960, when *Signposts for the Sixties*, deliberately crafted as a spur to unity, was adopted as policy. Its full triumph as party rhetoric came later, however, when Harold Wilson rode the call for greater technical competence in economic management to gain the leadership of the party in 1963 and victory at the general election in 1964. The 'scientific revolution' became 'the solvent of unity in the Labour party', and it somehow managed to paper over the differences that had seemed irreconcilable before 1960. As Richard Crossman, who managed Wilson's campaign for the leadership, put it, 'The question forced upon us is how we can become the masters, not the slaves, of technological change. Directly this question was asked . . . we realised that here was the new creative socialist idea needed to reconcile the Revisionists of the Right with the Traditionalists of the Left: Harold Wilson succeeded where Hugh Gaitskell failed.'[10]

That the superficialities of Harold Wilson could have appeared as 'the new creative Socialist idea' indicates more the underlying paucity of Labour party thought than the intellectual power of the notion. It indicates as well how far removed party debates were from the rank and file of the movement, for if there was one issue stimulating activism inside the outwardly very staid unions, it was the effect of technology in creating redundancies among workers. The revival of strikes and union organization in the late '50s, in fact, had been sparked off initially by temporary layoffs in the motor industry, and although other issues soon predominated, the animus towards technology remained strong.

Of course, the leaders of the party were hardly less out of touch with ordinary workers than were the officials of the unions. Moreover, the absence of any consciousness of the opportunities for the extension of union influence presented by the highly favourable conditions of the time was even more serious, for changes in the balance of tactical advantage between workers and employers have normally been registered more quickly and forcefully in union organization than in shifting political allegiances. It would have been logical to see some reflection in union strategy and activity of the increasing number of women in the workforce, of the growing importance of white-collar jobs, or of the potential enhancement of shop-floor organization. Yet on each of these issues the union movement was largely silent, and despite the favourable circumstances, membership just managed to keep abreast of employment and actually declined slightly as a percentage of the labour force.

On women's issues, for example, the TUC was quite unresponsive throughout the late 1940s and 1950s. The issue of equal pay had aroused considerable interest in 1944, and the upshot was a Royal Commission whose report, though extremely narrow, did nevertheless advocate equal pay in the public sector. Under presure from the Labour government to hold down wage increases, however, the TUC and its National Women's Advisory Committee in 1948 acquiesced in putting off its achievement to some indefinite future date. Though support for equal pay was reaffirmed in 1950, adoption lagged. The first breakthrough did not come until 1952, when the Labour-controlled London County Council agreed to it; other local councils followed in 1953, and in 1954 R. A. Butler was persuaded to support the introduction of equal pay into the Civil Service. By 1961, the campaign in the public sector had largely succeeded, but the success owed as much to Conservative desires to court women voters as to Labour's commitments, and it was won primarily by those unions of teachers, local government officers and civil servants which had substantial female memberships. The older, large, and more male-dominated unions in manufacturing had been thoroughly uninterested and the TUC as a body not much better.

Worse still, efforts to organize women workers in industry and the service sector were minimal, women's participation in union affairs probably dropped from its level in previous years, and technical change eroded the strongest bastion of women's trade unionism in textiles. The provision of welfare and nurseries during the war was allowed to disappear with little protest and it was not until women trade unionists pushed in 1962 for a *Charter for Women* that there was any serious progress. That programme called for equal pay, expanded opportunities for promotion, apprenticeship and other training, and for more and better health and welfare services. Needless to say, its formal adoption was a very late and highly inadequate recognition of the growing role of women in the workforce, and even this remained a formal rather than a real commitment.[11]

Since the issue of recruiting for the unions in the expanding white-collar occupations would have inevitably entailed evolving a serious strategy for enrolling women, it is no wonder that neither was seriously addressed during the 1950s and early 1960s. Rather more puzzling is why the unions were so reluctant to press for more extensive factory organization among male workers in manufacturing. Perhaps the critical factor was that wherever local organization improved, it placed more power in the hands of shop stewards, who were likely to be more militant than the officials and to contain a fair sprinkling of Communists and other left-wingers. The concern seems in retrospect slightly misplaced, for the Communists were very isolated, due to their own sectarianism, from 1947 into the mid-1950s, and their influence inside and outside the unions remained weakened until well after 1956. Still, the unions' heads looked askance at shop-floor organization and so had little to do with the one major achievement of these years, the warrening of manufacturing industry with a dense network of shop stewards between about 1956 and 1963.[12]

The growth of shop steward organization coincided with the revival of strikes. With full employment, the possibility of using localized bargaining and stoppages to push wages above the minimum laid down in national agreements became evident to ever-larger numbers of workers, but it required strong plant-level organization. In 1955, shop steward organization was surprisingly weak in engineering, and virtually non-existent elsewhere. The motor companies had striven to keep stewards out of their factories and to hold down the level of membership generally. Unionization at Morris Motors was a mere 25% in 1956, Vauxhall and Ford were under 50%; Austin's density was higher, but stewards' actions were restricted and ineffective. Only at the Coventry firms, such as Standard, was organization more or less complete. Outside Coventry it was not until after 1956 that shop steward organization became implanted.[13]

The upsurge of strikes and the flowering of local organization in the late 1950s were the product of several factors. One was surely the economy. Prosperity began to appear as more precarious, due to the onset of Britain's by now infamous 'stop-go' pattern of growth. The car industry was especially susceptible to fluctuations in demand. By 1956–7, many car workers became convinced that, 'since they have no way of knowing how long either their boom-time earnings or their jobs will last, their best policy is simply to go all out for what they can get while the companies' profits are high'.[14]

A second factor was more political. The Conservative government gradually became alarmed at the pace of inflation and, after the 1955 election, began to move away from their conciliatory policy towards the unions. Prior to 1955, Conservatives had sought above all to maintain industrial peace. Iain MacLeod, Tory Minister of Labour, explained that, 'We can afford strikes less than any other country in the world. We have got a knife-edge economy. . . .' After 1955, the mood shifted slightly and the government began to urge upon employers and unions something like a voluntary wage freeze. The employers responded by stiffening their opposition to wage demands. The Engineering Employers' were especially eager to stop the increase of wages and happy to take their cue from the government. After years of complaining about supposedly inflationary settlements in the public sector, the state seemed ready to back the employers against the unions.[15]

The EEF duly announced in June, 1956, that they would not offer any increase in wages for that year and proceeded to reject the unions' claim for 10%, submitted in October. A strike was called for March, 1957, to occur first among shipbuilders and then among engineers. When it became clear that the unions were prepared to wage a protracted strike, however, the government panicked, the emerging alliance with the employers collapsed, and the latter were forced to accept a Court of Inquiry. After several hearings and much negotiation, the unions won respectable increases; most important, their victory demonstrated vividly the changed balance of power in industry. As Clegg and Adams concluded, 'In 1940 the unions gained ascendancy over the British government in relation to decisions affecting wages. . . . this ascendancy was maintained until 1956. It was then challenged by the employers. The challenge was accepted and in the engineering and shipbuilding strikes the unions triumphantly reasserted their position.'[16]

The demonstration of the unions' latent power in 1957 impressed the rank-and-file of the unions as much as the employers, for while the bosses had long ago sensed the altered balance of power, the workers had not been so sure. Throughout the early 1950s, the unions were dominated by the most moderate of officials. Deakin and Feather, in particular, were reluctant to use the power that lay in their hands. In the 1940s, they restrained themselves out of loyalty to Labour; after that they were reluctant to face the consequences of militancy. And for at least a decade after 1945, ordinary workers did not dissent. Their expectations as to wages had apparently been shaped by memories of the interwar years, and the improvements of postwar appeared satisfactory. With the gradual fading of the old, cautious leadership and the awakening of workers to their new-found bargaining leverage and to higher expectations, prospects for industrial peace dimmed. When the dimensions of the change were fully revealed in 1957, the outcome was a major upsurge of strikes and a massive increase in local, shop steward organization. Within five years, labour relations in the motor industry were substantially transformed, and militancy and local organization began to spread throughout the economy.[17]

The creation of this strong shopfloor presence was the one solid organizational gain of the postwar years and pointed the way to further growth. From the late 1940s to the late 1950s, union membership had not quite kept pace with changes in employment. Overall union density reached 45.2% in 1948, but stood at 44.2% in 1960. This slight fall occurred entirely among men, with women's membership increasing just slightly. The losses were the result of the decline in the number of workers in well-organized, traditionally male jobs and the failure of membership to grow as fast as it could have in the newer industries. The most important of these was metal and engineering, of which motor cars formed a large part, and in this broad group density dropped from 54.5% in 1948 to 49.9% ten years later. The significance of the revival of shop stewards and strikes after 1956 lay in their impact on organization. Unions in this sector grew by almost 200,000 members between 1958 and 1962 and continued to expand for the next decade. The breakthrough in engineering spilled over into other manufacturing, where it affected women even more than men, and somewhat more slowly into white-collar work.[18]

Almost as soon as the growth of stewards' organization began to manifest itself, however, it was resisted by most of the established union leaders. Not only did they not use the emergence of the new movement as an occasion to advance ideas of industrial participation and workers' control, which might appear the next logical step; instead, they condemned the involvement of stewards in unofficial strikes and attempted to rein in their activities. However benign the daily practice of most stewards and however useful they might be in overcoming the fragmented structure of unionism at plant level, they were seen as a threat. They took root, therefore, in spite of the opposition of the established leaders and of many employers. In such a context, of course, when they were established they presented both with a serious problem of control.

In the political and trade union spheres, therefore, the labour movement largely stagnated during the years of Conservative rule. Its leaders developed no new strategies and relied instead on tired rhetoric and gestures. Even more damaging, they failed to extract from their vague perceptions of social change any sense of how the new structure of society might open up avenues of union recruitment or create additional reservoirs of socialist support. They reacted defensively and failed to take advantage of the opportunities it offered. These missed opportunities were scarcely noted in the 1950s and 1960s, given the fixation upon internal strife, and they did not translate in any immediate fashion into electoral liabilities. Indeed, Labour silenced its many critics by winning the election of 1964 and, two years after, increasing their majority still further. But the failures of omission of the previous decade and a half would become very evident in the course of the first Wilson government, whose troubled history revealed just how backward and inadequate were the inherited traditions of the Labour party and the unions, and just how poorly they served the working-class base from which they sprang.

Power and frustration, 1964–70

When Labour came to power in 1945, it claimed that its programme, though designed in its component parts to redress grievances and promote social justice, was overall a plan for national reconstruction. Labour made much the same claim in 1963–4, when it offered itself to the electors as the party that could successfully engineer growth by unleashing the pent-up forces of technology. It boasted that its unique relationship to the unions made it the rational choice to manage Britain's lagging economy, and brandished a 1963 Conference statement, moved and supported by the unions, calling for the development of 'an incomes policy to include salaries, wages, dividends, and profits (including speculative profits) and social security benefits'. The campaign reflected the note sounded earlier by Harold Wilson, that the Labour party would present itself 'as a national party and a nationally-based government', in opposition to the Conservatives whose 'great weakness . . .', was 'their failure to try to represent the nation'.[19]

There were crucial differences between 1945 and 1964, however, and the sum of these determined a markedly less successful outcome for the Labour government of 1964–70 than for its predecessor. At the top of the list was the matter of programme. Labour's programme of 1963–4 contained little more than pious promises about the future, and was noticeably lacking in the specifics that distinguished its pronouncements in 1945. 'Mobilizing the resources of technology' and 'harnessing our national wealth in brains' sounded good, but were pretty meaningless as policy. Even the emphasis on planning differed only minimally from what the Conservatives themselves had come to adopt in the early 1960s. Labour's primary selling point was its claim to be better able to plan and to govern because of its willingness to incorporate the unions. Labour's 'practical programme' 'for an active democracy' was especially vague; beyond promising new ministries of Economic Affairs and Technology, it offered few details.[20]

Closely related to this absence of specific proposals was a second set of political facts which differentiated 1964 from 1945. In 1945 Labour inherited a vast network of physical (i.e. direct) and fiscal controls over the economy. Its plans to nationalize key sectors of banking and industry and massively to increase spending on social services promised even greater leverage over the economy and the society. Its freedom to use these levers, moreover, was enhanced by the eclipse of the Treasury in the counsels of the state. The Chancellor of the Exchequer had been excluded from membership of the War Cabinet, and during the 1945–51 governments the Treasury's stranglehold over policy had not yet been reasserted.

The situation in 1964 was different indeed. Physical controls had become unpopular with voters and politicians in the late 1940s, and Labour had foresworn their future use in favour of less obstrusive means of managing the economy. Wilson, for example, argued in 1957 that Labour 'had relied too much on physical controls and made too little use of the monetary weapon'. Meanwhile, the Treasury gradually regained its old stifling influence over decision-making. The reassertion of Treasury control began as early as 1947 under Cripps, and progressed further under Gaitskell, but was restored thoroughly only with the return to power of the Conservatives. Despite this, Labour was quite unprepared upon resuming office for the crippling effect this would have on its plans. The party's previous experience of power had left a pleasant memory of administrative flexibility and led its leaders to minimize the difficulty of overcoming bureaucratic inertia or resistance. The state was seen as neutral, if not benevolent, and it was assumed that good policies needed only legislative enactment to be implemented.[21]

The third difference between 1964 and 1945 was the altered public perception of Britain's economic position. Though growth was sustained throughout the early 1960s, Britain's ability to maintain growth was called increasingly into doubt. Under the Conservatives, the economy had fallen into a cycle of 'stop-go', and with each successive upturn, it seemed that the rate of inflation and the balance of payments worsened, so that each successive deflation had to be more severe. The Conservatives had put the brakes on the economy very sharply during 1957–9, and they resolved to break out of the cycle after 1959. Thoughts turned to incomes policies, which led to the so-called 'pay pause' of 1961 and the establishment of the National Incomes Commission in 1962, and to planning.

Planning was not much in favour in Conservative circles during the 1950s. Having won the 1951 election on the promise of 'freeing the people' from controls, the Tories could not very well revert to planning very quickly after that. Nor was there much pressure to do so, for the economy surged ahead. Most economists were as concerned with stability and balance as with growth, which was seen largely as a by-product of full employment rather than something to be aimed at for its own sake. Only in the late 1950s, when the stop-go cycle began to trouble policy-makers and when Britain's relatively slow rate of expansion in comparison with other European countries became clear, did growth become the centrepiece of most political and economic debate.[22]

The drift of opinion back towards planning was a political windfall for Labour and for Wilson. It not only offered a solution to the debates of the 1950s, which combined the historic commitment to public enterprise with the new rhetoric of technical progress, but it also shifted partisan rivalry onto terrain particularly favourable to Labour. Once planning and growth became the objectives of government, the argument was over as to who could best do the job, and Labour made its claim for superior managing ability sound highly plausible. There was a price to be paid, however, and that was that Labour, having won the election, would subsequently be judged on how well it handled the economy. By furthering the debate on growth and planning, Labour helped to raise expectations and ensured that its record would be evaluated by a markedly higher standard than before. Just how dear the price would be was not evident in 1964, but after 1966 it became obvious that the pressure on Labour to manage growth was much greater than its resources to make it happen. From 1966 to 1970 Labour floundered in an increasing inability to make good its promises and presided over a major weakening of its working-class support.

These difficulties grew logically from the clash between the inherited policies of the party, and the altered context for the exercise of political power in the 1960s. Having failed to use the previous fifteen years of economic growth to extend the reach of its trade union allies, or to cement the bond between itself and its supporters, and having wasted its respite from office in sterile squabbling, Labour came to power in 1964 confronted with greater demands on its performance than it, or any previous goverment, had faced, and with fewer resources to marshal on its behalf. This imbalance virtually doomed the Wilson government to failure from the start, and guaranteed that as the party groped for solutions to its growing incapacity, it would more and more be forced to rely upon its one great source of strength, the allegiance of the organized working class, and in the process begin to diminish even that store of loyalty.

The troubled history of the 1964–70 government turned largely upon

185

this contradiction. The first two years witnessed several initiatives designed to make the commitment to growth and planning real, but none were crowned with success. A new Department of Economic Affairs, responsible for infusing dynamism into the economy by planning and selective intervention, was set up in 1964 with George Brown at its head. Its relationship to the Treasury was never made clear, and the latter's short-term management of expenditure overwhelmed long-term plans for growth. In the end, 'the Treasury dominated and the Department of Economic Affairs expired. . . .' The denouement was utterly predictable: Labour's National Plan for the economy was published in September, 1965 and passed by Parliament in November. It called for no less than a 25% increase in output by 1970. By the following July, when a balance of payments crisis hit, the plan was effectively abandoned; by 1969, the Department itself had been eliminated, its responsibilities transferred officially to the new Ministry of Technology or to the Treasury.[23]

The failure of planning pushed the government towards other expedients to accomplish the same objectives. In 1966, the Industrial Reorganization Corporation was set up to promote nationalization and in 1968 the Industrial Expansion Act was passed to allow the government wider discretion and the financial clout to promote investment in critical areas. But the efficacy of these measures was blunted by the situation in which they operated. The balance of payments problem continued to worsen and Treasury demands for fiscal restraint became more insistent. Cabinet frustration with the Treasury's dampening impact on virtually all its policy initiatives led to various plans for administrative reform, but nothing came of them during the tenure of the government. In the meantime, with the state either unwilling or unable to exercise firm direction over the implementation of industrial policies, planning became a kind of quasi-corporatist bargaining, and aid to industry became a subsidy rather than a spur to growth. Monies went to ailing firms or to the facilitating of mergers among healthy ones, productivity did not improve, and the entire project came to command diminishing levels of public support.[24]

Labour's growing impotence impelled Wilson and his colleagues to fall back upon their historic link with the unions not merely for political support, but as an instrument of policy. As the new mechanisms design to exert influence within the economy proved unworkable, the tired, old method of extracting wage restraint from the workers became more attractive. Success at that, it was felt, might at least provide the price stability necessary to allow advances in productivity to translate into increased exports and economic growth. The logic of the situation, with Labour's promises narrowing to a fixation upon growth, with expectations about economic performance escalating, and with the instruments designed to bring it about failing to do so, led the government to call upon its firmest supporters to make the sacrifices needed to achieve the party's goals in office.[25]

Once again, however, the context had changed to such an extent between the late 1940s and the mid-1960s that Labour's calls to its trade union allies went unanswered. Labour in the 1960s had little to offer in return for the unions' collaboration, for the party's objectives in office were so limited. The union leaders were being asked to clamp down on the wage demands of their members, but had nothing to hold out as inducements and a great deal to lose by disappointing their members. By the mid-1960s the days when Deakin, Feather, Lawther, Williamson and Carron could drag their members along with them behind unpopular policies were gone; gone, too, was the leaders' ability to label internal dissent as communist and in this way defeat it. In their stead was an engaged rank and file, increasingly organized through the network of shop stewards that permeated manufacturing industry by the mid-1960s. The will, the ability and the pay-off which had to be available to union leaders, if they were to go along with the government's requests for wage restraint, were all lacking. The effect was a growing estrangement between the unions and the party and, because the former seemed so unwilling or unable to discipline their own members, attempts by the state to reform unions and establish firmer control. This further exacerbated the relationship and led to a series of political battles.[26]

This sad tale has been told in great detail by others; for the present one need only highlight the main events.[27] In early 1965 the Labour government set up the National Board for Prices and Incomes. The NBPI lacked statutory powers and only passed on claims referred to it, often after a settlement was reached or a price rise announced. About the same time the government was able to agree to a 3–3½ per cent norm for pay rises with the TUC. The rate of wage increases accelerated, however, and the government developed a new 'early warning system' later in the year. The system was to be operated voluntarily, but was to be backed up by enabling legislation giving the state authority to mandate settlements if need be. Though this legislation lapsed in 1966, similar laws were put back on the books later. This system had mixed results through late 1965 and the first few months of 1966, but in May of that year the seamen's strike for a 17% increase flouted the government's aims. By July, the worsening balance of payments produced a sterling crisis. The government reacted with a stringent set of fiscal policies: a freeze on wages, prices and profits for six months, to be followed by six more months of 'severe restraint', as well as restrictions on consumer loans and cuts in state spending.

The trade unions responded to these policies in an increasingly negative manner. They objected strenuously to the wage freeze of 1966, with opponents garnering almost 4 million votes at Congress, and were especially hostile to the nil norm that the government attempted to enforce during the first half of 1967. Despite considerable grumbling, the policies stuck from mid-1966 to mid-1967. What really forced the breakdown of the government's incomes policies was the inflation following the devaluation of November, 1967.

As in 1966, the pressure on sterling was linked to industrial conflict, this time on the docks, but the key factor was the underlying weakness of the economy and the currency. Indeed, the real failure of the Labour government may well have been that it did not devalue sooner than in 1967. Even then, it was a decision taken against considerable resistance from the City and from the American bankers, both of whom would have preferred a further deflation of the economy and higher unemployment. The government opted for devaluation but, in return, came in with two highly restrictive budgets in 1968 and 1969 to stem the inflationary impact and move the balance of payments into surplus. This they succeeded in doing by 1969, but at a serious political cost, for by then both the unions and the Labour party were in open rebellion.

The government in response sought to impose legal restraints on the rank and file of the unions and to make the leaders responsible for their members' actions, but this, too, failed. Almost as soon as Labour took office, a Royal Commission on Trade Unions and Employers' Organizations (the Donovan Commission) was set up, with the aim of deciding whether there was any need to reform trade union law. The Commission's hearings and reports documented the extensive 'informal system' that had grown up inside British industry alongside the official union structures, and explained how this constituted a powerful base for shopfloor action, for local bargaining and for what was called 'wage drift'. The Commission did not conclude from this that industrial relations should be altered by law; rather, it saw the solution in terms of the elaboration of more integrated and sophisticated bargaining and personnel management at the level of the firm or the plant. The government went further, however, and used the diagnosis of Donovan as the rationale for a more interventionist set of policies, set out in January, 1969 in the White Paper, *In Place of Strife*.[28]

The Donovan report had called for the setting up of a Commission on Industrial Relations to review and improve procedures governing workplace relations on a voluntary basis. *In Place of Strife* would broaden the responsibilities of such a body, charging it with evaluating claims for recognition. Unions would also be assisted in getting information from employers and workers would be protected from 'unfair dismissals'. At the same time, there would be registration of the unions, which implied some degree of state supervision of their internal workings, and the government would be empowered to settle certain inter-union disputes, to declare a 28-day 'conciliation pause' in unofficial strikes and to order secret ballots for official strikes judged to pose a 'serious threat to the economy or the public interest'. Where the government's orders were not followed, fines or imprisonment could, at least in principle, ensue. The Labour government desperately wished to avoid that eventuality and no doubt saw the legislation as a means of forcing the unions to police themselves. Whatever the aim, *In Place of Strife* represented a substantial deviation from past practice and from the voluntarist traditions of British industrial relations.

The unions and the party's Executive opposed the plan, but the Cabinet decided to press ahead with legislation in the spring. This decision evoked an explosion of opposition and the TUC General Council called a special conference for 5 June 1969. Members of the Parliamentary Labour Party roused themselves as well, with Michael Foot accusing his colleagues of creating a situation with the potential 'to break the government and tear the movement to shreds'.[29] The General Council declared in April that it would not be party to a system involving penal sanctions on fellow unionists. They then proceeded to draft counter-proposals on industrial relations which appeared on 15 May as the TUC's *Programme for Action*. The unions ultimately prevailed and forced the government to withdraw the proposed legislation in return for a 'unanimous solemn and binding undertaking' on the unions' part to discourage unofficial strikes. By the middle of 1969, in short, the Labour government's last serious attempt to control the economy – this time through exerting control over the workers' attempts to push up wages – had come to naught. By 1970, wages were rising at a rate of 12–13% and the government was forced to fight the general election on a record of failure. They lost, of course, but the surprising thing, in view of their lack of policy success, was that they did not lose more heavily than they did.[30]

If the failure of the first Wilson government was inevitable, a quite predictable consequence of vacuous politics confronting novel problems in a new society, the precise circumstances of its demise were not so obviously predetermined. Nothing in the history of the unions and the party since the war gave any indication that the last two years of the Labour government were to witness an explosion of industrial militancy on a scale not seen since the 1920s; certainly none of the established leaders were prepared for such an outpouring of discontent, and none quite knew what to do about it.

The dimensions of the strike wave are best grasped statistically. In 1966–7, the average number of strikes was about 2,000 per year, involving approximately half a million workers annually. In 1967–8 the number of strikes grew to 2,378, and climbed still further, to over three thousand in 1968 and almost four thousand in 1969. More than two million workers struck in 1968, nearly a million and a half in each of the two following years. Almost 7 million working days were 'lost' in strikes in 1969, 11 million in 1970. The quantitative record was only part of the story, of course, for the strikes of 1968–70 also betrayed several qualitatively new features.[31]

First, there were the industrial and occupational distributions. No longer was conflict concentrated in mining or on the docks; it was much more widely diffused. Engineering and motor vehicles were much more prominent and no industry was immune. Especially important was the increase in the public sector. During 1964–8 there were only 135 strikes involving just over 35,000 workers in the public services, but from 1969–73 there occurred 347 strikes, bringing out 744,000 strikers for a total of 2,475,000 working days, an increase of more than seven times. This was symptomatic of a higher strike propensity amongst white-collar workers overall, and this in turn was correlated with major gains in white-collar unionization. Union density among white-collar workers jumped from 29.8% in 1966 to 34.3% in 1971, a growth in actual members of over 700,000. Many of these new recruits were women, it seems, for density among women increased from 25.9% to 31.2% over the same period. Unionism advanced in local government and education, in insurance, banking and finance and, most impressively, in national government and in the health services.[32]

Equally novel were the scope of demands and the tone of the militancy. Among the most prominent conflicts, for example, was the strike of sewing machinists at Ford in Dagenham in 1968. The dispute was directed against a new wage structure and classification scheme that pegged women's wages at 85% of men's and placed virtually all women in the two bottom grades of work. The 187 women involved translated their specific complaints into a broader claim for equal pay that galvanized large sections of the trade union movement into action. At the 1968 TUC a resolution was passed urging industrial action to obtain equal pay, and there were strikes to that end in London, Leeds and elsewhere. The pressure led ultimately to the Equal Pay Act of 1970, one of the Labour government's last and best efforts in office.[33]

The militancy of the late 1960s was different, too, in its aggressive and insurgent quality. Many workers undoubtedly took action out of defensive motives, to defend wages being eroded by inflation and by the increasing liability of workers to tax, and to protect their prerogatives at work from management encroachments.[34] Nevertheless, the forms their actions assumed involved the assertion of new rights and claims. Wage demands escalated dramatically, unofficial disputes proliferated, and more militant tactics spread throughout the movement. Strikes over issues concerning personal autonomy – over fights with foremen, for instance – became more common, as did other challenges to managerial authority. Sympathy strikes, though not large in number, seem to have entered into workers' expanded repertoire of struggle for the first time in decades.

As the movement progressed into the early '70s it broadened along two dimensions. Novel tactics, such as flying pickets among miners, especially during the strike of 1972, or factory occupations in situations where closures were threatened, caught on among the rank and file. At the same time, the resistance of the TUC and the leadership of various individual unions to state intervention led the leaders to look more favourably upon the militancy of the members. Throughout the course of the strike wave, moreover, there was growing evidence of a new emphasis upon equity and fairness. Numerous strikes occurred over differentials and comparisons between the wages of one group and another, usually in different plants within the same company, and nine in ten of these seem to have been for levelling up rather than for restoring or preserving differentials. Of course, the militancy often took a sectional form, but this was largely determined by the structure of bargaining, and cannot be read simply as an outburst of sectionalism.[35] Rather, it was a section-by-section insurgency through which trade unionists revealed just how broadly they had begun to define their rights and expectations as working-class citizens.

Arguably the strike wave of 1968–72, with its climactic aftermath in the winter of 1973–4, was the most important domestic event, or series of events, in postwar British history. Between 1968 and 1970, it weakened the link between Labour and the unions, provoked splits within the party, and revealed the essential bankruptcy of the social democratic vision. Its later phases were equally pivotal in turning the Conservatives away from the consensus-oriented, quasi-corporatist policies that they had adopted and practised from the 1950s to 1964, and that were not finally abandoned until the victory of Thatcher. But perhaps most important, it forced upon the whole of society the recognition that Britain in the 1960s and 1970s was a very different place from what it had been just after the war, and it therefore pushed politicians, union leaders and employers into beginning the search for new policies, new programmes and new forms of social and political organization.

11
Labour's Deepening Crisis, 1970–79

It was no accident that the industrial conflict of 1968–72 took the shape it did, for its contours conformed roughly to the new dimensions of Britain's evolving social structure. The stalemate of the shopfloor, so obvious in the various indices of industrial relations and in productivity, received its reflection in the enhanced role of shop stewards and their plant-wide 'combine committees' in the new militancy. The expansion of the service industries, of the public sector, of white-collar jobs and of working women, all translated directly into a greater participation by such industries and groups of workers in strikes and in union growth, and in demands and concerns appropriate to these new participants in the labour movement. However slow and stodgy the unions may have been, they adapted themselves more quickly to the changes in society of the postwar era than did the Labour party. It was thus fitting that Labour's losses in the general election of 1970 should have come from the abstentions of just those potential supporters – the better-paid industrial workers in the more affluent constituencies – who were in the forefront of the new militancy but to whom the Labour government appeared so unsympathetic.[1]

The overwhelming need for the Labour party and the unions to develop structures and programmes that would recognize the altered social relations of the late 1960s and 1970s was demonstrated most poignantly by Labour's failure first to govern effectively and then to be re-elected, but it was a lesson underlined daily by the accelerating and highly visible transformations occurring in British society. Commentators spoke of a social revolution before 1965; after 1965, it began to happen. Trends in occupation, in the structure of industry, in income and lifestyle that were modest and steady during 1950–64 took on greater dimensions and picked up speed from the mid-1960s.

The very lineaments of the economy began to shift markedly, as a new bout of mergers hit the business world. From 1960 to 1973, over 7,500 firms disappeared through mergers, an activity that consumed a quarter of investment capital. This occurred despite the setting up in 1965 of the Monopolies Commission; indeed, Labour's policy generally was to encourage concentration as a means to efficiency, and its Industrial Reorganisation Corporation played a major role in the creation of British Leyland and in the consolidation of the shipbuilding and electrical industries. The result was that, by the early 1970s, Britain had shot to the top of the league tables in industrial concentration. The median size of plants in Britain was by that date larger than in Germany or even the United States.[2]

Still, however, the increase in the size of plant and in concentration did not produce a comparable growth in productivity. As in the past, merger activity substituted for rationalization instead of promoting it, and in some of the very largest industries, such as machine tools, motor vehicles and metal production, plant size actually diminished, a clear indication of the unwillingness to invest in the latest technologies. On the other hand, Britain had by the early 1970s significantly fewer small, new firms that, it appears, have so often served as the 'seedbed' of innovation. The pattern, in brief, was for larger and larger companies to be formed by adding together medium-sized units of proven profitability, closing the least profitable and smaller plants, and then freezing in place the newly created, but not very new, structure. The pattern generated paper gains in productivity, but over the long run led to greater technical retardation and turned into actual retrogression or, as it came to be called, de-industrialization.[3]

For industrial workers, particularly men, this meant a heightened sense of insecurity. Between 1966 and 1979, the size of the Labour force remained constant but the percentage of men at work declined by more than 5%. From 1966 to 1979, 2.9 million jobs were lost in production industries, and about ¾ of these had been held by men. Nearly 600,000 had been employed in mining and quarrying in the mid-1960s; by the end of the 1970s there were less than 350,000. Manufacturing alone lost close to 2 million jobs. In motor vehicles the peak of employment came in 1960, the level then fell back to about 850,000 by 1965–6; after 1966 it began to drop steadily, until by 1979 another hundred thousand jobs were lost. Older industries fared even worse: textiles employed more than 800,000 in 1966, under 400,000 in 1979. The decisive point was that *most* industries contracted: approximately 170,000 jobs disappeared in clothing and footwear, close to half a million in construction, just over 140,000 in food and drink, 170,000 in metal manufacture, 90,000 in chemicals, and more than half a million in engineering and electrical goods.[4]

The decline in production was offset in aggregate terms by growth in services and in the public sector. Employment in the public services grew from 3.7 million in 1966, or 15.7% of the labour force, to over 5 million in 1976, or 27.3% of the working population. Other service industries continued to draw in new workers as well. The numbers employed in financial and professional services rose from just 2.5 million in 1960 to 4.9 million in 1979 – a doubling over just two decades. More than 300,000 were added in catering and hotels, a reflection of Britain's increased reliance on tourism, and lesser increases were registered in miscellaneous services. Overall, this meant that by 1966 services had come to employ 50.3% of the workforce, production industries 49.4%, and that by 1979 58% worked in services.

Many workers in the services remained in manual jobs, of course, but most of the increases came in white-collar work. In 1961, under 36% of employees were labelled white-collar; by 1979, it appears, 52% could be so classified. It seems, too, that the growth in these types of employment was disproportionately female. Women's employment in the service industries grew by about a third during 1966–79, men's by 3%; in 1979, women outnumbered men by a ratio of 7:6 in the services overall, the only exceptions being in transport and communication and in public administration. Even in the latter, almost all the growth in this period was accounted for by women, many of them part-time workers, but employed there nonetheless. Indeed, by 1979 over 36% of women worked part-time as compared to only 3% of the men, and many of the new jobs were filled by these part-time workers.

The movement of jobs into white-collar categories in service industries was thus largely accomplished through the increase in women's work. In 1961, the proportion of women over 15 who worked was 37.3%; five years on it was 42.4%, by 1977 it was 47.4%. By that point, 50.4% of married women were at work, and of those between ages of 20 and 59 no less than 6 in 10 worked for wages. The working wife was now the norm, not the exception. This was made possible by, and in turn made even more imperative, the continued drop in fertility and in family size. It also guaranteed progress towards a more equitable division of tasks within the household. By the early 1970s men and women in London were found to share housework and child-rearing more equally than ever before and to carry this over into a more thorough-going companionship in leisure and sociability as well. There were, of course, continuing inequities. A 1973 study of time budgets in Reading, for example, showed that the hours spent in work, domestic activities and childcare were on average one-sixth higher for working women than for men. Although the men tended to work at their jobs about 30% more time than did working women, the same women spent three times more time at housework and childcare than did the men. Genuine equality was still some distance away.[5]

The altered structure of the workforce had more visible, and less ambiguous, effects in the world of work. Among male manual workers, there seems to have been some deskilling. As the growth of the economy slowed after 1966, the impact of business cycles became more severe, and at the end of each cycle there were fewer skilled jobs to go around. In engineering, skill differentials declined by almost a third from the late 1960s to just 25% by 1977, as the poor labour market for skilled workers undermined their bargaining power. Between 1965 and 1976, moreover, the number of skilled craftsmen in engineering fell by a quarter of a million, and they decreased from 37.4% to 30.5% of the industry's workforce.[6]

Still, the main effect of industrial decline was to heighten the concern of all manual workers with the nature of their work. The survey evidence from the 1950s and 1960s showed that workers expected little from their jobs beyond a steady income, some long-term security and a reasonably humane environment. From the mid-1960s there was a marked intensification of criticism from workers about their jobs. As the very availability of work became more problematical, so its deficiencies became more obvious; and as the deepening of workshop organization gave workers greater leverage in the day-to-day affairs of production, so the constraints inherent in the organization of work began to chafe. Whether conditions of work actually deteriorated in the 1960s is doubtful; that there was a rising chorus of criticism about the quality of working life is not.

Sociologists and other investigators began in the late 1960s and 1970s to discover that the trade-offs accepted by workers in the 1950s were no longer accepted. The willingness to put up with intrinsically boring, arduous, perhaps hazardous jobs so long as they paid reasonably and were relatively secure seems to have disappeared, and more workers came to echo the complaints made by their more articulate and outspoken fellow workers about the monotony of jobs, the lack of opportunity for the exercise of skill, and the arbitrary power wielded by superiors. A collection of largely autobiographical essays published under the title *Work* in 1968–9, though hardly based on a random sample, contrasts sharply with earlier volumes published between the wars. The sense of pride in one's work is still there, but much diminished; fascination with the machine is still evident – 'The machines can appeal', was how one put it – but was coupled with a keener sense of its domination. The concern with money was much enhanced – 'a man's pay is a status symbol as well as a means of existence', it was claimed – and workers were less inclined to accept its relative absence.

But most significant was the pervasive sense that, for all the benefits of organization, the worker remained fundamentally lacking in effective power. An extensive survey done in Peterborough in the early 1970s documented in detail just how little job choice most manual workers had. Though 3 in 10 of the male workforce of the town were classed as skilled by the census, it turned out that very few were truly 'qualified' workers in the sense of having served a proper apprenticeship, and that most of those labelled skilled possessed few demonstrable skills but rather had been promoted within the firm through seniority and management discretion. For the bulk of the workers, opportunities were extremely limited, the scope for choice narrow; they understood their situation clearly, however, and responded with cynicism and a distinct lack of engagement. Such critical findings have been confirmed in detail in a variety of contexts, most notably in those high-wage and strike-prone industries like motor vehicles where it had previously been argued that workers had little concern with intrinsic work satisfaction.[7]

This waxing critique was linked to an intensified battle for the control of the shop floor. After Donovan, and before that in some industries, companies throughout the economy began to remould their own structures and policies to cope with the augmentation of workers' power in the shops. They initiated more sophisticated systems of company bargaining, devoted more management time and staff to personnel, and instituted more rational payment systems based upon job evaluation. Ford, for example, had promulgated a new wage structure just prior to the women's strike at Dagenham. British Leyland made an even more serious bid to re-assert control over wages and production by its introduction of Measured Day Work in 1971, aimed at curbing the negotiating function of the stewards and eliminating piecework bargaining. These and similar initiatives resulted in a shift in the locus of management/worker relations. By 1977–8, two-thirds of workers in manufacturing had their wages determined primarily by bargaining with their own employers, only a quarter by national or regional agreements. The employers' intention was to assert a more effective management role inside the plant, and by 1980, this had developed into an open hostility to unions and their prerogatives in the workplace. This only prompted workers to make their factory organization still more comprehensive. Between 1966 and 1971, union density among manual workers increased by almost 5%, and it kept on increasing throughout the 1970s. The numbers of shop stewards grew apace – there were an estimated 350,000 by 1975 – and efforts were made to integrate stewards more fully into the structure and routine operation of the national unions. Whatever the tendencies towards 'corporatism' at the level of national politics – and these were largely spent by the end of the 1970s – the trend in industry was towards a tightening of organization by management and workers and a deepening antagonism.[8]

Among workers in manufacturing, therefore, but especially among the men, the major factors causing changes in the experience of work were in a sense external. It was not increasing technology, but the drawing of battle lines over the control of production, that shaped workplace relations; at a broader level, it was not so much the changing character of work as its availability that predisposed workers to a sharper critical stance. The steady decline in manual jobs made the manual workers an increasingly homogeneous group of second and third-generation proletarians, sharing a common lot in a depressed labour market. Conversely, the growth in the numbers of white-collar workers made them an increasingly heterogenous group, whose expanding ranks required considerable recruitment from those sections of the working class best able to profit from the opening up of educational opportunities. Made up from diverse streams, divided sharply by sex and by sector, white-collar employees thus became highly fragmented in their social attitudes and behaviour. This fragmentation provided the social background for the substantial inroads made by union organization, and even Labour party support, among these workers.[9]

Among white-collar employees, therefore, as among manual workers, factors having to do with the job itself were less important in determining the experience of work than factors incidental to the workplace. For although the earlier trends towards 'bureaucratization' continued, the most dramatic change was the spread of collective organization and industrial conflict. The numbers of white-collar workers in unions grew from under three million in 1966 to over four million by 1974, and growth remained rapid after that as well. The jump in white-collar unionism was particularly concentrated among large firms in the private sector and, even more noticeably, in the public sector. In neither situation, however, does it appear that growth was produced by alterations in the status or conditions of the work. Rather, it was the cumulation of changes in the way wages and conditions were determined that was decisive. The reform of bargaining with manual workers at plant level led some firms to attempt a comparable institutionalization of relations with white-collar staff. More often, it was the staff themselves who saw the advantages to those who were well-organized during periods of incomes policies and then, perhaps even more dramatically, when they were abandoned. The lessons were particularly clear for those in the public sector, for one of the few levers governments had on the course of wages was the control of pay for those in public administration and in the nationalized industries. As both Labour and the Conservatives sought to hold down increases for these employees, the workers saw the need for stronger organization and created it.[10]

For most working people, then, the workplace became more and more an arena of conflict. Outside work, there were clashes and antagonisms as well. Race relations in particular became nastier from the mid-1960s. Still, the major change occurring outside production was the massive increase in the consuming power of ordinary citizens. Real wages, which had grown by less than 10% from 1956 to 1966, increased by 28% from 1966 to 1973, and increased a further 10% during 1974–9. Skill differentials lessened considerably, as did the gap between men's and women's wages. More working people thus shared in the improvements, and began to share in the possession of the things these increased incomes could buy. By 1979, 57% of all households had cars, 89% refrigerators and 76% washing machines. Between 1970 and 1978 the proportion of 'middle income' households having telephones more than doubled, car ownership reached three-quarters and nearly that many had colour televisions.[11]

An even more significant change occurred in housing. Expenditure on housing during the 1960s and 1970s not only rose, it was also redirected. In 1950, 53% of the population lived in privately rented accommodation, 18% rented from local authorities and 29% owned their own homes. By 1976, private rentals had declined to 15%, the proportion renting from local authorities had grown to 32%, while ownership reached 53% of households. According to the General Household Survey of 1979, almost 6 in 10 'junior non-manual' employees were home-owners, about half the skilled manual workers were, and almost 4 in 10 of the semi-skilled. These developments helped to create two relatively distinct groups of people, with potentially divergent interests concerning housing: the owner-occupiers who were able to purchase their homes only because of generous tax concessions or mortgage assistance, and those in council housing whose rents were subsidized by the authorities.[12]

It is doubtful whether emerging differences in housing tenure were serious enough by themselves to shift political alignments. What is clear, however, is that the lines of social division arising from consumption and life style no longer fitted neatly with those deriving from the workplace. The pattern of daily life, and the social attitudes embedded there, no longer reinforced, as they had in previous periods, those of production, of industry. Instead, there was a more varied, complex set of cleavages that resisted assimilation with the old, established alliances and antipathies.

The new pattern involved not merely a growing separation between work and non-work, but contradictory tendencies within both. At work, the old contrast between white-collar and manual workers lost at least some of its saliency as unionization spread among the former group. As the 1970s progressed, moreover, the lot of various sections of workers came to depend upon the fate of their particular industry and its relation to the state as much as upon such traditional considerations as skill levels. Equally significant were the aggregating or segregating effects of mass consumption. At a very general level, the achievement by ever-larger numbers of working people of the ability to become genuine consumers had a liberating and levelling impact. The culture of consumption was implicitly democratic, even if the exercise of consumer choice was limited by income. This was especially evident in the youth market of the 1960s, which was based on the visible, stylized consumption of rock culture and its accoutrements, and which, almost inevitably, was bound up with the rejection of the hierarchical, puritanical values that supposedly characterized the past. However confused the rhetoric of the youth revolt might have been, it was built upon a genuine social change. Most important, it was a change, and a culture, that seemed to cut across Britain's hitherto very rigid class boundaries.

Among workers, the capacity to possess and enjoy the rewards of material prosperity was reflected very broadly. Although working people continued to frame comparisons in relation to those much like themselves – a sign that class still mattered a great deal – most combined this restricted sense of social comparison with a much expanded sense of the possibilities of pecuniary gain for themselves and people of their sort. Thus, during the wage explosion of the early 1970s, Mark Abrams's 'subjective social indicators' showed that popular conceptions of personal well-being increased steadily, but that the distance between achievements and the sense of what one was due, of entitlement, was just as great in 1975 as in 1971. Shortly after this, in 1976–7, an attempt to replicate Runciman's findings on 'relative deprivation and social justice' showed a surprising intolerance among workers towards the persistence of inequality. Working men and women wanted increased incomes *and* less inequality. For most, of course, the path to equality was simply more pay. A variety of studies, in fact, showed that instrumental and pecuniary orientations, supposedly the distinguishing mark of the new affluent workers, were becoming widespread among extremely traditional groups like dockers and shipbuilders. The working class as a whole seems not to have harboured any particular disdain for monetary gain, only a resentment at their lack of it. Nor should its intensified pursuit be seen as an abandonment of the desire for class advancement; rather, it was the means by which working people sought to improve their standards and status individually and collectively.[13]

The transformation of popular attitudes towards a more material definition of personal and class interests ran directly counter to the thrust of Labour party policy as it emerged from 1964 to 1970. The result had been the almost inevitable weakening of working people's allegiance to Labour prior to the election of 1970. To their credit, the leaders of Labour and the unions learned from that defeat the necessity of recasting the party's programme to come to terms with the structural changes of postwar. Unfortunately, they did a much better job recognizing the new structure and composition of the working class than in understanding its newly-aggressive material demands. Thus the refashioning of Labour's programme succeeded well enough in its component parts, but did not couple these with a viable plan for economic growth, nor did the party's leaders manage to convince people that Labour as a party was capable of carrying out its policies.

Still, the most surprising fact about Labour politics after 1970 was how quickly the party moved to alter its programme. The inertia of the earlier postwar years was swept away, and in its place came the elaboration of a new, more radical programme that was put together and made party policy in a relatively short time. Although most of the leadership was carried over from office to opposition, moreover, its adoption was a smooth and uncontentious affair. The unions, the party apparatus and the PLP were eager to restore a sense of unity after the disagreements of 1964–70, and the common desire to oppose the Heath government's policies set up an opponent against whom to rally their forces. The mass movement against the Tories' new industrial policies also served to demonstrate the latent strength of the organized workers and the necessity, if government was to be effective, of co-opting rather than pressuring the unions.

The reconciliation was symbolized by a compact with the unions in 1973, which would grow over the next several years into the so-called 'social contract'. It would be further codified in *Labour's Programme 1973*, whose provisions were discussed amidst a rhetorical flourish of consensus and endorsed by massive majorities at Blackpool.[14] The new strategy for Labour had several parts. At the centre was an extension of public ownership. The concentration of industry, so the argument ran, had made economic power even less widely dispersed than before and less accountable to the public. A new phase of nationalization was called for, and, according to conference, would encompass the top 25 companies. Public ownership was to be supplemented by 'three major pillars' of planning: a new National Enterprise Board to give the state direct interests in private industry, a planning agreements system involving employers, workers and the state in the setting of goals for industry, and a new industry act that would extend control over the private sector. All these would together give the government the leverage with which to pursue a 'new economic strategy'. Implementation was to be guaranteed by the new relationship with the unions, whose support was secured by Labour's promise to repeal the noxious Industrial Relations Act of the Heath government, to refrain from incomes policies, and to effect the proposed 'fundamental shift in the balance of wealth and power in favour of working people and their families'.

Labour's Programme 1973 had significant social dimensions as well. The party proposed to take over private rental properties, to build 400,000 houses per year and create a publicly owned building society, to improve welfare benefits and remove prescription charges. There was support, too, for equal pay and for policies against racial discrimination. More controversial was a very explicit commitment to industrial democracy. Finally, to pay for all this there were proposals for a Wealth Tax and for other sorts of tax increases. *In toto*, it was a most impressive set of commitments, and it reflected a serious effort to grapple with the changing social context of politics. But was it serious enough?[15]

Reprospect would suggest a mixed verdict. Aspects of the new orientation show a great sensitivity to the underlying social realities. The commitment to equal pay, for example, seems a highly appropriate response to the growing presence of women in the workforce and the unions, even if it was rather limited. The stress on industrial democracy was also a genuine reflection of the growth of localized worker power. It reflected, too, the actual course of industrial struggles, as they had worked themselves out at places like GEC in Liverpool, Upper Clyde Shipbuilders, and perhaps another hundred locations. Yet, it was by no means clear that the thrust towards worker participation in management sprang from those on the shopfloor. It seems instead to have been the product of attempts by various leaders, especially Jack Jones, and enthusiasts, such as the Institute for Workers' Control, to develop structures in industry that might fit with the new relations at work but which, in their view, were worthwhile in themselves. The equivocal reception that ultimately greeted the Bullock Report on industrial democracy in 1977, and the lacklustre defence of it within the party and the unions were at least partly due to this lack of an organic link between its proposals and the needs and desires of the stewards or the rank and file.[16]

Other parts of the programme seem even less inspired. There was very little consideration given to workers' concerns over taxes or their aspirations towards home ownership, or to scepticism about nationalization, bureaucracy and the state. But, most important, there was a reluctance to come fully to terms with workers' increased material expectations. If, as seems to have been the case, workers measured social power by money, there was insufficient attention given to that by those who formulated the new programme. Stuart Holland, MP, even went so far as to hint that workers, especially the skilled, might be willing to trade off higher wages for increased participation: 'one of the strengths of the workers' control movement', he argued, 'is the extent to which it indicates how widening a worker's participation in the management of his own firm widens the identification with the job and reduces purely instrumental attitude [sic] to work'. The emphasis upon redistribution and participation may well have found resonance in workers' increased intolerance of inequalities at work and in society, but it was accompanied by a comparative neglect of the importance attached by working people to continually augmenting their incomes. Not surprisingly, the weakest link in the programme in 1973 was its vagueness on how all of its component parts would stimulate economic growth. The promise was there, but specific policy proposals were lacking.

Lacking too was any decisive break with the tired old rhetoric of the party. Wilson's verbiage about the harnessing of technology was gone, but nothing was put in its place. On the contrary, the new programme was interpreted and defended in terms that would have pleased the Bevanites, and that were modified very little to suit the 1970s. That traditional appeal, however, commanded less and less support among the populace. Since it did not truly distinguish the novel elements in Labour's revised programme anyway, it was also not necessary. Yet any new basis for appealing to the nation was not forthcoming. When put together with Labour's failure to change its leadership after 1974, it undermined the party's credibility and particularly its claims to have made a significant change in orientation.

A final and quite debilitating flaw in the new programme was its silence on how its proposals would become reality. Its numerous plans for reform were all premised on the notion that incorporating a proposal into the manifesto would lead sooner or later to its implementation. The record of the first Wilson government ought to have revealed the myopia of such a view, but it did not. Wilson himself, together with his former colleagues in Cabinet, presided over the formulation of Labour's new programme, and few questions were asked about its feasibility or about their will to carry it out. In particular, no more notice was taken of the power of the civil service and the Treasury, and there was no more thought given to overcoming the inevitable opposition from the City than there had been in the early 1960s. Nor were the enormous, presumably short-term, economic difficulties that would hinder implementation considered in any detail.[17]

The failure to think through the problem of making Labour's programme effective, and of meeting resistance to it, was to be demonstrated dramatically in the sorry history of the Labour governments of 1974-9. Within two years, most of the programme lay in ruins, wrecked by the economic crisis, the surge of inflation and the need to secure loans from the International Monetary Fund. Already in August 1974, the right within the Cabinet had watered down Tony Benn's White Paper 'The Regeneration of British Industry'. In January, 1975 the Industry Bill appeared, but also in a much weakened condition. Later that year a new incomes policy – the £6 limit – was negotiated with the unions, and the government began to revert to that overriding concern with inflation that had characterized the first Wilson government after 1966.

The battle over inflation intensified after 1975. Wages continued to increase and the Treasury proposed substantial cuts in expenditure, which prompted a rebellion by left-wing MPs. In March, Wilson resigned, and shortly after the pound began to decline. The crisis worsened in the summer and fall and Healey approached the IMF for a massive loan. In December, a deal was struck involving cuts of £2,500 million in government expenditure. The Cabinet caved in, and from then until May, 1979, the government's life was made miserable by the after-effects of the decision. It found itself presiding over sharp rises in unemployment and administering drastic cuts in social spending. It was also forced to adopt a harsh incomes policy which was rejected by the September, 1978, party conference. The unions' acquiescence was secured only with great reluctance and eventually it, too, disappeared. In January, 1979, there was a wave of industrial action by lorry drivers, railway workers and public service workers. The pay policy was destroyed and so was popular support for the government.[18]

The verdict of the voters on Labour in the election of 1979 was clear and harsh. The party received a mere 38% of the votes, its worst electoral result since the war. As Table 1 shows, the election was not only the climax of a steady decline in Labour support, it also revealed that the worst losses came from the very core of the party's historic strength.[19] Between 1966 and 1979 a sixth of Labour's supporters among the manual workers turned to some other party. The defections were not confined to the skilled, but affected the semi- and unskilled to exactly the same degree. Nor were they merely a reflection of the drifting away of non-unionized workers as the party became more

Table 11.1 *Electoral Support for Labour, 1964–79* (percentage of votes cast).

Election	Managerial, Administrative and Professional Employees	Lower White Collar	Skilled Manual	Semi- and Unskilled Manual	Women	OVERALL Labour	Cons
1964	9	25	54	59	39	44	43
1966	15	30	58	65	48	48	42
1970	10	30	55	57	45	43	45
1974 (Feb)	10	21	47	54	37	38	39
1974 (Oct)	12	24	49	57	38	39	36
1979	18	21	47	55	39	38	46

Source: See note 19.

closely associated with the unions, for between 1974 and 1979 the loss among trade unionists was marginally higher than among workers overall. Finally, data from the long-term series of British Election Studies show that the diminution of the Labour vote was paralleled by a decrease in those who 'identified' with the party and by a widening gap between the views of party supporters and its professed programmatic orientation.[20]

Interpreting the defeat has proved more difficult than describing it, however. From the various post-mortems on the election, it emerged that Labour had given the electors so many reasons to vote against it that it was impossible to discern the critical factor. The left maintained that it was due to the failure of Wilson and Callaghan to carry out the party's new programme, and there was truth in the charge.[21] The right among the party's leaders claimed, with perhaps less justice, that it was the radicalism of the party that drove away the voters. The centre, which was where most of the Parliamentary party liked to place themselves, focused upon external events, particularly the deteriorating economy, which forced the government to turn to the IMF and austerity, and eventually impelled workers themselves to reject the government's wage policy in the strikes of 1978–9.

However self-serving and superficial this perspective might sound, evidence could be adduced in its support. First, the decline in partisan support during the 1960s and early 1970s had not affected Labour any more than the Conservatives. Until 1974, it made more sense to talk of a broad dealignment and to chalk that up to the waning of deference and faith in politics generally, than to worry about Labour's specific fate.[22] Only after 1974 did the movement from party begin to affect Labour disproportionately, and even then it was possible to demonstrate that the party's losses came primarily in two specific moments – during the financial crisis of 1976 and the 'winter of discontent' of 1979.

Still, it is hard to credit such a narrowly conjunctural explanation, and the depth and breadth of the losses cries out for the identification of a more fundamental set of causes. So, too, does the prolongation of Labour's impasse into Thatcher's second term. Clearly, the unfortunate circumstances surrounding the 1974–79 regime blighted its prospects, just as the 'Falklands factor' militated against Labour four years later. But what allows such events at the surface of political life to take such a toll but the underlying weakness of the Labour party's link to its essential support among working people?

That weakening, moreover, cannot be properly understood as the product of recent events alone. However much Labour's flawed incomes policies or industrial relations initiatives may have alienated workers in the short term, the connections between Labour and working people have been becoming more tenuous since the early 1950s. The sharp class alignments of 1950–51, which had been based on the special conditions of war, war mobilization and reconstruction, persisted well into the 1960s, but well before then the numerous, non-political bonds linking Labour with the workers had begun to weaken. Up until the 1950s, working people had been largely excluded from British society and, in response, had evolved a highly separate style of existence organized through a complex set of class-specific institutions. Nearly all aspects of daily activity – shopping, saving, borrowing, insuring – were carried out locally or through groups formed by working men and women themselves. Much of what is now considered part of the social services was also provided from within the class, sometimes by the trade unions but usually by friends, neighbours and kin and with little or no public support. This dense network of class-based institutions, which was the hard reality behind the rather sentimental notion of 'working-class culture', was what working people left behind as they began to enjoy the benefits of the welfare state and the fruits of material prosperity.

Labour's ties with these formal and informal institutions had always been problematical: the link with the unions, for example, was generally stronger at the top than at the bottom; the party's leaders were often contemptuous towards the tastes of the workers in leisure and entertainment; the party as an organization was never very accessible to working-class women or to anyone working in the community; and so on. Nevertheless, the party had derived enormous positive advantage from the fact that working people lived in such an enclosed world, from the routine reinforcement of class identity provided by such an environment, and by Labour's unambiguous identification as the party of the working class. Indeed, for a time, giving one's support to Labour became the almost automatic political expression of being a member of the working class.

The trend of economic and social change since 1950, however, has been precisely such as to encourage working people to bypass such institutions, to escape from such networks into the broader community created by mass consumption, and to expand their horizons and expectations. The working class has not disappeared or become so affluent as to adopt a middle-class outlook on life, but it has come less and less to resemble that visage it had presented in the 1940s – culturally distinct, deprived, disenfranchised. Instead, working men and women have taken on a demeanour that is more self-confident and assertive, less inclined to accept the dismally low standards of the past and quite intolerant towards the pretensions and authority of employers, trade union officials and the state.

Unfortunately, neither the structure and organization, nor the ideology, nor the leaders of the Labour party were equipped to accommodate to this changed stance. The party thus failed to put its relationship with the workers on a new basis, but relied instead on the old rhetoric and on its alliance with the leadership of the unions. The result was a yet further loosening of Labour's ties to the workers and of the workers' allegiance to the party. Not very surprisingly, the party was equally unable to establish close and stable linkages with those new constituencies – immigrants, women, public sector workers, community activists, environmental groups – whose votes the party so desperately needed. By 1979, in consequence, Labour was left without that secure base of support which alone could have made up for the policy failures of 1974–9.

The defeats of 1979 and, perhaps to an even greater degree, of 1983, were in this sense long in the making, and they suggest that Labour's ensuing crisis transcends the mistakes of Callaghan and Foot, the personalities of Benn and Healey, and the good fortune of Margaret Thatcher. In essence, the crisis stems from the altered relation between Labour and the working class. The ties between the class and the party, nurtured over so many years, have atrophied. Since the process has been based upon a set of very real transformations in the way working people go about their daily lives, moreover, it cannot easily be reversed. Nor should it be, for, despite all the qualifications that need to be entered about the pattern of recent social change, there is little doubt that most working people have benefited a great deal. Nor is there reason to believe that any significant number of workers are so sentimentally attached to the older ways of living as to desire a return to the deprivations of the past. In sum, the conditions that produced 1945, or 1950, or even 1964, will not recur. This is not to say that Labour is destined never to win another general election. Rather, it is to argue that Labour's future will depend crucially upon its coming to terms with the changed realities of class, and of how class is lived and experienced, in contemporary British society.

Notes to the Text

Chapter One Pages 1–15

1 Raymond Williams, *The Long Revolution* (New York, 1961), pp. 329–35.

2 Eric Hobsbawm, 'The Forward March of Labour Halted?', *Marxism Today* (September 1978).

3 Ralf Dahrendorf, *On Britain* (Chicago, 1982), pp. 65–78.

4 Samuel H. Beer, *Britain Against Itself: The Political Contradictions of Collectivism* (New York, 1982), pp. 3–5, 12–15, 79–103.

5 Jeremy Seabrook, *What Went Wrong?* (London, 1978), pp. 31, 131, 133, 254–7; also *Working-Class Childhood* (London, 1982), *passim*.

6 See J. H. Goldthorpe, D. Lockwood, F. Bechhofer and J. Platt, *The Affluent Worker*, 3 Vols. (Cambridge, 1968–9). On the current state of the debate, see Howard Newby's SSRC proposal: 'Economic Stagflation and Social Change', 1982.

7 The methodological issues are discussed in greater detail in J. Cronin, 'Politics, Class Structure, and the Enduring Weakness of British Social Democracy', *Journal of Social History*, XVI, 3(1983), pp. 123–42.

8 Adam Przeworski, 'Social Democracy as a Historical Phenomenon', *New Left Review*, No. 122 (1980), pp. 27–58; Charles Tilly, 'Social Movements and National Politics', Center for Research on Social Organization, University of Michigan, Working Paper No. 197, May, 1979.

9 On this general process, see Alessandro Pizzorno, 'Interests and Parties in Pluralism', in S. Berger (ed.), *Organizing Interests in Western Europe* (Cambridge, 1981), pp. 247–84.

10 T. H. Marshall, *Citizenship and Social Class* (Cambridge, 1950). Despite occasional casual uses, the concept of citizenship elaborated by Marshall and its relationship to democracy, to legitimacy and to social class have not been developed in any serious fashion by subsequent scholars.

11   Martin Harrop, 'The Changing British Electorate', *Political Quarterly* (September, 1982), pp. 385–402.

12   R. Price and G. S. Bain, 'Union Growth Revisited: 1948–1984 in Perspective', *British Journal of Industrial Relations*, XIV (1976), pp. 339–55.

Chapter Two Pages 19–34

1   See Iain McLean, *The Legend of Red Clydeside* (Edinburgh, 1983), pp. 112–38; and also D. Englander and J. Osborne, 'Jack, Tommy and Henry Dubb: The Armed Forces and the Working Class', *Historical Journal*, XXI (1978).

2   H. B. Graham, *Relations between Employers and Employed – after the War* (London, 1918), 1, 3, *passim*; and Meyer Bloomfield, *Management and Men: A Record of New Steps in Industrial Relations* (New York, 1919), 153.

3   F. Dudley Docker, in S. J. Chapman (ed.), *Labour and Capital after the War* (London, 1918), pp. 132–4.

4   Docker, in *Labour and Capital after the War*, p. 132; Tom Jones, *Whitehall Diary, 1916–1925*, edited by K. Middlemas (London, 1969), p. 73. For Churchill's remark, see K. Middlemas, *The Politics of Industrial Society*, (London, 1979), pp. 143–4.

5   'The Labour Situation, Report . . . for the week ending 14th January, 1920', *PRO*, Cabinet Papers, CAB 24/96 C.P. 450, p. 21; Directorate of Intelligence (Home Office), 'Survey of Revolutionary Feeling during the Year 1919', *PRO* CAB 24/96 C.P. 462, pp. 4–5.

6   W. A. Orton, *Labour in Transition* (London, 1921), p. 205; B. Pribicevic, *The Shop Stewards' Movement and Workers' Control* (Oxford, 1959); and James Hinton, *The First Shop Stewards' Movement* (London, 1973), p. 169; Alan Clinton, *The Trade Union Rank and File* (Manchester, 1977), pp. 54–137; Ross McKibbin, *The Evolution of the Labour Party, 1910–1924* (Oxford, 1974); Middlemas, *Politics in Industrial Society*, p. 166; and J. Foster, 'British Imperialism and the Labour Aristocracy', in J. Skelley (ed.), *The General Strike 1926* (London, 1976), pp. 28, 56.

7   Carter Goodrich, *The Frontier of Control* (London, 1975, reprint of 1920 edition), p. 11; Clynes in Chapman, *Labour and Capital*, pp. 17–18; Orton, *Labour in Transition*, p. xiv; Ministry of Labour, cited in Middlemas, *Politics in Industrial Society*, p. 159.

8   On the arbitrariness of virtually all classifications according to

skill levels, see the discussion in Charles More, *Skill and the English Working Class* (London, 1980). Moreover, reliable statistics on the 'rise of the semi-skilled' are very hard to come by. Still, we do have information about certain classes of workers who could reasonably be labelled 'semi-skilled'. The numbers grow substantially:

Number of workers in

Occupation	1881	1891	1901	1911
Cotton manufacture	156,971	176,991	173,139	210,697
Miners of coal and shale	355,262	482,525	609,402	843,681
Porters and other railway workers	37,187	65,029	88,874	106,644
Engine drivers	65,643	81,268	105,351	110,249
Metal machinists	14,828	16,773	28,219	35,916
Tramways service	2,591	6,723	17,996	41,219
Steel smelting	22,905	25,304	30,178	39,087

Census data overall reveal a marked growth in the category of 'semi-skilled' and a stabilisation – after 1901, a slight but actual decline – in the category that approximates the distinction 'unskilled'. For the actual data, see J. A. Banks, 'The Social Structure of Nineteenth Century England as seen through the Census', in R. Lawton (ed.), *The Census and Social Structure* (London, 1978), pp. 179–223; and for a more elaborate argument J. Cronin, 'Strikes, 1870–1914', in C. J. Wrigley (ed.), *History of British Industrial Relations* (Brighton, 1982), pp. 74–98.

9 L. Macassey, *Labour Policy – False and True* (London, 1922), pp. 17–18, 211–19. On Macassey himself, see Hinton, *First Shop Stewards' Movement*, p. 144.

10 Arthur Gleason, *What the Workers Want* (London, 1920), esp. p. 153.

11 Whiting Williams, *Full Up and Fed Up: The Worker's Mind in Crowded Britain* (New York, 1921), pp. 208, 217, 229.

12 *Ibid.*, pp. 130–1, 135, 145.

13 *Ibid.* pp. 36, 54–7, 71–6.

14 *Ibid.*, pp. 55, 70, 78, 84.

15 *Ibid.*, pp. 42–4.

16 Directorate of Intelligence, 'Revolutionary Feeling during 1919'; 'Revolutionary Movements in 1920', *PRO* CAB 24/118 C.P. 2455.

17 St Philip's Settlement Education and Economics Research Society, *The Equipment of the Workers* (London, 1919). References organized by category and respondent.

18   R. McKibbin, 'Social Class and Social Observation in Edwardian England', *Transactions of the Royal Historical Society*, 5th Series, XXVIII (London, 1978), pp. 175–199. The alternative popular tradition is captured in John Burnett, *Destiny Obscure: Autobiographies of Childhood, Education and Family* (Harmondsworth, 1982).

19   *Equipment of the Workers*, p. 14; on Sheffield's uniquely rich working-class culture, see Dennis Smith, *Conflict and Compromise: Class Formation in English Society, A Comparative Study of Birmingham and Sheffield* (London, 1982); and David J. Hakken, 'Workers' Education: The Reproduction of Working-Class Culture in Sheffield . . .', Ph.D. Dissertation, American University, 1978.

20   On culture and community before the war, see Standish Meacham, *A Life Apart* (London, 1977), esp. pp. 184–220; and, more recently, Ellen Ross, 'Survival Networks: Women's Neighbourhood Sharing in London before World War One', *History Workshop* No. 15 (Spring, 1983), pp. 4–27.

21   G. D. H. Cole, *The World of Labour*, 4th edition (1919, reprinted New York, 1973), p. xiii.

22   M. Swenarton, *Homes Fit for Heroes* (London, 1981); David Englander, *Landlord and Tenant in Urban Britain: The Politics of Housing Reform, 1838–1924*, (Oxford, 1983).

23   Marion Kozak, 'Women Munition Workers in the First World War', PhD Dissertation, University of Hull, 1976; Harold Smith, 'The Issue of "Equal Pay for Equal Work" in Great Britain, 1914–1919', *Societas – A Review of Social History*, VIII (1978), pp. 39–52; and Gail Braybon, *Women Workers in the First World War* (London, 1981).

24   Commission of Enquiry into Industrial Unrest, 'Report . . . for the North-Eastern Area' (Cmnd. 8662) and 'Report . . . for the West Midlands' (Cmnd. 8665), and 'Summary' (Cmnd. 8696), *Parliamentary Papers* (1017–18), XV, Pt. II.

25   Middlemas, *Politics in Industrial Society*, pp. 120ff.

Chapter Three Pages 35–48

1   C. Delisle Burns, *The Principles of Revolution. A Study in Ideals* (London, 1920).

2   Murphy's report is cited in Roderick Martin, *Communism and the British Trade Unions, 1924–1933* (Oxford, 1969), p. 23. See also

Sidney Webb, 'The British Labour Movement and the Industrial Depression', *International Labour Review* II (1923), p. 216; and James Hinton and Richard Hyman, *Trade Unions and Revolution: The Industrial Politics of the Early British Communist Party* (London, 1975), p. 18.

3   *Working Days, Being the Personal Accounts of Sixteen Working Men and Women*, edited by Margaret A. Pollack (London, 1926), pp. 24, 94–5, 149–50, 188.

4   R. M. Fox, *The Triumphant Machine: A Study in Machine Civilization* (London, 1928), pp. 19–20, 115.

5   H. G. Matthew, R. McKibbin and J. A. Kay, 'The Franchise Factor in the Rise of the Labour Party', *English Historical Review*, XCI (1976), p. 747; McKibbin, *The Evolution of the Labour Party* (Oxford, 1974), pp. 88–123; Stanley Pierson, *British Socialists: The Journey From Fantasy to Politics* (Cambridge, Ma., 1979); Kirk Willis, 'The Introduction and Critical Reception of Marxist Thought in Britain, 1850–1900', *Historical Journal* XX, 2(1977), pp. 417–60; R. H. Tawney, *British Labour Movement* (New Haven, 1925), pp. 150–54, 158–62; and Stephen Yeo, 'The Religion of Socialism', *History Workshop*, No. 4(1977).

6   Whiting Williams, *Full Up and Fed Up* (New York, 1921); J. R. Clynes, quoted in F. Bealey, *The Social and Political Thought of the British Labour Party* (London, 1970), p. 97.

7   Stuart MacIntyre, 'British Labour, Marxism and Working Class Apathy in the Nineteen Twenties', *Historical Journal*, XX, 2(1977), pp. 479–96; and *A Proletarian Science* (Cambridge, 1980); and on the infusion of middle class support after 1918, see Catherine Cline, *Recruits to Labour* (Syracuse, 1963).

8   G. D. H. Cole, cited in A. W. Wright, *G. D. H. Cole and Socialist Thought* (Oxford, 1979), p. 84 and *passim*; Burns, *The Philosophy of Labour* (London, 1925), p. 26; Sidney & Beatrice Webb, *A Constitution for the Socialist Commonwealth of Great Britain*, introduction by Samuel Beer, (Cambridge, 1975), reprint of 1920 edition, pp. XLI–XLII, 213–14. H. A. Deane, *The Political Ideas of Harold Laski* (New York, 1954), also shows the importance of the growth of unionism in Laski's early writings (pp. 29–30).

9   A fuller discussion of this process is contained in J. Cronin, 'Coping with Labour, 1918–1926', in J. Cronin and J. Schneer (eds.), *Social Conflict and the Political Order in Modern Britain* (London, 1982), pp. 113–45.

10   Employers' association official quoted in Williams, *Full Up and*

Fed Up, p. 252; remarks of Arthur Beck appear in the Transcript of the Meeting, National Union of Manufacturers' Deputation to the Ministry of Labour, 12 October 1926, *PRO*, LAB 10/4,3.

11   Lloyd George to Bonar Law, reported in R. Lowe, 'The Failure of Consensus in Britain: The National Industrial Conference, 1918–21', *Historical Journal*, XXI (1978); *Beatrice Webb's Diaries, 1918–24*, (London, 1952), p. 208; Lloyd George to Thomas, cited in Foster, 'British Imperialism and Labour Aristocracy', p. 35.

12   John Lovell, 'The TUC Special Industrial Committee, January–April, 1926', in A. Briggs and J. Saville (eds.), *Essays in Labour History 1918–1939* (London, 1977), pp. 36–56.

13   G. A. Phillips, *The General Strike* (London, 1977); A. Mason, 'The Government and the General Strike', *Internation Review of Social History*, XIV(1968).

14   Steel-Maitland's view is discussed in Middlemas, *Politics in Industrial Society*, p. 204. See also C. L. Mowat, *Britain Between the Wars* (Chicago, 1955), p. 330, and the TUC General Council, *The Mining Crisis and the National Strike, 1926. Official Reports* (London, 1927).

15   R. Scally, *The Origins of the Lloyd George Coalition* (Princeton, 1975); G. D. Phillips, *The Diehards: Aristocratic Society and Politics in Edwardian England* (Cambridge, Mass., 1979); G. Searle, 'Critics of Edwardian Society: The Case of the Radical Right', in A. O'Day (ed.), *The Edwardian Age: Conflict and Stability* (London, 1979), pp. 79–96.

16   See G. R. Searle, *The Quest for National Efficiency* (Oxford, 1971); Lloyd George to Philip Lloyd Greame in January, 1921, quoted in Gilbert, *British Social Policy*, p. 27.

17   K. Morgan, *Consensus and Disunity: The Lloyd George Coalition Government, 1918–1922* (Oxford, 1979), p. 280; R. G. Hawtrey, *The Exchequer and the Control of Expenditure* (London, 1921), p. 71; B. Gilbert, *British Social Policy* (London, 1970), pp. 46–8.

18   F. D. Klingender, *The Condition of Clerical Labour in Britain* (London, 1935), V. L. Allen, *Trade Unions and the Government* (London, 1960), pp. 71–89, and J. Melling, 'Non-Commissioned Officers: British Employers and their Supervisory Workers', *Social History*, V,2(1980). On the middle classes, see Frederick Guest to Lloyd George, noted in D. Englander, *Landlord and Tenant in Urban Britain* (Oxford, 1983). The opposite, perhaps more typical, reaction was exemplified by Lord Rothermere's 'Anti-Waste' movement which led to the appointment of the

Geddes Committee in 1921. See Morgan, *Consensus and Disunity*, pp. 243–5.

19   Morgan, *Consensus and Disunity*, p. 300; J. A. Ramsden, *The Age of Balfour & Baldwin* (London, 1978), esp. pp. 244–64.

20   M. Cowling, *The Impact of Labour* (Cambridge, 1971), p. 1.

21   S. J. Hurwitz, *State Intervention in Great Britain* (London, 1947), p. 41; R. Davidson and R. Lowe, 'Bureaucracy and Innovation in British Welfare Policy, 1907–1945', in W. J. Mommsen (ed.), *The Evolution of the Welfare State in Britain and Germany* (London, 1981), pp. 269–95.

22   D. E. Moggridge, *The Return to Gold, 1925* (Cambridge, 1969), esp. pp. 45–60.

23   Transcript of Meeting between Ministry of Labour and National Union of Manufacturers, 12 October 1926, *PRO*, LAB 10/4, 3.

24   Reports on Trade Union Reactions to Proposed Trade Union Legislation, January 1927, *PRO*, LAB 10/5.

25   G. W. McDonald and H. F. Gospel, 'The Mond-Turner Talks, 1927–1933: A Study in Industrial Co-operation', *Historical Journal*, XXI(1973); Martin Jacques, 'The Emergence of "Responsible" Trade Unionism: A Study of the "New Direction" in T.U.C. Policy, 1926–1935', PhD thesis, University of Cambridge, 1975; R. Martin, *Communism and the British Trade Unions* (Oxford, 1968), pp. 78–101; L. J. Macfarlane, *The British Communist Party* (London, 1966), pp. 166–94.

26   M. Kinnear, *The British Voter. An Atlas and Survey since 1885* (London, 1968), pp. 49–49. The evidence from cohort surveys suggests that most of this increase came not from conversions from the Liberals or the Conservatives but from Labour's ability to mobilize 'the support of manual workers who grew up in relatively non-political homes'. See D. Butler and D. Stokes, *Political Change in Britain* (London, 1969), pp. 255–6, whose findings indicate that less than a quarter of their sample of working-class voters remember fathers whose allegiance was to Labour before 1918. The percentage would rise steadily to 40% or more by the later 1920s and continue rising to over two-thirds by 1945–51. See also William Miller, *Electoral Dynamics in Britain since 1918* (London, 1977), pp. 146–54.

27   Carl Brand, *The British Labour Party* (Stanford, 1974), pp. 132–3; Robert Skidelsky, *Politicians and the Slump* (London, 1967), pp. 51–61.

Chapter Four Pages 51–69

1   Leslie Hannah, *The Rise of the Corporate Economy* (London, 1976), pp. 116–41; Alan Armstrong and Aubrey Silverston, 'Size of Plant, Size of Enterprise and Concentration in British Manufacturing Industry, 1935–1958', *Journal of the Royal Statistical Society*, Series A, Vol. 128 (1965) Pt. 3, pp. 395–420; and Derek Aldcroft, *The Inter-War Economy, 1919–1939* (London, 1970), Chapters 5–7.

2   See Political and Economic Planning (P.E.P.), *Report on the Location of Industry in Great Britain* (London, 1939).

3   S. Lewenhak, *Women and Trade Unions* (London, 1977), pp. 225–6; R. Strachey, *Careers and Openings for Women* (London, 1934), pp. 58–60.

4   G. Routh, *Occupation and Pay in Great Britain, 1906–1979* (London, 1980), pp. 6–7.

5   Morris Ginsberg, 'Interchange between Social Classes', *Economic Journal* (December, 1929), pp. 556–7; Francis Klingender, *The Condition of Clerical Labour in Britain* (London, 1934), p. 64; David Lockwood, *The Blackcoated Worker: A Study in Class Consciousness* (London, 1958), pp. 106–16.

6   Eric Wigham, *The Power to Manage* (London, 1973); G. W. MacDonald, 'The Role of British Industry in 1926', in Margaret Morris, *The General Strike* (London, 1976), pp. 289–317.

7   Harold Cox, speaking to the Institute of Civil Engineers, quoted in Wayne Lewchuck, 'Technology, Pay Systems and the Motor Companies', in Howard F. Gospel and Craig Littler (eds.), *Managerial Strategies and Industrial Relations* (London, 1983).

8   Urwick on scientific management in 1946; president of the Institute of Automotive Engineers, 1920; Austin's management, 1930, 1934, reported in Lewchuck, 'Technology, Pay Systems and the Motor Companies'.

9   Sidney Pollard, *The Development of the British Economy, 1914–1967* (London, 1969), pp. 110–25.

10   Roger Penn, 'Skilled Manual Workers in the Labour Process, 1856–1964', in S. Wood (ed.), *The Degradation of Work?* (London, 1982), p. 97.

11   Len Holden, 'Think of Me Simply as the Skipper: Industrial Relations at Vauxhall, 1920–1950', *Oral History* IX, 2 (Autumn, 1981); Arthur Exell, 'Morris Motors in the 1930s', *History Workshop*, Pt. I, No. 6 (Autumn, 1978), pp. 52–78, Pt. II No. 7 (Spring, 1979), pp. 45–65; Lewchuck, 'Technology, Pay Systems

and the Motor Companies'; Roy Church, *Herbert Austin. The British Motor Car Industry to 1941* (London, 1979), pp. 96–102.

12   Craig Littler, 'Taylorism in Britain in the Interwar Years', in Gospel and Littler, *Managerial Strategies*; 'Deskilling and Changing Structures of Control', in Wood (ed.), *The Degradation of Work?*, pp. 122–45; and Trades Union Congress, *The TUC Examines the Bedaux System of Payment by Results* (London, 1933).

13   W. F. Watson, *Machines and Men. An autobiography of an Itinerant Mechanic* (London, 1935), p. 190.

14   *Ibid.*, 213–18; see also Watson's 'A Working Mechanic's View', in *The Workers' Point of View. A Symposium*, preface by C. T. Cramp (London, 1933), pp. 15–46; and William Ferrie, 'The Engineer', in H. Williams (ed.), *Man and the Machine* (London, 1935), pp. 73–82.

15   Alfred Barratt Brown, *The Machine and the Worker* (London, 1934), pp. 43–52 and *passim*. Though Barratt Brown quotes frequently from his students' essays, these potentially very valuable sources do not appear to have survived.

16   John Hilton, *et al.*, *Are Trade Unions Obstructive? An Impartial Inquiry* (London, 1935); see also Richard Price, 'Rethinking Labour History: the Importance of Work', in J. Cronin and J. Schneer (eds.), *Social Conflict and the Political Order in Modern Britain* (London, 1982), p. 182.

17   Walter Greenwood, *How the Other Man Lives* (London, 1939).

18   Jack Common, *Seven Shifts* (New York, 1938), pp. 9–10, 101.

19   G. M. Broughton, E. M. Newbold and E. C. Allen, 'A Statistical Study of Labour Turnover in Munition and Other Factories', *Report* of the Industrial Fatigue Research Board (London, 1921).

20   M. Culpin and M. Smith, 'The Nervous Temperament', Industrial Health Research Board, *Report* No. 61 (London, 1930).

21   S. Wyatt and J. N. Langdon, 'The Machine and the Worker. A Study of Machine-Feeding Processes', IHRB *Report* (London, 1938); Wyatt and Langdon, 'Fatigue and Boredom in Repetitive Work', IHRB *Report* No. 77 (London, 1937).

22   Marie Jahoda, 'Some Social-Psychological Problems of Factory Life', *British Journal of Psychology*, XXXI, Pt. 3 (1941), pp. 191–206. See also Pearl Jephcott, *Rising Twenty. Notes on Some Ordinary Girls* (London, 1948), pp. 118–28.

Chapter Five Pages 70–92

1 H. Llewellyn Smith (ed.), *New survey of London*, Vol. VII (London, 1934), p. 36.

2 John Hilton, *et al., Are Trade Unions Obstructive?* (London, 1935), p. 7.

3 Henry Durant, *The Problem of Leisure* (London, 1938), p. 30.

4 Jack Common, *The Freedom of the Streets* (London, 1938), p. 56.

5 Innis Pearce and G. Scott Williamson, *The Case for Action* (London, 1931), p. 43. For less sympathetic instances, see D. Caradog Jones (ed.), *The Social Survey of Merseyside*, Vol. III., (London, 1934), pp. 265–7; and Constance Harris, *The Use of Leisure in Bethnal Green* (London, 1927), pp. 14, 33, 54, 69.

6 Common, *Freedom of the Streets*, pp. 106–8.

7 On Mass-Observation itself, see Tom Jeffery, 'Mass-Observation – A Short History', Birmingham University, Centre for Contemporary Cultural Studies, 1978.

8 The responses are contained in the files of the Mass-Observation Archive at the University of Sussex among the 'Replies to Directives' for June, 1939. The class distribution for the 349 completed questionnaires was as follows:

Class Identification	Men	Women	Total
Upper	8	5	13
Upper Middle	33	19	52
Professional	18	15	33
Middle	62	38	100
Lower-middle	58	25	83
Farmers	2	–	2
Lower-middle/upper working	12	7	19
Upper working	21	11	32
Working	41	–	41
Total	225	124	349

These totals are obviously insufficient for detailed analysis within specific groups, but quite useful for analysis at various levels of aggregation, at least for men. For specific quotations, see 'Replies' Nos. 1245, 1257, 1442, 1126, 1616, 1235, quoted in that order.

9 Hoggart, *The Uses of Literacy* (London, 1957), p. 32.

10 Margery Spring Rice, *Working-Class Wives* (London, 1939, reprinted 1981), p. 14.

11 Mark Abrams, *The Condition of the British People, 1914–1945*

(London, 1946), pp. 83–4.

12   Jane Lewis, *The Politics of Motherhood* (London, 1980), esp. pp. 196–218; Angus McLaren, *Birth Control in Nineteenth-Century England* (London, 1978), Mass-Observation, *Britain and her Birthrate* (London, 1945); Carr-Saunders, (1924), quoted in Eva Hubback, *The Population of Britain* (New York, 1947), p. 53; Diana Gittins, *Fair Sex: Family Size and Structure, 1900–1939* (London, 1982).

13   Margaret Llewelyn Davies, *Maternity: Letters from Working Women* (London, 1915); Margery Spring Rice, *Working-Class Wives, passim*; Lewis, *Politics of Motherhood*, pp. 35, 197–200.

14   Spring Rice, *Working-Class Wives*, pp. 28, 37–40, 155, 188.

15   *Ibid.*, p. 94.

16   'A Worker's Family Life from the Inside', in *The New Survey of London Life and Labour* ed. by H. Llewellyn Smith, Vol. IX, *Life and Leisure* (London, 1935), pp. 415. See also K. Brown, *The English Labour Movement, 1700–1951* (New York, 1982), pp. 280–1.

17   *New Survey of London Life and Labour*, Vol. IX, pp. ix., 396, 402, 404, 408.

18   Workers' views reported in E. Wight Bakke, *The Unemployed Man, A Social Study* (New York, 1934), pp. 160–2.

19   Noreen Branson and Margot Heinemann, *Britain in the Nineteen Thirties* (London, 1973), p. 70.

20   Pilgrim Trust, *Men Without Work* (Cambridge, 1938), pp. 51, 320; *New Survey of London*, Vol. IX, p. 254.

21   Pilgrim Trust, *Men Without Work*, pp. 189–93; A. L. Beales and R. S. Lambert (eds.), *Memoirs of the Unemployed* (London, 1934, rep. 1973), pp. 69–70, 203, 112, 105.

22   Pilgrim Trust, *Men Without Work*, pp. 90–1, 68–9, 273–7, 74, 312. See also, for evidence on social life in 'distressed areas': James Hanley, *Grey Children: A Study in Humbug and Misery* (London, 1937); E. Ginzberg, *Grass on the Slag Heaps* (New York, 1942); E. Wilkinson, *The Town That Was Murdered* (London, 1939); Philip Massey, 'Portrait of a Mining Town', *Fact* (London, 1937); and J. B. Priestley, *English Journey* (London, 1934).

23   Terence Young, *Becontree and Dagenham* (London, 1934), p. 25; Spring Rice, *Working-Class Wives*, p. 17; Karl Silex, *John Bull at Home* (New York, 1931), p. 44.

24   Young, *Becontree and Dagenham, passim*.

25   Ruth Durant, *Watling: A Survey of Social Life in a New Housing Estate*, p. 253.

26   Durant, *Watling*, pp. 3–4, 124; J. Burnett, *A Social History of Housing* (Newton Abbot, 1978), p. 253.

27   Mass-Observation, *People's Homes* (London, 1943), *passim*; and Mass-Observation, *The Pub and the People* (London, 1943, reprinted 1970), p. 334.

28   Durant, *Problem of Leisure*, pp. 71–5; Caradog Jones, *Social Survey of Merseyside*, Vol. III, pp. 265–71; Branson and Heinemann, *Britain in the Nineteen Thirties* 91–4; J. A. R. Pimlott, *The English-man's Holiday* (London, 1948), pp. 211–37; M. A. Bienefeld, *Working Hours in British Industry* (London, 1972), pp. 145–50.

29   Abrams, *Condition of the British People*, pp. 82–6; 'Weekly Expenditure of Working-Class Households in the United Kingdom in 1937–8', *Ministry of Labour Gazette*, XLVIII (December, 1940), pp. 300–5. The 18% figure for 'other' expenditure comes from an American study of British budgets in 1890. See the *Seventh Annual Report of the U.S. Commissioner of Labour* (Washington, D.C., 1892), pp. 2000–2007.

30   Common, *Freedom of the Streets*, p. 71. It is also clear that a considerable portion of working-class expenditure, even when spent on novel items, was organized and experienced through established, class-specific institutions, thus reinforcing class awareness and loyalties. See Paul Johnson, 'Credit and Thrift and the Working Class, 1870–39', in J. M. Winter, ed., *The Working Class in Modern British History* (Cambridge, 1983), pp. 147–70 and M. Tebbutt, *Making Ends Meet* (New York, 1983).

31   R. B. Ainsworth, 'Earnings and Working Hours of Manual Wage-Earners in the United Kingdom in October, 1938', *Journal of the Royal Statistical Society* (1949), Pt. 1, pp. 40–2; A. C. Pigou and Colin Clark, 'The Economic Position of Great Britain (1935)', *Royal Economic Society Memorandum* No. 60 (1936), pp. 29–33; E. D. Smithies, 'The Contrast between North and South in England, 1918–1939', PhD thesis, (University of Bradford, 1974).

32   C. Chisholm (ed.), *Marketing Survey of the United Kingdom* (London, 1937).

33   Brian Simon, *The Politics of Educational Reform* (London, 1974), pp. 225–50; S. Humphries, *Hooligans or Rebels*, pp. 28–61, 113–20; Hoggart, *Uses of Literary*, pp. 100–109; Caradog Jones, *Social Survey of Merseyside*, Vol. III, pp. 274–6; Kirsten Drotner, 'Schoolgirls, Madcaps, and Air Aces: English Girls and their Magazine Reading between the wars', *Feminist Studies*, LX (Spring, 1983), pp. 33–52.

34   Richard Stone and D. A. Rowe, *The Measure of Consumers'
      Expenditure and Behaviour in the United Kingdom, 1920–1938*,
      Volume II (Cambridge, 1966), pp. 17, 21, 25; A. H. Halsey (ed.),
      Trends in British Society Since 1900 (London, 1972), p. 564, 571.

35   Mass-Observation, *The Pub and the People*, pp. 17, 20, 38–41,
      76–9, 106–7, 109–11, 142–3; *New Survey of London*, IX, pp. 251–7;
      Durant, *Problem of Leisure*, pp. 95–7; and H. M. Vernon, *The
      Shorter Working Week* (London, 1934), p. 169.

36   Mass Observation, *The Pub and the People*, pp. 305–7; *New Survey
      of London*, IX, pp. 121–30.

37   *New Survey of London*, IX, p. 257; Caradog Jones, *Social Survey of
      Merseyside*, III, pp. 281–3, Durant, *Problem of Leisure*, p. 92, John
      Hilton, *Rich Man, Poor Man* (London, 1944), pp. 123–8.

38   Durant, *Problem of Leisure*, pp. 87–94; Halsey, *Trends in British
      Society*, pp. 558–9; see also Madeleine Rooff, *Youth and Leisure: A
      Survey of Girls' Organizations in England and Wales* (Edinburgh,
      1935).

Chapter Six Pages 93–110

1   Robin Page Arnot, *The Miners: Years of Struggle* (London, 1953),
      pp. 457–519.

2   A. R. Griffen and C. P. Griffin, 'The Non-Political Trade Union
      Movement', in Asa Briggs and John Saville (eds.), *Essays in
      Labour History, 1918–1939* (London, 1977), pp. 133–62; Page
      Arnot, *The Miners in Crisis and War* (London, 1961), pp. 194–240;
      and H. Francis and D. Smith, *The Fed* (London, 1980).

3   G. W. MacDonald and H. F. Gospel, 'The Mond-Turner Talks,
      1927–1933: A Study in Industrial Cooperation', *Historical Journal*,
      XVI (1973), pp. 807–29.

4   L. J. MacFarlane, *The British Communist Party: Its Origin and
      Development until 1929* (London, 1966); Stuart MacIntyre, *A
      Proletarian Science* (Cambridge, 1980); and *Little Moscows* (Lon-
      don, 1981).

5   Wal Hannington, *Unemployed Struggles* (London, 1936) pp.
      219–97.

6   Roderick Martin, *Communism and the British Trade Unions,
      1924–1933* (Oxford, 1969), pp. 150–91. The reorientation towards
      work within the unions rather than in opposition is best seen in
      the pages of the various factory, shop and pit newsletters which
      party members started. These factory sheets are available at the

Modern Records Centre, University of Warwick, Renshaw Papers MSS104, Militant Textile Workers Collection, MSS80, and the Militant Miners Collection MSS88, and at the Working-Class Movement Library in Manchester.

7   Ralph Miliband, *Parliamentary Socialism* (London, 1961).

8   Ross McKibbin, 'The Economic Policy of the Second Labour Government', *Past and Present*, (August, 1975), pp. 95–123; Robert Skidelsky, *Politicians and the Slump* (London, 1967).

9   Snowden, in R.W. Hogue, ed. *British Labour Speaks* (New York 1924), p. 29. J. H. Thomas, in *The Labour Magazine*, December, 1929, p. 339.

10   Carl Brand, *The British Labour Party* (Stanford, 1974), pp. 134–57.

11   H. W. Drucker, *Doctrine and Ethos in the Labour Party* (London, 1974); Clement Attlee, *As It Happened* (London, 1954), p. 107.

12   R. Dowse, *Left in the Centre* (London, 1966).

13   Ben Pimlott, *Labour and the Left in the 1930s* (Cambridge, 1977), pp. 48–9.

14   *Ibid.*, pp. 14, 52, 63–7.

15   John Saville, 'May Day 1937', in *Essays in Labour History*, pp. 232–84.

16   Patrick Seyd, 'Factionalism within the Labour Party: the Socialist League, 1932–37, in *Essays in Labour History*, pp. 204–31; Pimlott, *Labour and the Left*, pp. 52–6, esp. quote on pp. 55–6.

17   See G. D. H. and M. I. Cole, *The Condition of Britain* (London, 1937); and J. Zeitlin, 'The Emergence of Shop Steward Organization and Job Control in the British Car Industry: a Review Essay', *History Workshop*, No. 10 (Autumn, 1980).

18   Roy Church, *Herbert Austin. The British Motor Car Industry to 1941* (London, 1979), pp. 147–53; R. P. Hastings, 'The Birmingham Labour Movement', *Midland History* (1980), pp. 78–92; T. J. Claydon, 'The Development of Trade Unionism among British Automobile and Aircraft Workers, c. 1914–1946', PhD thesis (University of Kent at Canterbury, 1981), pp. 80–1, 105–7.

19   R. C. Whiting, 'The Working Class in the "New Industry" Towns: The Case of Oxford,' Oxford University, D Phil thesis, 1978; and, for details of the Pressed Steel dispute, see *The Conveyor*, No. 7 (September, 1934), in 'The Factory Papers Collection', R9 Box 13, Working Class Movement Library, Manchester.

20   F. W. Carr, 'Engineering Workers and the Rise of Labour in Coventry', Warwick University, PhD thesis, 1978; Ronald

Edsforth, 'Divergent Traditions: Union Organization and the Automobile Industries in Flint, Michigan and Coventry, England', *Detroit in Perspective* V, 3 (Spring, 1981), pp. 2–20.

21 Nina Fishman, 'The Communist Party and the Trade Union Revival', thesis in progress, University of London; Claydon, 'The Development of Trade Unionism . . .', pp. 84–9.

22 R. Croucher, *Engineers at War* (London, 1982), pp. 37–42; *Fairey Battle*, No. 4 (February, 1939), in Factory Papers, R9 Box 12, Working Class Movement Library; Claydon, 'The Development of Trade Unionism . . .', pp. 181–95.

23 Croucher, *Engineers at War*, pp. 45–57.

24 John Rowett, 'The Labour party and Local Government: Theory and Practice in the Inter-War Years', DPhil thesis, Oxford University, 1979, chapter 4, esp. p. 247, where he quotes Joe Westwood, MP, to the effect that 'the greatest successes of our Movement in the political field since 1931 has been in the sphere of municipal government'. On London, see K. Young and P. Garside, *Metropolitan London: Politics and Urban Change, 1837–1981* (New York, 1982), pp. 173–218; G. W. Jones and Bernard Donoughue, *Herbert Morrison: Portrait of a Politician* (London, 1973), pp. 44–128.

25 Pimlott, *Labour and the Left*, pp. 111–40 on the Constituency Parties Movement, and pp. 143–54 on the Popular Front.

Chapter Seven Pages 111–132

1 Roger Opie, 'The Political Consequences of Lord Keynes', in D. E. Moggridge (ed.), *Keynes: Aspects of the Man and His Work* (London, 1974), pp. 75–90; Paul Addison, *The Road to 1945* (London, 1977) esp. 270–8; Arthur Marwick, 'Middle Opinion in the Thirties', *English Historical Review* (April, 1964); Roger Eatwell, *The 1945–1951 Labour Governments* (London, 1979), pp. 43–4, 155–9; Donald Winch, *Economics and Policy. A Historical Study* (New York, 1970), pp. 255–94, 339–50; and Pat Thane, *The Foundations of the Welfare State* (London, 1982), pp. 12–14.

2 J. T. Murphy, *Victory Production* (London, 1942), pp. 12–14.

3 George Orwell, 'England Your England', (1941) reprinted in *Inside The Whale and Other Essays* (Harmondsworth, 1962), p. 78; Tom Wintringham, *New Ways of War* (London, 1940), p. 122; and David Fernbach, 'Tom Wintringham and Socialist Defence Strategy', *History Workshop*, No. 14 (Autumn, 1982), pp. 73–82.

4   Margaret Gowing, 'The Organization of Manpower in Britain during the Second World War', *Journal Of Contemporary History*, VII, 1–2 (1972), p. 151; Richard Croucher, *Engineers at War, 1939–1945* (London, 1982), pp. 95–8; P. Inman, *Labour in the Munitions Industries* (London, 1957).

5   W. K. Hancock and M. Gowing, *British War Economy* (London, 1949), p. 209.

6   *Ibid.*, pp. 143–50, 281–314, 438–65; Richard Stone, 'The Use and Development of National Income and Expenditure Estimates', in D. N. Chester (ed.), *Lessons of the British War Economy* (Cambridge, 1951), pp. 83–101; and Alan Booth, 'The "Keynesian Revolution" in Economic Policy-Making', *Economic History Review* (1983), pp. 103–23.

7   Sheila Lewenhak, *Women and Trade Unions* (London, 1977), pp. 235–41; G. S. Bain and R. Price, *Profiles of Union Growth* (Oxford, 1980), pp. 37–8.

8   Nina Fishman, 'The Communist Party and the Trade Union Revival, 1930–1945', PhD thesis in progress, University of London, chapter on Dagenham.

9   Alan Bullock, *The Life and Times of Ernest Bevin*, Vol. II (London, 1967), chapters 2, 4 and 6; Angus Calder, *The People's War* (London, 1971), pp. 452–3. Steven Tolliday, 'Government, Employers, and Shopfloor Organisation in the British Motor Industry, 1939–69', King's College, 1982, correctly points out Bevin's aloofness in many particular instances, however, including Ford.

10   Croucher, *Engineers at War*, pp. 147, 162–67. See also James Hinton, 'Coventry Communism: A Study of Factory Politics in the Second World War', *History Workshop*, No. 10 (Autumn, 1980).

11   Calder, *People's War*, pp. 280–4; Hinton, 'Coventry Communism', pp. 91–118; Croucher, *Engineers at War*, pp. 174–6, 285–92.

12   Penelope Summerfield; 'Education and Politics in the British Armed Forces in the Second World War', *International Review of Social History*, XXVI (1981) Pt. 2, pp. 133–58; Mass-Observation, 'Report on Some Opinion Trends in the Forces', File Report 1617, February 1942, and 'Report on Reconstruction – Jobs and Security', File Report 1389, August 1942, which found women to be far less optimistic than men and the soldiers and sailors most cynical of all.

13   George H. Gallup, *The Gallup International Public Opinion Polls.*

Great Britain, 1937–75, 2 Vols. (New York, 1976), p. 79. Hereafter simply cited in the text as Gallup Polls, with the appropriate date; Hinton, 'Coventry Communism', pp. 108–11; and Mass-Observation, 'Report on Manchester Industrial Atmosphere', File Report 839, August 1941, and 'Bolton's Industries', File Report 856, September 1941.

14   Mass-Observation, *War Factory* (London, 1943), pp. 9, 45; S. Wyatt, 'A Study of Women on War Work in Four Factories', Industrial Health Research Board Report, February, 1945, pp. 28–9; H. Smith, 'The Problem of "Equal Pay for Equal Work" in Great Britain during World War II', *Journal of Modern History*, LIII, (December 1981), pp. 652–67; Lewenhak, *Women and Trade Unions*, pp. 237, 247–52; Denise Riley, 'The Free Mothers: pronatalism and working mothers in industry at the end of the last war in Britain', *History Workshop*, No. 11 (Spring 1981), pp. 59–118; G. Thomas, *Women at Work: The Attitudes of Working Women towards Post-War Employment and Related Problems* (London: Wartime Social Survey, 1944).

15   David Howell, *British Social Democracy. A Study in Development and Decay* (London, 1976), pp. 107–34.

16   A useful overview is contained in the essay by the Cultural History Group at Birmingham, 'Out of the People: The Politics of Containment, 1939–1945', *Working Papers in Cultural Studies*, IX (1976), pp. 29–50.

17   Priestley's speeches were published simply as *Postscripts* (London, 1940), and *Out of the People* (London, 1941); Wintringham's series appeared as *New Ways of War* (London, 1940). On the *Mirror*, See A. Smith, *Paper Voices: The Popular Press and Social Change, 1935–1965* (London, 1975), pp. 62–113.

18   Calder, *People's War*, pp. 343–8. At the same time, G. D. H. Cole discovered widespread pessimism among working people concerning the prospects of postwar social reform. See José Harris, 'Did British Workers Want the Welfare State? G. D. H. Cole's Survey of 1942', in J. M. Winter, ed., *The Working Class in Modern British History* (Cambridge, 1983), pp. 200–214.

19   Mass-Observation, 'Report on Attitudes to Socialism and Communism', File Report 1050, January, 1942; Hinton, 'Coventry Communism', pp. 103–8.

20   Mass-Observation, 'Public Reactions to the Beveridge Report', File Report 1568, January, 1943; Calder, *People's War*, p. 609; Orwell, noted in 'Out of the People', p. 43.

21   Calder, *People's War*, pp. 612–14; Summerfield, 'Education and Politics in the British Armed Forces', pp. 144–5; Addison, *The Road to 1945*, pp. 211–28.

22   British Institute of Public Opinion, *The Beveridge Report and the Public* (London, 1943).

23   G. Routh, 'Civil Service Pay, 1875–1950', *Economica*, N.S., XXI, (August, 1954); Robert Sinclair, *The Big City, A Human Study of London* (New York, 1938), pp. 288–96; Walter Greenwood, *How the Other Man Lives* (London, 1939); Mass-Observation, 'Report on Post-War Jobs', File Report 857, September 1941.

24   Tom Jeffery, 'Mass-Observation – A Short History', Centre for Contemporary Cultural Studies, University of Birmingham, 1978; Don MacPherson (ed.), *Traditions of Independence: British Cinema in the Thirties* (London, 1980); and Ralph Bond, 'Cinema in the Thirties: Documentary Film and the Labour Movement', in J. Clark, *et al.*, *Culture and Crisis in Britain in the 30s* (London, 1979), pp. 241–56; and Lancelot Hogben, 'Marxism and the Middle Classes', in *Dangerous Thoughts* (New York, 1940), pp. 194–208. See also Evan Durbin, *The Politics of Democratic Socialism* (London, 1940), and, on the distinct interests of the shopkeepers, Neil Killingback, 'The Politics of Small Business in Britain during the Nineteen Thirties', PhD thesis, Sussex University, 1980.

25   James Hinton, *Labour and Socialism* (Brighton, 1983), p. 167; Calder, *People's War*, pp. 631–5; Addison, *Road to 1945*, pp. 225–6, 249–50; Henry Pelling, *The British Communist Party* (New York, 1958), pp. 131–2.

26   Summerfield, 'Education and Politics in the British Armed Forces', pp. 151–3; Mass-Observation, *The Journey Home* (London, 1944), p. 116. On women, see Smith *et al.*, *Paper Voices*, pp. 118–27; and also Mass-Observation, 'Women and the Vote', File Report 2179, November 1944.

27   R. B. McCallum and Alison Readman, *The British General Election of 1945* (Oxford, 1947), pp. 233–65; Mass-Observation, 'Youth and the Election', File Report 2257, June 1945; Eatwell, *The 1945–1951 Labour Governments*, pp. 37–44.

28   D. Winch, *Economics and Policy*, pp. 269–73; Booth, 'The "Keynesian Revolution" in Economic Policy-Making', pp. 111–17; William Beveridge, *Full Employment in a Free Society* (London, 1944); J. Tomlinson, *Problems of British Economic Policy, 1870–1945* (London, 1981), pp. 120–34.

29　Centre for Contemporary Cultural Studies, *Unpopular Education: Schooling and Social Democracy in Britain since 1944* (London, 1981), pp. 57–9; Rodney Barker, *Education and Politics, 1900–1951* (Oxford, 1972); and R. G. Wallace, 'Labour, the Board of Education and the Preparation of the 1944 Education Act', PhD thesis, University of London, 1980.

30　Pat Thane, *The Foundations of the Welfare State* (London, 1982), pp. 230–54, 266; Samuel Beer, *Britain Against Itself* (New York, 1982), p. 7.

31　This account of the reforms of 1945–48 is based largely upon Eatwell, *The 1945–51 Labour Governments*; but see also Thane, *Foundations of the Welfare State*, pp. 223–69; and I. Pinchbeck and M. Hewitt, *Children in English Society*, Vol. II (London, 1973), pp. 638–56.

32　Raymond Williams, *The Long Revolution* (London, 1961), p. 329.

Chapter Eight Pages 134–145

1　Leslie Hannah, *The Rise of the Corporate Economy* (London, 1976), pp. 142–63, esp. p. 156; *British Labour Statistics. Historical Abstract* (London, 1972), p. 408.

2　G. Routh, *Occupation and Pay in Great Britain, 1906–1979* (London, 1980), pp. 4–7, 11–12, 24–6, 28–39; Robert A. Brady, *Crisis in Britain* (Berkeley, 1950), pp. 495–8; A. A. Rogow, *The Labour Government and British Industry, 1945–1951* (Ithaca, 1953), pp. 75–6.

3　R. Fletcher, *The Family and Marriage in Britain* (Harmondsworth, 1973), pp 122–5; A. H. Halsey (ed.), *Trends in British Society Since 1900* (London, 1972), pp. 31, 40–1, 51.

4　E. Slater and M. Woodside, *Patterns of Marriage. A Study of Marriage Relationships Among the Urban Working Classes* (London, 1951), pp. 33–8, 41–5, 116–18; Cynthia White, *Women's Magazines, 1693–1968* (London, 1970), pp. 123–37. See also Geoffrey Gorer, *Exploring English Character* (New York, 1955), pp. 125–161.

5　Pearl Jephcott, *Rising Twenty. Notes on Some Ordinary Girls* (London, 1948), 37–8, 42–6, 65–7, 85; Mass-Observation, *Britain and Her Birth-Rate* (London, 1945), pp. 96–105.

6　Department of Employment, *Family Expenditure Survey 1980* (London, 1982), pp. 9–12; Sidney Pollard, *The Development of the British Economy* (London, 1969), pp. 398, 501–2; C. Chisholm (ed.), *Marketing Survey of the United Kingdom* (London, 1948).

7   Arthur Marwick, *British Society Since 1945* (Harmondsworth, 1982), pp. 42, 75; B. Seebohm Rowntree and G. R. Lavers, *English Life and Leisure. A Social Study* (London, 1951), esp. p. 355.

8   Mass-Observation, Directive Replies on Class, September 1948, M-O Archive, Sussex University. Comparable findings were made by Gorer three years later: see *Exploring English Character*, pp. 34–42, though he found less bitterness than did the earlier survey.

9   D. V. Glass, *Social Mobility in Britain* (London, 1954), pp. 38–42, 180–8, 51–75, esp. 59–60. See also the follow-up to the LSE study by M. Young and P. Willmott, 'Social Grading by Manual Workers', *British Journal of Sociology* (1956).

10   Harry Hopkins, *The New Look* (London, 1963), p. 153; Glass, *Social Mobility in Britain*, p. 3; Roy Lewis and Angus Maude, *The English Middle Classes* (New York, 1950), p. vii.

11   G. D. H. Cole, 'The Conception of the Middle Class', *British Journal of Sociology*, I (1950), and *Studies in Class Structure* (London, 1955), pp. 77, 98; Mass-Observation, 'Middle-Class: Why?', File Report No. 3073, January 1949.

12   Mass-Observation, 'It Isn't There. An Interpretation of Political Trends Based on M-O Material', File Report No. 2415, August, 1946; Mark Jenkins, *Bevanism. Labour's High Tide* (Nottingham, 1979), pp. 113–20; and, on cynicism more generally, Mass-Observation, *Puzzled People* (London, 1947).

13   R. Eatwell, *The 1945–1951 Labour Governments* (London, 1979), pp. 125–31, 151–4; John Bonham, *The Middle-Class Vote* (London, 1955), 30–5, 167–77.

Chapter Nine Pages 146–172

1   The following discussion is based upon Sidney Pollard, *The Development of the British Economy, 1914–1967* (London, 1969) pp. 408–9, 413–14, 422–3; C. H. Feinstein, *National Income, Output and Expenditure, 1855–1965* (Cambridge, 1972), pp. T51–2, T129–30; A. H. Halsey (ed.), *Trends in British Society Since 1900* (London, 1972); Richard Brown, 'Work', in P. Abrams (ed.), *Work, Urbanism and Inequality* (London, 1978), pp. 66–7; G. Routh, *Occupation and Pay in Great Britain, 1906–79* (London, 1980), Chapter 1; I. Katznelson, *Black Men, White Cities* (Chicago, 1976), pp. 123–88.

2   Routh, *Occupation and Pay*, pp. 123–7.

3   A. Marwick, *British Society Since 1945* (Harmondsworth, 1982), p. 47.

4   An additional factor worth noting parenthetically was the peculiar slant of scholarly studies on work in the 1950s. The most influential stemmed either from Liverpool University or the Tavistock Institute, and these shared a case-study method and a taste for broad theorizing about 'the culture of the factory' or the workplace as a social system, which combined in such a fashion as to minimize divisions internal to the workforce. On this research, see Richard Brown, 'Participation, Conflict and Change in Industry', *Sociological Review*, XIII, 3 (1965), pp. 273–95; 'Research and Consultancy in Industrial Enterprises', *Sociology*, I (1967), pp. 33–60; and Michael Rose, *Industrial Behaviour: Theoretical Development Since Taylor* (London, 1975).

5   Ferdynand Zweig, *The British Worker* (Harmondsworth, 1952), pp. 33–45, 96–114, 201–8; *Productivity and Trade Unions* (Oxford, 1951), pp. 37–44, 61 ff. See also W. H. Scott *et al.*, *Technical Change and Industrial Relations. A Study of the Relations Between Technical Change and the Social Structure of a Large Steelworks* (Liverpool, 1956).

6   Zweig, *The British Worker*, p. 34; Liverpool University, Department of Social Science, *The Dockworker* (Liverpool, 1956), pp. 66–7; D. F. Wilson, *Dockers* (London, 1972).

7   S. Melman, *Decision-making and Productivity* (Oxford, 1958); Andrew Friedman, *Industry and Labour* (London, 1977), pp. 205–24.

8   S. Wyatt and R. Marriott, 'A Study of Attitudes to Factory Work', Medical Research Council, Special Report Series, no. 292 (London, 1956).

9   F. Zweig, *Women's Life and Labour* (London, 1952), pp. 33–43, 121–4; Richard Brown, 'Women as Employees: Some Comments on Research in Industrial Sociology', in D. L. Barker and S. Allen (eds.), *Dependence and Expoloitation in Work and Marriage* (London, 1976), pp. 21–56.

10 David Lockwood, 'Sources of Variation in Working-Class Images of Society', *Sociological Review* XIV (1966), pp. 249–57. Martin Bulmer (ed.), *Working-Class Images of Society* (London, 1975), reprints that essay together with critiques, several case studies, and an extensive bibliography. Undoubtedly, Lockwood's view was shaped by the tradition of community studies as much as by industrial findings. On these, see below, pp. 00.

11   It should be noted, of course, that maintainaing the *status quo* in industry meant preserving differentials between men and women. Indeed, it is clear that the situation for women had changed very little from 1950 to the early and mid-sixties: see J. H. Smith, 'Managers and Married Women Workers', *British Journal of Sociology* XII (1961); T. Lupton, *On the Shop Floor* (London, 1963), p. 191; P. Jephcott *et al.*, *Married Women Working* (London, 1962); Viola Klein, *Britain's Married Women Workers* (London, 1965); and Sheila Cunnison, *Wages and Work Allocation* (London, 1966), pp. 82–6.

12   Friedman, *Industry and Labour*, pp. 216–18; L. Hannah, *Rise of the Corporate Economy* (London, 1976), pp. 165–6.

13   Joan Woodward, *Industrial Organization: Theory and Practice*, Second Edition (Oxford, 1980), pp. 35–49; Trevor Noble, *Modern Britain: Structure and Change* (London, 1975), p. 150; Board of Trade, *Report on the Census of Production 1963*, (London, 1970), table 1. On skill levels, see Routh, *Occupation and Pay*, pp. 28–32; Halsey, *Trends in British Society* p. 113; and Department of Employment, *The Metal Industries* (London, 1965), pp. 15–17. On piecework, see R. Marriott, *Incentive Payment Systems* (London, 1957), pp. 48–53; J. Cronin, *Industrial Conflict in Modern Britain* (London, 1979), pp. 174–6; William Brown, *Piecework Bargaining* (London, 1973) and, from a rather different perspective, Hilde Behrend, 'Financial Incentives as the Expression of a System of Beliefs', *British Journal of Sociology*, X (1959), pp. 137–49.

14   R. M. Blackburn, *Union Character and Social Class* (London, 1967), pp. 71–5.

15   David Lockwood, *The Blackcoated Worker. A Study in Class Consciousness* (London, 1958), pp. 93–4; Routh, *Occupation and Pay*, p. 25; A. A. Murdoch and J. R. Dale, *The Clerical Function* (London, 1961); A. J. M. Sykes, 'Some Differences in Attitudes of Clerical and of Manual Workers', *Sociological Review*, XIII (1965), pp. 297–310; and A. Stewart, K. Prandy and R. M. Blackburn, *Social Stratification and Occupational Structure* (London, 1981).

16   Lockwood, *Blackcoated Worker*, p. 95.

17   G. S. Bain, *The Growth of White-Collar Unionism* (Oxford, 1970).

18   Richard Price, 'Rethinking Labour History: The Importance of Work', in J. Cronin and J. Schneer (eds.), *Social Conflict and the Political Order in Modern Britain* (London, 1982), p. 196; David Lee, 'Beyond deskilling: skill, craft and class', in S. Wood (ed.), *The Degradation of Work?* (London, 1982), pp. 146–62.

19   Pollard, *Development of the British Economy*, p. 502; F. Zweig, *The Worker in an Affluent Society* (London, 1961), pp. 8–9; Michael Young and Peter Willmott, *The Symmetrical Family* (London, 1973), p. 23; Cole, *Post-War Condition of Britain*, pp. 79–98; 'Family Expenditure', *Department of Employment Gazette* (February, 1978), p. 139; John H. Goldthorpe *et al.*, *The Affluent Worker in the Class Structure* (Cambridge, 1969), pp. 21–2, 39; Mark Abrams, *The Teenage Consumer* (London, 1961); Graham Murdock and Robin McCron, 'Youth and Class: the career of a confusion', in *Working Class Youth Culture*, edited by Geoff Mungham and Geoff Pearson (London, 1976), pp. 15–16; and John Barron Mays, *The Young Pretenders* (New York, 1965), pp. 32–3.

20   Chas Critcher, 'Sociology, Cultural Studies and the Post-War Working Class'; Richard Johnson, 'Culture and the Historians'; and Jon Clarke, 'Capital and Culture: the Post-War Working Class Revisited', in Clarke, Critcher and Johnson (eds.), *Working-Class Culture: Studies in History and Theory* (New York, 1979), pp. 13–40, 41–71, 238–53.

21   Richard Hoggart, *The Uses of Literacy* (London, 1957).

22   Raymond Williams, *Culture and Society, 1780–1950* (London, 1958); and *The Long Revolution* (London, 1961); E. P. Thompson, *The Making of the English Working Class* (London, 1963).

23   A. C. H. Smith *et al.*, *Paper Voices: The Popular Press and Social Change, 1935–1965* (London, 1975) and Stuart Hall and Paddy Whannel, *The Popular Arts* (New York, 1965). Both of these, it should be noted, were undertaken under Hoggart's direct influence.

24   Norman Dennis, Fernando Enriques and Clifford Slaughter, *Coal is Our Life* (London, 1956, reprinted 1969); Elizabeth Bott, *Family and Social Network* (London, 1957), Second Edition (1972).

25   See John Burnett, *A Social History of Housing, 1815–1970* (Newton Abbot, 1978), p. 279..

26   Peter Townsend, *The Family Life of Old People* (London, 1957); M. Young and P. Willmott, *Family and Kinship in East London* (London, 1957); Willmott and Young, *Family and Class in a London Suburb* (London, 1970). On the group's politics, see Michael Young, 'The Planners and the Planned: The Family', *Journal of the Town Planning Institute*, XL (1954). Patrick Dunleavy, *The Politics of Mass Housing in Britain, 1945–1975* (Oxford, 1981), pp. 141–3; and Elizabeth Wilson, *Only Halfway to Paradise: Women in*

Postwar Britain, 1945–1968 (London, 1980), pp. 61–9, make useful critiques.

27   Young and Willmott, *Family and Kinship in East London*, p. 133.

28   The two most comprehensive of such reviews are Josephine Klein, *Samples from English Cultures*, 2 vols., (London, 1965); and R. Frankenberg, *Communities in Britain* (Harmondsworth, 1966).

29   C. C. Harris, *The Family* (London, 1969), *passim*; Noble, *Modern Britain: Structure and Change*, pp. 96–131.

30   Willmott, *The Evolution of a Community* (London, 1963). See Roy Greenslade, *Goodbye to the Working Class* (London, 1977), for confirmation of this depiction of Dagenham.

31   Noble, *Modern Britain: Structure and Change*, pp. 124–28; J. and E. Newson, *Patterns of Infant Care* (London, 1965) and *Four Years Old in an Urban Community* (London, 1968); Zweig, *The Worker in an Affluent Society*, p. 208; Young and Willmott, *The Symmetrical Family* (London, 1973); and Brian Jackson, *Working Class Community. Some General Notions Raised by a Series of Studies in Northern England* (London, 1968), pp. 162, 165–6.

32   Hopkins, *The New Look*, pp. 432–8; MacInnes, *English, Half English*, pp. 11–16; Bernice Martin, *Sociology of Contemporary Culture Change* (Oxford, 1981), pp. 136–32; Paul Rock and Stanley Cohen, 'The Teddy Boy', in V. Bogdanor and R. Skidelsky, *The Age of Affluence* (London, 1970), pp. 288–320.

33   Rock and Cohen, 'The Teddy Boy'; Jackson, *Working Class Community*.

34   This new ethnographic literature is exemplified by Stuart Hall and Tony Jefferson (eds.), *Resistance Through Rituals: Youth Subculture in Post-War Britain* (London, 1975); Mungham and Pearson, *Working Class Youth Culture*; Paul Willis, *Profane Culture* (London, 1978); Dick Hebdige, *Subculture: The Meaning of Style* (London, 1979); and with a slight twist, S. Daniel and P. McGuire (eds.), *Paint House* (Harmondsworth, 1972). For a useful critique, see Chris Waters, 'Badges of Half-formed, Inarticulate Radicalism', *International Labour and Working Class History*, No. 19, (Spring 1981), pp. 23–37. A major weakness is the exclusive focus on young men. On this, see Angela McRobbie, 'Working Class Girls and the Culture of Femininity', in Women's Studies Group, Centre for Contemporary Culture Studies, *Women Take Issue* (London, 1978), pp. 96–108.

35   See Jack Common, *Freedom of the Streets*; S. Humphries, *Hooligans or Rebels* (London, 1981); James Patrick, *A Glasgow*

Gang Observed (London, 1973), pp. 144–54.

36   See D. H. Allcorn, 'Young Men With Money', PhD Thesis, Manchester University, 1954, summarized in Max Gluckman, 'Preface' to Bott, *Family and Social Network*, p. xxviii; Willmott, *Adolescent Boys of East London* (Harmondsworth, 1968), p. 174.

37   W. G. Runciman, *Relative Deprivation and Social Injustice* (London, 1966); Goldthorpe *et al.*, *The Affluent Worker*, 3 vols., (Cambridge, 1968–9).

38   Robert McKenzie and Allan Silver, *Angels in Marble. Working Class Conservatives in Urban England* (London, 1968); and Eric Nordlinger, *The Working-Class Tories* (London, 1967).

39   For critical reviews of these studies, see J. H. Westergaard, 'The Rediscovery of the Cash Nexus', in J. Saville and R. Miliband (eds.), *The Socialist Register 1970* (London, 1970), pp. 111–38; and R. Hoggart, *Speaking to Each Other*, Vol. 1 (Oxford, 1970), pp. 45–68.

Chapter Ten Pages 173–192

1   Hugh Gaitskell, 'The Economic Aims of the Labour Party', *Political Quarterly* XXIV (January–March, 1953).

2   Crosland, 'The Transition from Capitalism', in R. H. Crossman (ed.), *New Fabian Essays* (London, 1952), pp. 33–68, esp. pp. 38–42, 68.

3   H. L. Beales, 'The Labour Party in its Social Context', *Political Quarterly*, XXIV (1953), 90–8.

4   Crosland, *The Future of Socialism* (London, 1956), pp. 515–29.

5   Crossman, 'Towards a Philosophy of Socialism', in *New Fabian Essays*, pp. 1–32.

6   Michael Gordon, *Conflict and Consensus in Labour's Foreign Policy, 1914–1965* (Stanford, 1969), pp. 118–52, 222–47; T. Brett, S. Gilliatt, and A. Pople, 'Planned Trade, Labour Party Policy and US Intervention: The Successes and Failures of Post-War Reconstruction', *History Workshop*, No. 13 (Spring, 1982), pp. 130–42.

7   David Coates, *The Labour Party and the Struggle for Socialism* (Cambridge, 1975), pp. 190–7; David Howell, *British Social Democracy* (London, 1976), pp. 181–202; Gerhard Lowenberg, 'The Transformation of British Labour Party Policy Since 1945', *Journal of Politics*, XXI (1959), pp. 234–57.

8   Howell, *British Social Democracy*, pp. 221–7. For a more detailed analysis, see Lewis Minkin, *The Labour Party Conference* (Harmondsworth, 1980), p. 151 and *passim*.

9   Rita Hinden, 'The Lessons for Labour', in Mark Abrams and Richard Rose, *Must Labour Lose?* (Harmondsworth, 1960), pp. 100–1, 104–8.

10   Vernon Bogdanor, 'The Labour Party in Opposition, 1951–1964', in Bogdanor and R. Skidelsky (eds.), *The Age of Affluence, 1951–1964* (London, 1970), pp. 105–7.

11   S. Lewenhak, *Women and Trade Unions* (London, 1977), pp. 244–76.

12   J. Hinton, *Labour and Socialism* (Brighton, 1983), p. 176. There is need for a serious study of the CP's industrial strategy since the war. These brief comments are based largely upon material on rank-and-file movements at the Modern Records Centre. See the Renshaw Papers MSS 104, for copies of rank-and-file papers among transport workers; and the Etheridge Papers, MSS 202, esp. files labelled CP8, and Boxes 8 and 11.

13   Steven Tolliday, 'Government, Employers and Shopfloor Organization in the British Motor Industry, 1939–1969', King's College, September 1982.

14   H. A. Turner, G. Clack and G. Roberts, *Labour Relations in the Motor Industry* (London, 1967), pp. 82–3.

15   H. A. Clegg and R. Adams, *The Employer's Challenge* (Oxford, 1957), Leo Panitch, *Social Democracy and Industrial Militancy* (Cambridge, 1976), pp. 44–5; see also Nigel Harris, *Competition and the Corporate Society* (London, 1972); and K. Middlemas, *Politics in Industrial Society* (London, 1979), pp. 421–2.

16   Clegg and Adams, *The Employers' Challenge*, pp. 155–6.

17   J. Cronin, *Industrial Conflict in Modern Britain* (London, 1979), pp. 139–41.

18   G. S. Bain and R. Price, *Profiles and Union Growth* (Oxford, 1981), pp. 37–42, 47, 49, 50, 63; W. E. J. McCarthy, *The Role of Shop Stewards in British Industrial Relations*, Royal Commission on Trade Unions and Employers' Organizations, Research Papers No. 1 (London, 1967); and A. I. Marsh and E. Coker, 'Shop Stewards Organization in the Engineering Industry', *British Journal of Industrial Relations*, I (1963), pp. 170–90.

19   Panitch, *Social Democracy and Industrial Militancy*, pp. 52–62.

20   'Let's Go with Labour for the New Britain', Labour Manifesto 1964, reprinted in F. W. S. Craig, *British General Election Manifestos* (Chichester, 1970), pp. 229–46.

21   Gaitskell, 'The Economic Aims of the Labour Party', pp. 12–13; Harold Wilson, *Post-War Economic Policies in Britain* (London:

Fabian Tract 309, 1957), p. 14; F. T. Blackaby (ed.), *British Economic Policy, 1960–74* (Cambridge, 1978) pp. 402–15; Peter Oppenheimer, 'Muddling Through: The Economy in 1951–1965', in *The Age of Affluence*, pp. 118–20, 112–9; Frank Longstreth, 'The City, Industry and the State', in Colin Crouch (ed.), *State and Economy in Contemporary Capitalism* (London, 1979), pp. 157–90; and Bob Jessop, 'The Transformation of the State in Post-War Britain', in R. Scase (ed.), *The State in Western Europe* (London, 1980), pp. 23–93.

22   T. W. Hutchinson, *Economics and Economic Policy in Britain, 1946–1966* (London, 1968); and Roger Opie, 'Economic Planning and Growth', in Wilfred Beckerman (ed.), *The Labour Government's Economic Record, 1964–70* (London, 1972), pp. 157–64.

23   Blackaby, *British Economic Policy, 1960–1974*, p. 31; T. Balogh, *Planning for Progress: A Strategy for Labour* (London, 1963).

24   Blackaby, *British Economic Policy*, pp. 431–9; Hugh Heclo and Aaron Wildavsky, *The Private Government of Public Money* (Berkeley, 1974), pp. 266–7.

25   On expectations concerning growth, see James Alt, *The Politics of Economic Decline: Economic Management and Political Behaviour in Britain Since 1964* (Cambridge, 1979).

26   On the altered internal balance in various unions in the 1960s, see Minkin, *The Labour Party Conference*, pp. 90–115, 175–206; Ross Martin, *TUC: The Growth of A Pressure Group, 1868–1976* (Oxford, 1980), pp. 299–324; Irwin Richter, *Political Purpose in Trade Unions* (London, 1969).

27   Panitch, *Social Democracy and Industrial Militancy*, chapters 6 and 7; and Colin Crouch, *Class Conflict and the Industrial Relations Crisis* (London, 1977).

28   Royal Commission on Trade Unions and Employers' Organizations, *Report*, Cmnd 3623 (London, 1968); Department of Employment and Productivity, *In Place of Strife*, Cmnd 3888 (London, 1969).

29   *Tribune*, 18 April 1969.

30   Blackaby, *British Economic Policy*, p. 377.

31   Cronin, *Industrial Conflict in Modern Britain*, chapter 6; C. T. B. Smith *et al., Strikes in Britain* (London, Department of Employment, 1978) and J. Durcan, W. McCarthy & G. Redman, *Strikes in Post-War Britain* (London, 1983), pp. 132–171.

32   Patrick Dunleavy, 'The Political Implications of Sectoral Cleavages and the Growth of State Employment: Part 2, Cleavage

Structures and Political Alignment', *Political Studies* XXVIII, 4 (1980), p. 534; Bain and Price, *Profiles of Union Growth*, pp. 39–42.

33   Henry Friedman and Sander Meredeen, *The Dynamics of Industrial Conflict* (London, 1980); S. Lewenhak, *Women and Trade Unions*, pp. 284–6. More generally, see J. H. Goldthorpe, 'The Current Inflation: Towards a Sociological Account', in Fred Hirsch and Goldthorpe (eds.), *The Political Economic of Inflation* (Oxford, 1982), pp. 186–212; and R. Taylor, *Workers and the New Depression* (London, 1982), pp. 46–9.

34   D. Jackson, H. A. Turner and F. Wilkinson, *Do Trade Unions Cause Inflation?*, 2nd ed. (Cambridge, 1975); and D. Hibbs, 'On the Political Economy of Long-Term Trends in Strike Activity', *British Journal of Political Science*, VIII (1978), pp. 153–75.

35   As Ian Maitland seems to do in *The Causes of Industrial Disorder* (London, 1983). On the structure of bargaining see Hugh Clegg, *The Changing System of Industrial Relations in Great Britain* (Oxford, 1979); and W. A. Brown, *Piecework Bargaining* (London, 1970).

Chapter Eleven Pages 193–208

1   D. Butler and M. Pinto-Duschinsky, *The British General Election of 1970* (London, 1971), pp. 337–51; Ivor Crewe, 'The Politics of "Affluent" and "Traditional" Workers in Britain: An Aggregate Data Analysis, *British Journal of Political Science*, 111 (1973), pp. 29–52.

2   L. Hannah, *The Rise of the Corporate Economy* (London, 1976), pp. 214–16; and S. J. Prais, *Productivity and Industrial Structure* (Cambridge, 1981), p. 27.

3   Prais, *Productivity and Industrial Structure*, pp. 17–32, 270–2; F. Blackaby (ed.), *De-Industrialization* (London, 1979); Sidney Pollard, *The Wasting of the British Economy* (London, 1982); and Robert Bacon and Walter Ellis, *Britain's Economic Problem: Too Few Producers* (London, 1976).

4   *Annual Abstracts of Statistics*, 1967, 1981, *Social Trends*, 1971 and 1981.

5   Michael Young and Peter Willmott, *The Symmetrical Family* (London, 1973), pp. 65–101; N. Bullock *et al.*, 'Time budgets and Urban Activity Patterns', *Social Trends*, 1974, pp. 57–8. Ann Oakley, in *The Sociology of Housework* (Oxford, 1974), pp. 135–65, also presents a mixed picture. See also E. Wilson, *Women and the*

Welfare State (London, 1977).

6   A. R. Thatcher, 'Labour Supply and Employment Trends', in Blackaby, *De-Industrialization*, pp. 38–9; D. Robinson (ed.), *Local Labour Markets and Wage Structures* (London, 1970), pp. 58–60; D. Lee, 'Beyond Deskilling: skill, craft and class', in S. Wood (ed.), *The Degradation of Work?* (London, 1982), p. 156.

7   Ronald Fraser (ed.), *Work*, 2 vols (Harmondsworth, 1968, 1969), especially the contributions by Dennis Johnson, Bryan Slater, Mike Taylor, Phillip Higgs, and Edward Sutcliffe; R. M. Blackburn and M. Mann, in *The Working Class in the Labour Market* (Cambridge, 1979), report on the Peterborough survey. The best case study is undoubtedly Huw Beynon, *Working For Ford* (Harmondsworth, 1973). For general reviews, see Maria Herszowicz, *Industrial Sociology* (Oxford, 1981), and Stephen Hill, *Competition and Control at Work. The New Industrial Sociology* (London, 1981), as well as David Weir (ed.), *Men and Work in Britain* (London, 1973).

8   William Brown (ed.), *The Changing Contours of British Industrial Relations* (Oxford, 1981), esp. pp. 5–25, 10–15; H. A. Turner, G. Roberts and D. Roberts, *Management Characteristics and Labour Conflict* (Cambridge, 1977), pp. 35–9; M. Poole *et al.*, 'Managerial Attitudes and Behaviour in Industrial Relations', *British Journal of Industrial Relations* XX (1982), pp. 285–307; Robert Taylor, *The Fifth Estate* (London, 1978), pp. 125–46; Joe England, 'Shop Stewards and Transport House: a comment upon the incorporation of the rank and file', *Industrial Relations Journal* XII (1981), pp. 16–29; and S. G. Ogden, 'Bargaining Structure and the Control of Industrial Relations', *BJIR*, XX (1982), pp. 170–85.

9   The homogeneity of working-class life chances in stressed by J. H. Goldthorpe, *Social Mobility and Class Structure in Modern Britain* (Oxford, 1980), esp. Chapter 5; and Blackburn and Mann, *The Working Class in the Labour Market*. The impact of education and mobility in the formation of both the middle and working class is discussed in A. H. Halsey, A. F. Heath and J. M. Ridge, *Origins and Destinations. Family, Class and Education in Modern Britain* (Oxford, 1980). On changes in the work situation of white-collar employees, see Rosemary Crompton and Stuart Reid, 'The deskilling of clerical work', in S. Wood (ed.), *The Degradation of Work?*, pp. 163–78; on unionization among such workers, see R. Price and G. S. Bain, 'Union Growth Revisited: 1948–1974 in Perspective', *BJIR*, XIV (1976).

10   K. Roberts *et al.*, *The Fragmentary Class Structure* (London, 1977), pp. 123–43; Brown, *Changing Contours of Industrial Relations*, pp. 51–79.

11   'Women in the Labour Force', *New Society*, 20 August 1982; *Annual Abstract of Statistics*, 1981; *Social Trends*, 1981; *Family Expenditure Survey*, 1980.

12   *Social Trends* 1981; P. Dunleavy, 'The Urban Basis of Political Alignment: Social Class, Domestic Property Ownership, and State Intervention in Consumption Processes', *British Journal of Political Science*, IX (1979), p. 411.

13   W. W. Daniels showed the persistence of narrow reference groups in *The PEP Survey on Inflation*, Broadsheet No. 553 (London, 1975), pp. 18–28, though the implications of the finding for the stability of workers' expectations seems questionable. On the persistence of class attitudes more generally, see R. Scase, *Social Democracy in a Capitalist Society* (London, 1977); and the compilation of survey data in Ivan Reid, *Social Class Differences in Britain* (London, 1977). On expectations among the entire population, see Mark Abrams, 'Subjective Social Indicators', *Social Trends*, 1975, p. 48, and, more theoretically, Alan Marsh, 'The "Silent Revolution", Value Priorities and the Quality of Life in Britain', *American Political Science Review*, LXIX (1975), pp. 21–30. For the attempt to replicate Runciman, see M. Harrop, 'Democracy and Inequality: Mass Conceptions of Stratification in Britain', PhD thesis, Yale University, 1979. The findings on the dockers and shipbuilders are from S. Hill, *The Dockers: Class and Tradition in London* (London, 1976), and R. Brown and P. Brannen, 'Social Relations and Social Perspectives Amongst Shipbuilding Workers', *Sociology*, IV (1970). On pecuniary orientations and class attitudes more generally, see W. F. Moorhouse, 'Attitudes to Class and Class Relationships in Britain', *Sociology* X (1976), pp. 469–96.

14   The context is described clearly in Michael Moran, *The Politics of Industrial Relations* (London, 1977).

15   The new programme is reviewed in Geoff Hodgson, *Labour at the Crossroads* (Oxford, 1981), pp. 64–88; and defended vigorously in Stuart Holland, *The Socialist Challenge* (London, 1975).

16   John Elliott, *Conflict or Cooperation? The Growth of Industrial Democracy* (London, 1978), pp. 207, 241–63.

17   Holland, *The Socialist Challenge*, p. 171. On Labour's blindness on the issue of centralization, see L. J. Sharpe, 'The Labour Party

and the Geography of Inequality: A Puzzle', pp. 137–70 and, on the lack of resonance of the old appeals, Ivor Crewe, 'The Labour Party and the Electorate', pp. 26–38, in Dennis Kavanagh (ed.), *The Politics of the Labour Party* (London, 1982).

18 David Coates, *Labour in Power?* (London, 1980), is the best general account.

19 This table was compiled from the studies by David Butler and a succession of co-authors on the British general elections from 1964 to 1974, and from data presented by Ivor Crewe in 'The Disturbing Truth Behind Labour's Rout', *The Guardian*, 13 June 1983, p. 5. The designations in the table correspond to NOP class categories AB, C1, C2, DE respectively. For a comparison of these with other classifications, see P. Pulzer, *Political Representation and Elections in Britain* (London, 1972), p. 104.

20 Ivor Crewe, Bo Sarlvik and James Alt, 'Partisan Dealignment in Britain, 1964–74', *British Journal of Political Science*, VII (1977), pp. 129–90; and Crewe, 'The Labour Party and the Electorate', and P. Whiteley, 'The Decline of Labour's Local Party Membership and Electoral Base, 1945–79', in Kavanagh (ed.), *Politics of the Labour Party*, pp. 9–49, 111–34.

21 See K. Coates (ed.), *What Went Wrong?* (Nottingham, 1979).

22 Samuel Beer, *Britain Against Itself* (New York, 1982), pp. 110–20; Dennis Kavanagh, 'Political Culture in Great Britain: The Decline of the Civic Culture', in G. Almond and S. Verba, *The Civic Culture Revisited* (Boston, 1980), pp. 124–76; and Vivien Hart, *Distrust and Democracy: Political Distrust in Britain and America* (Cambridge, 1978).

Appendix

Table A. 1 *Britain's Changing Labour Force, 1911–71.*

	1911	1921	1931	1951	1961	1971
Total Occupied Population (000s)	18,347	19,333	21,029	22,514	23,639	25,021
Female Participation Rate (%)	35.3	33.7	34.2	34.7	37.5	42.7
Percentage classed as:						
Employers and proprietors	6.7	6.8	6.7	5.0	4.7	4.2
Managers and administrators	3.4	3.6	3.7	5.5	5.4	8.2
Higher professionals	1.0	1.0	1.1	1.9	3.0	3.3
Lower professionals and Technicians	3.1	3.5	3.5	4.7	6.0	7.8
Foremen, inspectors and supervisors	1.3	1.4	1.5	2.6	2.9	3.9
Sales	5.4	5.1	6.5	5.7	5.9	9.0
Clerical	4.8	6.7	7.0	10.7	13.0	13.9
Manual: Skilled	30.6	28.8	26.7	24.9	25.3	21.6
Semi-skilled	39.5	33.9	35.0	32.6	25.4	25.2
Unskilled	9.6	14.2	14.8	12.0	8.6	11.9

Sources: These data were drawn primarily from G. Routh, *Occupations and Pay in Great Britain, 1906–79* (London, 1980), pp. 6–7, 11, supplemented by data from G. S. Bain, 'The Labour Force', in A. H. Halsey, ed., *Trends in British Society* (London, 1972), pp. 113, 118. The main gap in Routh's data is for the census year 1961. For this information, Bain's figures are used. Bain's figures are also used for the numbers engaged in 'sales', which Routh for some reason omits, except that Routh's estimate for 1971 is included. Routh adopts a somewhat broader definition of clerical workers than Bain, so Bain's 1961 figure had to be adjusted slightly.

Table A.2 *Industrial Conflict and Union Organization, 1910–1981*

Year	Industrial Conflict: Strikes*	Workers Directly* Involved (000s)	Working Days** Lost (000s)	Union Organization: Union Membership (000s)	Union Density %
1910	521	384	9,867	2,565	14.6
1911	872	824	10,155	3,139	17.7
1912	834	1,232	40,890	3,416	19.1
1913	1,459	497	9,804	4,135	23.1
1914	972	326	9,878	4,145	23.0
1915	672	401	2,953	4,359	24.1
1916	532	235	2,446	4,644	25.6
1917	730	575	5,647	5,499	30.2
1918	1,116	923	5,875	6,533	35.7
1919	1,352	2,401	34,969	7,927	43.1
1920	1,607	1,779	26,568	8,348	45.2
1921	763	1,770	85,872	6,633	35.8
1922	576	512	19,850	5,625	31.6
1923	628	343	10,672	5,429	30.2
1924	716	558	8,424	5,544	30.6
1925	603	401	7,952	5,506	30.1
1926	323	2,724	162,233	5,219	28.3
1927	308	90	1,174	4,919	26.4
1928	302	80	1,388	4,806	25.6
1929	431	493	8,287	4,858	25.7
1930	422	286	4,399	4,842	25.4
1931	420	424	6,983	4,624	24.0
1932	389	337	6,488	4,444	23.0
1933	357	114	1,072	4,392	22.6
1934	471	109	959	4,590	23.5
1935	553	230	1,955	4,867	24.9
1936	818	241	1,829	5,295	26.9
1937	1,129	388	3,413	5,842	29.6
1938	875	211	1,334	6,053	30.5
1939	940	246	1,356	6,298	31.6
1940	922	225	940	6,613	33.1
1941	1,251	297	1,079	7,165	35.7
1942	1,303	349	1,527	7,866	39.0

Table A.2 cont.

Year	Industrial Conflict:			Union Organization:	
	Strikes*	Workers Directly* Involved (000s)	Working Days** Lost (000s)	Union Membership (000s)	Union Density %
1943	1,785	454	1,808	8,174	40.4
1944	2,194	716	3,714	8,087	39.8
1945	2,293	447	2,835	7,875	38.6
1946	2,205	405	2,158	8,803	43.0
1947	1,721	489	2,433	9,145	44.5
1948	1,759	324	1,933	9,363	45.2
1949	1,426	313	1,807	9,318	44.8
1950	1,339	269	1,389	9,289	44.1
1951	1,719	336	1,694	9,530	45.0
1952	1,714	303	1,792	9,588	45.1
1953	1,746	1,329	2,184	9,527	44.6
1954	1,989	402	2,457	9,566	44.2
1955	2,419	599	3,781	9,741	44.5
1956	2,648	464	2,083	9,778	44.1
1957	2,859	1,275	8,412	9,829	44.0
1958	2,629	456	3,462	9,639	43.2
1959	2,093	522	5,270	9,623	44.0
1960	2,832	698	3,024	9,835	44.2
1961	2,686	673	3,046	9,916	44.0
1962	2,449	4,297	5,798	10,014	43.8
1963	2,068	455	1,755	10,067	43.7
1964	2,524	700	2,277	10,218	44.1
1965	2,354	673	2,925	10,325	44.2
1966	1,937	414	2,398	10,259	43.6
1967	2,116	552	2,787	10,194	43.7
1968	2,378	2,074	4,690	10,200	44.0
1969	3,116	1,427	6,846	10,479	45.3
1970	3,906	1,460	10,980	11,187	48.5
1971	2,228	864	13,551	11,135	48.7
1972	2,497	1,450	23,909	11,359	49.5
1973	2,873	1,103	7,197	11,456	49.3
1974	2,922	1,161	14,750	11,764	50.4
1975	2,282	570	6,012	12,026	51.0

Table A.2 cont.

Year	Industrial Conflict:			Union Organization:	
	Strikes*	Workers Directly* Involved (000s)	Working Days** Lost (000s)	Union Membership (000s)	Union Density %
1976	2,016	444	3,284	12,386	51.9
1977	2,703	785	10,142	12,846	53.4
1978	2,471	725	9,405	13,112	54.2
1979	2,080	4,121	29,474	13,447	55.4
1980	1,330	702	11,964	12,947	53.6
1981	1,338	1,326	4,266	12,182	51.0

* Refers to stoppages beginning in year
** Refers to all stoppages in progress in year

Source: Bain, 'The Labour Force', pp. 127–8; 'Stoppages caused by industrial disputes in 1982', Employment Gazette (July, 1983), p. 303; Bain and R. Price, Profiles of Union Growth (Oxford, 1980), pp. 37–8; and Price and Bain, 'Union Growth in Britain: Retrospect and Prospect', British Journal of Industrial Relations (1983), pp. 46–7.

Index